Gasmasks and Garston
A Liverpool Childhood (1937–1953)

BEATRICE SMITH

First impression: 2015

© Copyright Beatrice Smith and Y Lolfa Cyf., 2015

The contents of this book are subject to copyright, and may
not be reproduced by any means, mechanical or electronic,
without the prior, written consent of the publishers.

Cover design: Y Lolfa

ISBN: 978 1 78461 203 0

Published and printed in Wales
on paper from well-maintained forests by
Y Lolfa Cyf., Talybont, Ceredigion SY24 5HE
website www.ylolfa.com
e-mail ylolfa@ylolfa.com
tel 01970 832 304
fax 832 782

Acknowledgments

FIRST I WOULD like to thank my family.

'Why spoil a good story with the truth?' Tom used to say of Mam's tales. She was a wonderful storyteller in the Irish tradition.

Dad, on the other hand, would quote time, date and place with pinpoint accuracy and pedantry.

Listening to them reminiscing I heard the stories from the childhoods of my parents, the tales of my older brothers and sisters before I was born, and the histories of grandparents, great-grandparents, great aunts and great uncles.

Over a lifetime my siblings added to the great fund of knowledge that has made this book possible.

The extended family has also played its part. Cousins from the Smith family and the McCarten family recently added their memories, as have some of the older grandchildren of Alf Smith and Martha McCarten.

I would like to thank all those who provided photographs. In particular, I want to thank Joe and James Dillon, children of Mary and grandchildren of Nell Stockton. She was the eldest sister of my mother. Most of the studio photographs of the McCarten family at the beginning of the 20th century come from their family collection. Other McCarten studio photographs come from Richard McCarten (born 1928), son of Richard McCarten (1908–75) and from Sheila Cartwright, daughter of Johnny Blain and granddaughter of Frances McCarten, née Blain.

Garston Historical Society supplied most of the photographs of Garston buildings and events.

Dave Thompson, a Runcorn historian, donated photographs

5

of the Runcorn-Widnes Transporter Bridge, and the technical information about the bridge.

The Youth Hostel Association archivists, Mr Martin and Jo Ferguson, very helpfully provided photographs and information about specific YHA hostels.

Most of the family photographs, including Alf Smith's studio photographs, are from the Smith family archive that was started by Alf Smith and continued by the author.

Sketches are by Harry Smith. My thanks go to Wendy Lewis and Tad Davies for their cartoons.

Special thanks go to Margaret and Bernard Brett and Barbara Price of Garston Historical Society. The following articles from GHS archives were also used: (1) 'Industrial development from the 18th century'; (2) 'The Blackburn's and the Norris's'; (3) 'Landmine in Garston Gasworks'. (This information came from Jimmy (surname unknown) in the society archives, and my brother Richard Smith.)

I am also grateful to Rachel Rich of the Liverpool schools' website, Mike Royden (for medieval landscape of Liverpool, monastic lands), Revd J.M. Swift (for Garston and its church), Mike Axworthy (for Garston riots), the archivist from Speke Hall (National Trust), Garston public library and the archivists of Liverpool Record Office and Liverpool Central Library.

I was particularly grateful to the steward of Rushill Social Club, near Ledbury, Herefordshire. The club was adjacent to the YHA hostel in 1953, where the family stayed en route to the Coronation. His stewardship of the club included that period. He showed me around the building that had been the hostel. The information he gave me on agriculture, particularly the road I would have taken to see red soil and a man using a single plough, was invaluable. One of the sheds outside still bore the word 'Bikes' in flaked white paint. I wish to take this opportunity to congratulate him for winning a ploughing competition in Hale, Merseyside.

Youth hostels were in isolated places. I would not have been able to revisit them without the help of my brother, Richard, who acted as my chauffeur. He was also a mine of information, particularly on horticultural and agricultural matters. Amongst his other great gifts he had a phenomenal memory. He knew the names of every teacher who had ever taught him. Poetry was a great love and he knew at least twenty to thirty poems by heart.

It would be remiss of me not to mention Google but it would be impossible to name any specific source as I dipped into it so often for information and clarification.

The author has not knowingly failed to thank anybody who has contributed towards this publication or knowingly used copyright material. She apologises for any omissions.

Once more the author wishes to thank her sister-in-law, nephews and nieces, and all their children, grandchildren and great-grandchildren. Without their continual encouragement this book would not have been written.

Joan Thomas and Gill Court deserve their places in the galaxy for volunteering to proofread the book. They carefully read through the book pointing out grammatical errors, spelling mistakes and repetition of the same stories.

Beatrice Smith
November 2015

Contents

INTRODUCTION

A brief history of Garston

IN 1811 GARSTON was a sleepy fishing village of 597 inhabitants. Most of the fishermen and their families lived on an island in the Mersey river while the rest of the population lived in St Mary's Road, known as 'The Village'.

The Mersey teemed with fish. There was such an abundance that the surplus was fed to the pigs and used as manure. Even in 1793 there were forty-four kinds of fish, including salmon and sturgeon.

In the 1790s the Blackburn brothers built a salt refinery for salt from Cheshire. The Blackburn family had been landowners in Garston since the 14th century. In the 1950s they still owned a metallurgical works near the corner of King Street, Banks Road and Church Road, where the corn mill had once stood. Two tidal docks were built. One was called the Salt Dock and the other the Rock Salt dock. Blackburn House, the Liverpool townhouse of the Blackburn family became a girls' grammar school in the 19th century.

The really dramatic change in Garston came with the building in 1850/51 of the first enclosed dock by the St Helen's Canal and Railway Company.

The population had risen to 2,756 by 1861, but Mr Sam Tickle still described it as a small fishing village surrounded by farms.

Forty years later the industrial revolution had changed the village beyond recognition. A railway company had filled up the shore between the island and the mainland and built a seawall. Within a few years the island was lost beneath three docks and eight miles of rail tracks.

When was the name Garston first recorded, and what did the name mean?

The two most popular explanations of the name come from Old English. The first is Gaerstun, meaning meadow or grazing farm, while the second is Grestan, meaning great or big stone. The mainland was a grassy area where sheep grazed, while the island was said to have had a large stone at one end that resembled a whale. The stone prevented erosion of the island.

The earliest mention of Gerston was in 1094, shortly after the Norman Conquest. It appears in *Oxford Dictionary of Place Names*.

The first vicar of Garston was Henry, who was a parson in 1225. The church is referred to by one authority as St Winifred's and by another as St Michael's. A possible explanation is that St Michael's was the church while St Winifred's was a chapel which stood at the south side of the church. St Michael's stands on a sandstone cliff. In the Middle Ages it was a popular custom to give the name St Michael to churches built on cliffs near the sea, as in St Michael's Mount, Cornwall, and Mont St Michel in Normandy. Throughout the centuries it was a landmark for sailors. Today's church is a landmark for aeroplanes.

In 1264, when Henry III had been reigning for forty-eight years, and Adam was Lord of the Manor of Gerstan, a brook flowed down towards the Mersey, close to present-day Church Road. The corn mill and dam were near King Street, where Banks Road and Church Road now meet King Street to form a corner. During recent rebuilding of the area, the mill was excavated and carefully examined and photographed by archaeologists.

Adam also had a fulling (woollen) mill, somewhere between the bottom of St Mary's Road (The Village) and Horrocks Avenue. In the 1940s there was a brook running parallel to Speke Road between Horrocks Avenue and Vineyard Street in a green area called 'The Willows'. This brook possibly came from where the woollen mill once stood. It is thought that this was probably the first woollen mill in Lancashire.

In 1264 Adam, Lord of Gerstan, gave Garston to the Benedictine monks at the Priory of St Thomas the Martyr in Upholland. They never built a monastery in Garston. Tithes (taxes) were collected for the priory from tenant farmers at Grange Farm, Garston Hall, from the corn mill, the woollen mill and the fishery.

In 1334 a Benedictine monk, William of Doncaster, was sent to live in Garston Hall by the monks of the Upholland priory because he had been causing dissention amongst them. The monks were commanded by the bishop to recall William. The bishop threatened to excommunicate all of them if they refused.

In the reign of Henry VIII the monasteries were suppressed. The priory of St Thomas the Martyr in Upholland, one of the smaller establishments, went in the first wave in 1536/7.

The Cistercian Stanlaw Abbey on the Wirral peninsula also owned land in Garston before the monasteries were suppressed.

After the dissolution Garston became the property of the Duchy of Lancaster; then it was owned by the bishops of Chester. It was then leased to the Anderton family and the Gerard family. Both families appear to have followed the Roman Catholic religion. There were two other families whose name crop up often in the story of Garston and her borders. In 1265, Adam de Gerstan had a dispute with Alan le Norreys regarding fishing rights in the pool in Garston. The home of the Norrises of Speke was Speke Hall,[1] a timber and wattle building, now in the care of the National Trust. Robert de Blackburn, who died in 1332, held parcels of land in the area for forty years and acquired the fishery in Garston from Simon, son of John de Garston.

Although the village was no longer owned by the Benedictine priory, life for the villagers doesn't appear to have altered.

Through the violent swings from Roman Catholicism to Protestantism and back again during the Tudors, then the Civil War during the Stuarts, followed by the Commonwealth, then back to the Stuarts, and on through the rise of the middle-class tradesmen and the Whigs at the start of the Industrial Revolution, the people of Garston continued to fish and farm, to mill the corn, tan the hides into leather and prepare the wool for making cloth.

Within three decades, at the end of the 19th century, Garston changed from a rural idyll into an industrial town that rivalled Liverpool in the coal exporting trade. Trade increased so rapidly that by 1867 the North Dock had to be built and eventually, in 1909, the much larger Stalbridge Dock. In 1902 the ancient village had been swallowed up (incorporated) into Liverpool and her history forgotten.

Francis Morton Iron Works,[2] established in 1880, made and exported pre-fabricated iron and corrugated buildings all over the world. They made everything from stations and schools to the Liverpool overhead railway.

Joseph Rawlings and Sons Ltd[3] started in Garston in 1900. They built most of the railway stations on the north Wales line and those from Edge Hill to Speke.

Shipbuilding developed alongside the first dock in the 18th century. Then came Garston Iron and Steel Company, and the copper works owned by John Bibby and Sons. They made copper sheets for covering the hulls of sailing ships. Later, they made copper parts for trains and then for steamships. Garston Tanning Company (1899) replaced the 13th-century tanning works. Bibby's copper works moved to Seacombe and the site was sold to Mersey Docks and Harbour Board.

Another copper works, the Crown Copper Mills,[4] developed on the opposite side of Window Lane and was opened in 1880 by two sons of the manager of the Bibby Copper Works. Their produce went to China, India, Australia, South America, South Africa, Egypt, and other eastern countries. Many of their workers came from Swansea in south Wales. ICI bought out

14

the Crown Copper Works in 1933 and closed the factory to stop the competition.

Wilson Brothers Bobbin Company Ltd (1893) was the largest bobbin and shuttle manufacturer in the world at the peak of their production. They had a fleet of schooners to bring the specialised timber in from all over the world and take bobbins and shuttles across the globe wherever they were required for the cotton industry.

Elders and Fyffes, the banana importers, moved from Manchester to Garston in 1912. At their peak Elders and Fyffes had twenty-two ships and were handling 12,000 bunches of bananas a year. In 1965 they moved to Southampton.

Matches had been manufactured in Garston since about 1887, first by Bell and Company who were taken over by Maguire, Paterson and Palmer in 1919. They built a new factory on the American daylight factory model. It is a Grade II listed building, designed by the architect Sven Bylander. Bryant and May took over in 1922. The factory closed in 1994. It is now the administrative office of the Speke-Garston Development Company.

Garston Gasworks[5] (1892) has one of the largest gas holders in the country with a capacity of four million cubic feet. It is now a major distributor of North Sea gas for south Liverpool.

A vineyard appears an unlikely business in 19th-century Garston but a Mr Meredith had a thriving business. He is remembered in two attractive rows of railway cottages, Meredith Street and Vineyard Street, on the opposite side of Speke Road to Bryant and May.

From 1884 to 1902 the only hospital Garston possessed was a portion of a building above a shop. It had six beds. A number of local doctors had been holding meetings to discuss how they could raise money for a purpose-built hospital.

In 1906, James Wilson, a grocer, left £5,000 in his will for the maintenance of the proposed new accident and emergency hospital.

Alfred Lewis Jones,[6] ship owner, who had a monopoly on

the Congo-Antwerp mail traffic and considerable territorial interests in the Congo, left £10,000 for maintenance of the proposed hospital. The 'gift' from Alfred Lewis Jones was conditional upon the hospital being named the Alfred Jones Memorial Hospital. This gave the impression that his donation paid for the building, which it didn't. Alfred Lewis Jones is remembered today for the part he played in subjugating the people of the Congo.

Liverpool Corporation was reluctant to make a contribution for the hospital building.

The working people of Garston raised £2,000 for the building. Eventually Parliament donated £7,500. The foundation stone was laid in 1914. Two years later, in 1916, the new hospital was opened.

The period 1911 to 1912 was one of industrial turmoil. Throughout Britain workers were organising themselves into unions. Dockers, railway workers and miners were demanding better pay and working conditions.

'You need not attach great importance to the rioting in Liverpool last night,' said one Winston Churchill in 1911. 'It took place in an area were disorder is a chronic feature.'

There were 2,000 workers in Wilson's bobbin factory. They started work at 6am. The work was sometimes dangerous. Men were on low pay even by 1912 standards, but it was even lower for the women.

Management refused to negotiate with the leaders of the five unions. The Council of Trades in the shuttle and bobbin turning industry called a strike.

The strike began on 4 May 1912 and lasted fifteen weeks. This was remarkable, as the alternative to accepting pay and conditions was the workhouse.

The Garston carters and dockers supported the strike by refusing to carry any cargo to or from Wilson's bobbin works.

Office staff and other none-manual workers, such as the matron, were not unionised and didn't support the strike. There were some none-unionised tradesmen and other manual workers. The management brought in casual workers (scabs or blacklegs) from outside Garston, particularly from The Dingle.

There were angry scenes when the scab workers were escorted by the police to the trams going back to The Dingle when they had finished work each day. Large crowds would gather to follow them. The police would charge into the crowd with batons.[7]

According to the *Liverpool Echo*, 'A large crowd made a hostile demonstration and charged the police batons with their heads.' Amongst those who attacked the police batons was a seven-month-old baby.

The majority of the Garston population supported the strikers. They also had financial support from the other trades unions from Liverpool and nationwide.

The Garston women set up a distress fund. Contributions and donations came from local shops, public houses and factories. Many individuals also made donations.

After three months both sides agreed to submit to binding arbitration. It was agreed on 17 August 1912 that all those who had been on strike would be reinstated.

Councillor W.A. Robinson was the first Labour councillor for Garston on Liverpool City Council. Later he became the leader of the Labour Group.[8]

According to folklore Winston Churchill visited Garston with his wife and children during the depression of the 1930s. They were in an open carriage. The women wore the latest 1930s fashion while Winston and his son Randolph wore morning dress including top hats. They were pelted with rotten fruit. The few tomatoes the people possessed were too precious to waste.

After the 1918 Reform Act most men had the vote. By 1928 women also had the vote. Despite this, the Liverpool electorate, who were predominantly working-class, kept Conservatives in power until the late 1950s.[9]

For many years Garston ward, and its successor, St Mary's

ward, were marginal seats, swinging each election between the Labour Party and Conservative Party candidates. Most of the electorate were artisans or manual workers up until the 1950s. The bobbin works strike split the community. It appeared that many of those who voted Conservative had been strike breakers during the bobbin works strike, or were the children of strike breakers. For the naïve it was surprising how many members of Banks Road Methodist chapel were Conservatives. The matron from the bobbin works turned up at a social event in the 1970s. There were notable exceptions, i.e. Frank Mason and Arthur Goodall, both exemplary trade unionists.

Alfred Smith came from Ainsdale to Garston during the bobbin works strike of 1912, when he was ten years old. In 1925, when he was working in Crown Copper Works, he married Martha McCarten from The Dingle. They started their family life in The Dingle. With changing fortunes, the 1930s depression, self-employment followed by unemployment, they moved between Garston and The Dingle for over a decade before settling in Garston in the late 1930s.

By the time Beaty was born in 1937, the history of Alfred and Martha Smith had become interwoven with the history of Garston.

---

1   Martha Smith (née McCarten) told a vivid story of Miss Watt, the last owner of Speke Hall, walking down St Mary Street with a horsewhip in hand. 'The villagers jumped off the pavement to let her pass and the men doffed their caps.' Martha didn't meet Alf until 1923. Miss Watt died in 1921. This story must be hearsay.

2   Alf Smith worked in Francis Morton ironworks in 1916 at fourteen years of age, starting at six in the morning and working at least twelve hours a day. It is said that during his fourteenth year, prior to working at Morton's, he went to sea as a merchant seaman. This might not be correct. Another version of the story is that he was doing some work on a ship in Garston docks when the ship sailed out of the harbour. He asked where it was going and was told Buenos Aires. It went into one of the Liverpool docks. A year or two later he was a merchant seaman on a ship to South America. There was a violent storm during the return voyage.

[3]   Alf Smith told his children that Joseph Rawlings used to ride a wooden bicycle, sometimes called a hobbyhorse, without pedals. Perhaps he made it and rode it for fun on one occasion.

[4]   Alf Smith worked in the Crown copper works in the 1920s. He became interested in the Welsh language and attempted to master it, but without success.

[5]   A bomb landed on the gas holder on 29th November 1940. Six thousand people were evacuated. Eight of the workers were given awards for bravery. Lieutenant Newgass RNVR was awarded the George Cross.

[6]   Alfred Jones Memorial. See *King Leopold's Ghost*; Elder Dempster, a Liverpool shipping firm. Also, Edmund Dene Morel (1873–1924), whistleblower and founder of the Congo Reform Association.

[7]   Martha Smith (née McCarten) told the story of Winston Churchill coming to Garston wearing a top hat during the depression of the 1930s. Randolph Churchill would have been 21 years old in 1932. Winston Churchill was blamed for causing the General Strike of 1926, when, as Chancellor of the Exchequer in 1925, he returned Britain to the Gold Standard. He did this on the advice of experts in economics. The coal owners cut the pay of the miners because the profits from coal went down, which led to the General Strike. In 1932 Churchill admitted in parliament that he had been ill advised.

[8]   In the summer of 1912, when the bobbin works strike was at its height, Alf Smith, aged ten, moved from the quiet village of Ainsdale, near Southport, to the home of his Uncle Harry in Garston. His uncle, who was a bread roundsman and drove a horse and bread van around the village, was not directly affected by the strike. Alf remembers the friction between Roman Catholics and the Orange Lodge very clearly. He appears to have been unaware of the strike.

[9]   In the 1980s Martha Smith broke off her holiday with her daughters, who were living in Wales, to return to Garston. There was a council election. Postal votes were not available at that time except in dire circumstances. She remembered the struggle of the suffragettes to get the vote for women. In particular the image of Emily Wilding Davison being trampled by the king's horse lived in her memory. Nothing was more important than going to cast her vote.

1

Gasmasks and Garston, 1937–45

ON THE DAY I was born four chicks hatched and Evelyn brought them in for Mam to see. Minutes later my plump maternal grandmother arrived from The Dingle. The July sun filtered through the lace curtains of the terraced house. It was summer 1937. 'How did it go?' she said smiling tenderly at me as she drew a chair to the bedside.

'They've only just hatched, but they all look fine. Aren't they a pretty yellow,' answered my mother holding out one of the fluffy chicks nestling in her eiderdown.

'Jesus, Mary and Joseph, I'm asking about the baby.'

When I was about nine months old Mam found work as a maid in the Isle of Man for a season. Dad and the older girls looked after me. When Mam saw all the shoes outside the rooms of the guests each night she decided that they weren't allowed to wear them inside. It was a few days before she discovered she was expected to clean them.

A family of five teenage girls and their mother and father came to stay for two weeks. The girls wore pretty, fashionable dresses. They never went anywhere from the time of their arrival until they went home. It soon became clear to Mam that they were as poor as church mice. They weren't the class that used buses and they had no car. They were very careful not to crush or snag their clothes if they sat on benches or deckchairs in the garden. Mam wondered if the clothes were made on a sewing machine at home, out of sight of the housemaid.

When I was two, my brothers (redhead Tom, six, and fair Richard, five) bounced me on a blanket between them as they skipped along the sea wall and grassy headland overlooking the Mersey. I laughed with joy tinged with terror, holding tightly on to the blanket. As they gambolled along they were singing 'My name is McManara. I'm the leader of the band.'

We had spent the day by the Mersey and the family surrounded me, their precious baby girl, as we made our way back to Garston. The sun glistened on the brown river, the mud banks and the multicoloured glass from the bottle works.

We lived in a six-roomed terraced house in an area known locally as 'Under the Bridge'. The crowded streets, some with only two rooms upstairs and two downstairs, were hemmed in by the river with docks and factories, the gasworks with gas tanks that towered above St Michael's parish church and churchyard, the Bryant and May matchworks, the Roman Catholic church and school, the aerodrome with a barn converted into an aircraft hangar and, of course, the railway bridge spanning the road from the sandstone outcrop known as Spion Cop to the docks. The bridge was the demarcation line between our community and the rest of the world.

I was two years old and the fourth girl in the family. Dolly was thirteen, solidly built with an unruly mop of fair, wavy hair. When I grew up I was her image but didn't have her personality. Her abrasive tongue lashed teachers who tried to put her down. Dad received his share of it too when she grew older. She was a second mother to us and the responsible eldest while I was, and always will be, one of the spoilt little ones.

Cousin Mary recently described our hair as strawberry blonde. She had always been envious of it. It would have made a great difference to my self-esteem had she told me when I was young. I always thought of it as light mouse. Nine-year-old Evelyn had a head of gleaming red curls. She was round and comfortable like our maternal grandmother rather than solid.

Eleven-year-old Freda looked totally different from the other sisters. Slim built with straight black hair, fair complexion, rosy cheeks and blue eyes, she was once dressed as an Irish colleen for a float in Garston carnival and hated every minute of it. She has never liked to draw attention to herself. The village gossips were convinced she was the eldest child and of dubious parentage, while she thought she had been found on the doorstep and adopted by my parents. She waited anxiously during each pregnancy, hoping mother would produce another dark-haired Celt.

There were six chapels dotted around St Mary's Road for the Welsh-speaking residents of Garston. One of the chapels ran a Sunday school 'Under the Bridge' for some years but it folded for lack of congregation. An independent Baptist minister hired it from them. It was named Bethel.

The minister attracted people to his chapel with concerts and a soup kitchen. Dad was in a high state of excitement on the evening that a well-known pianist was performing.

'When he plays the piano talks,' he enthused.

Banks Road County Primary School playground about 1940. Dorothy, aged 14, centre right; Freda, aged 12, centre left; Richard, aged 6, Beaty aged 3. Evelyn, aged 10, and Tom, aged 8, were also there.

Bethel, Canterbury Street

Freda couldn't rest until he came home. Hearing his footsteps on the street she rushed out of the house to meet him.

'Dad, the piano,' she said breathlessly. 'Did it talk tonight? What did it say?'

She began her own love affair with music in the Liverpool Philharmonic Hall. In her seventies she travelled to Saint Petersburg year after year to the Mariinski Theatre to watch Valery Gergiev conduct.

When Dad heard about the soup kitchen in Bethel he was delighted. There were five children, and I was due in the summer. Mam wouldn't take soup from the chapel unless Dad joined the congregation with her. Nothing he said would move her. With great reluctance he began attending the Sunday evening services.

Dad had been raised in the Church of England and attended a Anglican church school until he was fourteen. He said with pride that school taught him how to learn. He drifted away from the church and by the time the two eldest girls were school age he had taken a stand against the Church of England. Dad wouldn't allow the children to go to the church school across the road. Mam had to walk a mile with them to the county primary school each day. During the depression of the 1930s his greengrocery business failed and then his ice cream business collapsed. He collected scrap iron on Garston shore and signed on at the unemployment exchange to receive his dole.

He heard Christianity presented in a new way by the Baptist preacher. He was won over and became a committed Christian for life.

On Sundays the congregation paraded through the streets 'Under the Bridge' to attract more people to the chapel. Three-year-old Richard marched along, swinging his arms as he joined in the singing.

> We're marching to Zion,
> Beautiful, beautiful Zion;
> We're marching upward to Zion,
> The beautiful city of God.

On Monday morning Dad went to sign on at the labour exchange. He carried Richard on his shoulders. All the way Richard sang lustily:

> We're marching to sign on,
> Beautiful, beautiful sign on;
> We're on our way to sign on
> The beautiful city of God.

Imagine Richard's disappointment when they arrived at a redbrick Victorian building, entered a yellow ochre room, and joined a queue of unemployed men. This wasn't how he had pictured the beautiful city of God.

The council re-housed the family in a new block of tenements in 1939, soon after my blanket ride. It was a fortunate move for us, but not for the new occupants of number 5 Saunby Street. The Second World War started on 1 September 1939. The house where I had been born was almost obliterated by

German bombs during an attack on the docks. One wallpapered wall stood alone amongst the rubble.

The front door of the flat opened on to a wide hallway of cardinal red tiles that continued into the bathroom and kitchen, making it easy to keep clean. The walls were painted cream. Windows were everywhere, filling our home with light.

In the hall there was a picture of Jesus holding a lantern and knocking at a door. The verse beside it was by M. Louise Haskins: 'And I said to the man that stood at the gate of the year: Give me a light.'

Fifteen years later it became the target of our silly teenage jokes; 'I've run out of matches' or 'Sorry mate, I don't smoke.' But never within earshot of Mam or Dad.

In the living room was a large sepia picture of Ruth and Naomi with the caption 'Beseech me not to leave thee'.

Dad was a pacifist, so he signed up for the Auxiliary Fire Service in 1938 in preference to being conscripted into the armed forces. On his first day he forgot his helmet and Freda had to run after him. He was stationed at a temporary fire station, close to the bobbin works and bottle works near Garston shore.

Dad was earning a wage again. He bought a tent for our family expeditions along the shore. We would stay throughout the school holidays except for Sunday when we returned to the house so that the children could attend Sunday school at the Methodist chapel, next to the county school, in the afternoon, and Bethel in the evening with Mam and Dad.

Playing waist deep in the water one day I took a step and found the river over my head. I thrashed about trying to find the sandbank without success. Each time I came up I shouted and waved but Mam and Dad thought I was playing and waved back. Everything went into slow motion as I watched the seaweed and thought about my seven years of life passing before me.

Tom was an excellent swimmer. He could swim a full length of the swimming pool underwater. He realised I was not waving

Speke Road Gardens

Garston shore, 1948. Alf and Martha pretending to be in deep water. Harry, aged 9, standing behind them.

but drowning and came to my rescue. I don't remember Mam and Dad coming to comfort me or showing any concern. Perhaps they did come to me and I have forgotten or maybe they were unaware that I had nearly drowned. Tom might not have told them they almost lost a daughter.

Sometimes Freda and Tom would become so involved in the games they were playing on their way to Sunday school that they would arrive too late to go into the junior hall unnoticed. The first time this happened they returned to the swing park to continue their games. They had a problem. What were they going to do with their pennies for the Sunday school collection? They bought a cigarette. The next time they were late they thought of buying a cigarette but decided there was no pleasure in spending the money. They had suffered pangs of conscience. The money was for God. Opening the door to the hall they threw their pennies in and ran away.

The sun shone endlessly throughout those summer days as we played in the shade of the trees or ran across the glutinous sucking mud to cool in the river. Rain was so unusual that we all remember the storm. The deluge drenched everything. Food was ruined, clothes and blankets were saturated. Fortunately, Dad was with us and had weathered more than one storm as a merchant seaman. Mam and Evelyn took the soaking babies

Banks Road Methodist Church and church hall

home while he organised the rest of the dripping band. They wrung the water from bedding and jumpers to make them lighter to carry. Tinned food, jars and cooking utensils were hidden until they could be collected later. Dad tied small bundles to their backs. The soggy tent, pegs, groundsheet and poles were packed with difficulty into the tent bag. He had the strength of an ox. He carried the tent and all the rest of the gear. The bedraggled dripping crew sang 'Onward Christian Soldiers' and other marching hymns to keep up their spirits on the two-mile trek back to Garston.

Bethel was a homely little chapel. Heating was from two coal fires on each side of church. Dad asked permission to dry the tent in the raised area between the altar rail and the pulpit. The following Sunday we all winked and nudged each other when the hymn was announced 'We pitched our tent in Bethel'.

In the living room of the flat, sitting on my mother's lap, I heard pacifism debated for the first time.

'If your wife and children were being attacked here in your kitchen you would fight tooth and nail to defend them,' Charlie Winkles said. He was Dad's best friend and best man at his wedding.

'Fighting never solved anything,' Dad replied.

Mam muttered in an undertone to Mrs Winkles, 'He would fight.'

She was right. He was talking about principles, theories and world politics. In a personal situation he would react aggressively if he or his loved ones were under threat.

Putting out fires on burning ships in the docks, in the homes of the Liverpool community and in factories was no easy option. From neighbours we heard about the fire in the Tate and Lyle sugar warehouse, where the firemen had to walk through molten syrup to rescue people. The family heard nothing from Dad of his war. Others in the community told us of his quiet bravery and physical strength in terrifying situations. Throughout his life he never talked about work when he came

28

home. He often hated what he was doing, hated the routine, the restrictions having to kowtow to those over him but he bit the bullet.

Mam was giving us dinner (the midday meal in the north of England) when the announcement was made on the radio: 'We are at war with Germany.'

'Has your Dad got his axe? Did he remember his helmet?' said Mam.

'The war will be over before we have our pudding,' grumbled five-year-old Richard. Food was always his first priority. At fifteen he wanted to join the Merchant Navy as a trainee cook, in hope of satisfying his hunger, but Dad wouldn't sign for him to go. Four years later he found himself working in the canteen of an Australian army barracks. It wasn't by choice. He was on washing up fatigues, endlessly. Looking smart in uniform or obeying rules weren't his strongest points. Whether he had access to extra food during this punishment was never revealed, but it was his good fortune that his unit went to Korea without him.

Mam said that if he fell in the river he would come up with a pocket full of fish.

On Halloween Mam was in labour and the ambulance arrived to take her to hospital. Our flat was on the first floor. As she was carried into the ambulance Freda shouted to her over the balcony, 'How many ducking apples should I buy.'

After more than two years as the baby of the family I lost my special position to Harry. All the girls in the family were born at home while the boys were born in hospital. This was added to my store of knowledge of how the world worked. Girls are born at home but boys in hospital is on a par with the statement by my godson, that women can't pee because they don't have a penis. Both theories appear rational but don't stand up to vigorous tests.

Evelyn pushed me three miles from Garston to The Dingle in the family pram, to stay with Mam's best friend, while Mam was in hospital. It is one of my earliest memories.

Pram Ride

Feathered deep in cushions
Framed in steel and split cloth
Caught, in snapshot glimpses,
Was the road that's gone.

Smiled back, as my sister
Sent me off, free wheeling,
Spun a space between us
Room to trust, and fear.

Grey stone, net drawn houses
Taller than the dock cranes
Solid as our mother
Marshalled the wide street
down to the river.

War was a normal part of life when I was a child. I had no concept of life without war. As I played with my friends on the grass embankment near the tenements we watched wingless aeroplanes, chained together in groups of half a dozen, being pulled to the airport by lorries. In the school playground we formed into two lines, German and English. The lines would dance towards each other, alternately singing:

Are you ready for a fight, for a fight, for a fight
Are you ready for a fight
We are the Germans.

(And finally, jumping with both legs together, arms stiffly at their side, and both eyes closed they sang:)

Now we've got no legs at all, legs at all, legs at all.
Now we've got no legs at all.
We are the English.

Early in 1942 sixteen-year-old Dolly was a trainee dressmaker. Dad didn't want the girls to work in factories. He was afraid of the kind of people they would mix with. But he wouldn't let

Freda work in an office because she might get above herself. She trained as a confectioner. Later Evelyn followed Dorothy into the rag trade.

Mam was blind in one eye. When she was about six months into her pregnancy with Dianne she became totally blind for a short time.

Eight-year-old Richard became her guide, leading her everywhere.

One day he had been particularly attentive and had taken her from shop to shop in St Mary's Road, which everyone in Garston called 'The Village'. Mam rewarded him by giving him two pennies. Delighted, he let go of her hand and ran into a cake shop. She walked into a bus-stop post.

About this time Dad decided to have a talk with Dolly. He was concerned that she was reaching an age when she might take up seriously with a young man (as he would have delicately put it). In the course of this conversation he told her that she must be absolutely certain that she loved a man before she married him.

'I am speaking from my own experience,' he told her gravely. 'I didn't love your mother.'

Mam heard every word of this conversation. If he wasn't out fire fighting that night he probably slept on the sofa. There were no more pregnancies.

When Dianne was born she had no hand-me-downs. She had a complete layette. Out went the battered old pram with the ripped hood to be replaced by a classic carriage. In came a beautiful cot with brightly coloured nursery rhymes to the delight of Harry and me. It was adorned with a pink coverlet. At two she had the latest coat and matching red hat that was beyond my wildest dreams. I was never envious of her. I loved to see her beautiful clothes.

For the rest of his life Dad tried to mollify Mam with kindness and with gifts, tokens of his love. Gradually she allowed him back but he had to watch his step.

A woman is obliged to have sex with her husband, she

would have said. As a child she opposed much that she was taught or observed in the Roman Catholic Church and rejected it completely when she married my father, a nominal Anglican, but duty had been instilled into her. Her cousin had not consummated her marriage until weeks after her wedding. This cousin was totally unaware that the sexual act was a normal part of marriage and came to Mam for advice. She thought her new husband had turned into a brute.

'I told her that having sex was her duty,' Mam said. 'If she didn't he would go to another woman.'

Lie back and think of England.

Mam didn't relate this story in front of four-year-old Beaty. Even when I reached thirty she said I shouldn't know about sex or contraceptives because I wasn't married.

In her eighties she giggled when telling Dianne: 'I always knew what was coming if Dad brought me Toblerone.'

Neither Mam nor Dad ever hugged or kissed us. They found physical expressions of affection embarrassing. They passed this reticence onto us and we have had to unlearn this crippling social behaviour. We started by hugging the nephews, nieces and grandchildren. Gradually we have learned to hug and kiss each other. Mam would have liked a hug – she needed hugging often – but there was a steel fence all around her and she couldn't take it away. She used to comb my hair, putting it in rags to make ringlets. This gave her an excuse to make physical contact with me.

As the air-raid siren was blaring Mam would be taking out the rags and curling my hair around her finger. Dianne and I would be dressed in pretty calico nightdresses before going down to the shelter. The nightdresses were taken off as soon as we were back in the house. They weren't for sleeping in.

In the shelter the residents were partying. An accordion would be playing and people were singing, flirting, smoking and dancing. They were probably drinking too but we were God-fearing folk who knew nothing of such matters. Mam and Dad didn't smoke, drink or swear. She gathered us to her, as far away from this frivolity as possible. We would have loved to be a part of it. Harry always associated the sound of the air-raid siren with comfort. It was the only time Mam sat him on her knee and he was allowed to cuddle her. Whenever he heard factory sirens or ships sounding their horns in the fog or to celebrate a New Year he was filled with a warm glow.

Gasmasks were carried with us to school. Older children had hideous black ones but Harry's and Dianne's looked like Mickey Mouse. They were suffocating and smelt of rubber.

I said Dad didn't swear. When angry he would shout 'Damn and blast.' Under extreme provocation it would be 'Hells fire and damnation.' That was usually reserved for street vendors peddling their wares in the street when he was working nights.

My best friends and most constant companions were my brothers and sisters but, as I played on the landings and stairwell in the tenements, I also made friends of my own age. I learned to join in when the group showed intolerance to children who were different. The difference we wouldn't tolerate was a Standard English accent. There was a boy in the tenements who lived with his aunt. In Liverpool this is pronounced 'Ant' as in the insect. His unforgivable error was to call her 'Aarnty'. Another boy was nicknamed Green Graarse throughout his schooldays because he sang 'and the green graarse grew all around, all around, and the green graarse grew all around.' Though we couldn't put a name to it, this was class war.

The unpardonable sin in Garston was to get above your station and put on airs and graces. Fifty years later I met a woman who had been brought up with one working-class parent and one middle class. Her Standard English accent had caused her confusion and pain throughout her life. At about the same time as I met her I met two native Welsh speakers cursed with this same social impediment. Other Welsh-speaking friends told me that when these women with cut-glass English accents were speaking Welsh their personalities came across as warm and friendly. Later in life I shed one of the notions learned in childhood or, rather, I began to question it.

The Garston community, including young children were sympathetic to people with physical deformities such as rickets, which was not uncommon. Dirty houses or lack of personal hygiene were the subject of gossip so I sensed that my mother looked down on one swearing, dirty girl I befriended, but she didn't say anything. Snobs, on the other hand, were teased until they modified their behaviour to the social norm.

The hair of my friend Annie was crawling with lice, but so was mine. Hers were easier to see because she had black hair. Saturday night was bath night. After having our hair washed we would kneel over a stool covered in newspaper while Mam combed out the head lice with a fine-tooth comb. The lice would be killed by squashing them between thumbnails. This practice didn't appear to have any effect, as the family left their classes every week to go to the school clinic and be treated by the nit nurse.

I had seen ballet and tap dancing at a concert in Bethel. Dad's favourite programme on the wireless was *Friday Night is Music Night* with the Palm Court Orchestra. Hearing classical music on the radio I danced joyfully around the living room. My brothers rolled on the floor laughing. They said I was a fairy elephant.

That could have been the end of my dancing career but my friend Annie told me we could go for dancing lessons.

'It costs five shillings,' she told me. 'Ask you Mam for the money and I'll take you.'

Gullible, I ran to Mam brimming with excitement.

She dismissed my request without any discussion and I returned to Annie empty-handed.

Not prepared to accept that her ruse hadn't worked Annie said 'Go back and tell her the teacher charges only half a crown if you dance on one leg.'

We had a wind-up gramophone and Mam bought old gramophone records at the spring and Christmas fairs held in the Methodist church hall. My lack of grace was a source of sadness to me until I heard the song about Wilhemina. I was gratified to learn that being plump didn't mean you were ugly and ungainly.

Wilhelmina is plump and round
Plump and round, plump and round
Jacob and Peter and Fritz and Hans
Ask her permission to put up the banns
All she said is 'Nein, nein, nein
No wedding bells for me'.

I knew when I was four years old that one day my prince would come. He would love me above all others, not in spite of being plump and round but because of it. When, in puberty, I became hirsute as well as ungainly, I was convinced that my prince would see past my outward appearance to my beautiful, intelligent mind.

Beside Annie, the one-legged dancer, another friend in infancy was Margaret, the youngest of three girls. Thelma, the middle girl, was about seven years old. She felt very badly done to by her family. Mam asked her to give an example.

'Mrs Smith, I always get the gooseberries with the hairs on,' she whined.

This entered the Smith family vocabulary, particularly in relation to Richard. He, like Thelma, always got the gooseberries with the hairs on.

Dolly, my eldest sister, would say, 'Here he comes, the voice of spring.'

Dad's brother Tom had joined the army when he was seventeen. In the 1930s he had served on the Khyber Pass in India, in the Sudan and in Egypt.

When he was on the Khyber Pass the army camp was protected by a double barbed wire perimeter fence. He found it incredible and almost admirable that Indians were so insolent and crafty that they were able to sneak up during the night and steal the barbed wire. They put it to many uses including making children's toys. He remained an unrepentant, self-opinionated bigot and defender of the British Empire until the day he died, but he often showed generosity to his brother's family.

Malta was under siege from 1941 when he was there as a sergeant in the Cheshire Regiment. He asked the army to have a photograph taken for him of the family in 1942.

When he came home on leave he married his childhood sweetheart, Mamie. She was a singer held in high regard in the north of England who would have gone far as a performer. She gave it all up to be with the love of her life and live in army quarters. In 1944 she gave birth to Elaine.

Dad isn't in the family photograph. He might have been on duty at the fire station. Beaty is leaning against a drainpipe. Dianne at six months old is in the centre on Mam's knee.

She is holding a golliwog twice her size with a pillar-box red jacket and yellow trousers. Twenty years later golliwogs were politically incorrect. I thought he was wonderful. My dolly and constant companion was 'baldy shivers,' christened by Freda. I thought nothing of the name until talking about her when I was an adult. She was a rag doll with no clothes and most of her hair missing.

Freda told us a saga called *Adam and Eve and the Prehistoric Monster* as our night-time story. This was based around a woollen animal knitted by Dorothy that probably started life as a kangaroo. It was Harry's. The stuffing had gone from the centre due to Harry squeezing it. Mam told us stories from memory, usually *Tom Thumb*. Dad would read to us. He treated books with reverence, holding them carefully and turning the pages as though they were delicate. When we were tiny most of the stories were from *Bread and Butter Tales*. Later we listened in wonder to *The Pilgrim's Progress*. He held the red leather-bound book on his knees. The pictures caught our imagination as he turned the gold-edged pages.

Every night we would kneel beside the bed to say our

The Smith family, 1942, at 57a Speke Road Gardens. The photograph was taken by an armed forces photographer for Alf's brother, Tom. Uncle Tom was a regular soldier, caught up in the siege of Malta. L–R, back row: Evelyn, aged 12; Dorothy, aged 16; Freda, aged 14; paternal grandma Susanna; middle row: Richard, aged 8; Martha, aged 36; Dianne, aged 5 months, with full-size golliwog; Tom, aged 10; front row: Harry, aged 3; Beaty, aged 5.

Evelyn, Dorothy and Freda with paternal grandma Susanna

prayers. Then Dad would say 'Good night and go' bless.' Gob in Liverpudlian is the mouth, as in shut your gob. I thought go' bless was an instruction to stop talking.

One of our usual prayers was 'Gentle Jesus, meek and mild'. When Dianne was about five she asked Dad, 'Where is Plicity?'

'Plicity?' Dad asked. 'I don't think I've ever heard of it.'

'Yes, you have,' she said earnestly. 'You know. The place with the poor mice in the prayer.'

Totally bewildered he asked her to say the prayer for him.

Gentle Jesus, meek and mild,
Look upon a little child;
Pity mice in Plicity
Suffer me to come to Thee.

'Now I understand,' he said seriously. 'I'm sorry to have misled you. I haven't been reciting the words correctly. There are no mice in the prayer. The words are 'Pity my simplicity'.

Although he could be thoughtful and understanding he wasn't sweetness and light by any standard. He had a very loud voice and sudden bursts of temper. I never knew why or when these outbursts would come so lived in constant anticipation.

The wireless was on almost constantly except on Sundays. Often we would sit quietly listening to a programme. Naturally, we regarded news bulletins as an interval, when we took the opportunity to talk. He would go ballistic as he had been waiting for the news.

A short prayer was said before all meals. 'For what we are about to receive, may the Lord make us truly thankful.'

Sunday lunch was a real trial. Dorothy said she always avoided sitting on Dad's right. If his irritation reached boiling point he would strike out with his right arm. What we were about to receive was a tongue-lashing, a thick ear and overboiled cabbage. Harry and I didn't sit during this family meal. We were told it was because we would grow better standing. If Dad was next to me I was too nervous to ask him to pass anything for fear of being told, 'Don't talk with food in your mouth.' When I reached across the table I would knock over whatever was in my path, usually a bottle of milk or the spoon in the sugar bowl. When I graduated to sitting down, 'Take your elbows off the table' was added to the endless catechism.

We were not allowed dessert until every scrap of the main course had been eaten.

'There are thousands dying in the gutters in India and Africa. They are dying of starvation.'

'Let's send this tasteless mess to them,' we would mutter rebelliously under our breath.

I would try to gulp it down without tasting it but one Sunday lunchtime I balked at every mouthful. I had no dessert and was banished to the bedroom, grounded as they say today. Dad said I would be given the food I had left at lunchtime for my tea. If it wasn't eaten then I would have it for breakfast. After a couple of days Mam started bringing milk up to the bedroom. Dad returned to work and I returned to the meal table. After that Mam gave me a minuscule portion of vegetables and Dad either didn't notice or he turned a blind eye to it.

Talking of blind eyes Freda, like Mam, was blind in one eye. Freda always missed what she intended to do by a fraction. When pouring tea she would miss the cup. She heard Dad saying to Mam that she couldn't help it. When he had time to reflect he was empathetic, as I discovered over far more important matters later in life. As a child his unexpected temper tantrums and threats to bring the strap to me were a constant cause of fear and trembling.

Raised by his grandmother and surrounded by grown-up uncles until the age of nine, he was a late Victorian. Spare the rod and spoil the child was deeply embedded in his psyche. The leather strap he used to sharpen his razor hung from a nail in the kitchen.

Shortly after Dianne was born I discovered a new game. Left alone while Mam looked after the new baby, I began climbing on the armchair and jumping off. There was a hammering on the front door. Mam went to open it. She stood open-mouthed with shock as the man who lived below us raved at her. He was working nights.

'Who's making all that bloody noise.'

I stepped in front of her.

'It was me Mr Wibbly,' I said.

He softened immediately. 'You didn't mean it chuck,' he said, patting my head. He went away pacified.

Mam and Dad had always told me to confess if I had done anything. Stand up and be counted. It was a lesson I took with me through life.

Mam liked to take us three babies out for a picnic in the afternoon. The shore was too far as she made a point of being home when the other children returned from school. We used to go over a railway footbridge to the Willows, a path beside the stream which once ran through Garston. We were always thrilled with the idea of a picnic, but I can't imagine what we ate. Mam was no cook or pastry chef, but she made passable apple or jam tarts and rice pudding you would die for. If we had sandwiches they probably had spam in them, gelatine doted with tiny pieces of meat. Bread and milk were our staple diet. Babies were weaned on pobs, lumps of bread in warm milk. As an adult I fed it to patients who were unable to eat solid food. I improved the taste by adding a teaspoon of margarine and

Alf Smith, aged 14, with his maternal grandmother and a baby

sugar. By then I had realised that pobs was an acronym for Pieces of Bread. The family loaves were about half a metre long and we ate three or four a day. We drank six to eight pints of milk.

The stream from the Willows ran under a culvert behind the tenements and ended in a ditch beside our block of flats. There must have been soil around it, for all of the children gathered there to make mud pies. There were large grassed areas between the tenement blocks but we weren't allowed to play on them. Opposite the fire station and airport on the main road to Speke, there was a grass verge. We would lie for hours in the grass, watching ants busily carrying their wares. Many of our schoolteachers came from Wales and returned to the verdant hills during the school holidays. We were amazed when one of these teachers told us that there were places in the world where the people had never seen grass. We saw it through the railings of the airport. Running down the centre of the dual carriageway between the tenements and the Bryant and May matchworks was a grass verge. Mam told us to keep to the path when crossing it. The grass would be ruined if we walked across it.

Many years later I stood looking in horror when a respected member of the community, a county councillor who was a very large man, walked across a grass verge.

'I never walk on grass verges,' I told him. 'It kills the grass and we are left with hard brown soil. There is a path less than two yards away.'

'I'll walk on tiptoes,' he replied, with a twinkle in his eye.

Dorothy was Brown Owl for Speke church Brownie pack and deputy lieutenant of Banks Road Methodist Guides. Tom, Richard and Harry were in St Michael's church Cubs and Scouts.

Church parade in old Speke church stirred the soul. Standard bearers stood to attention as we filed past them in the pews. The whole building reverberated as the organ played 'Onward Christian Soldiers'. The standard bearers processed up the aisle with the Union Jack, St George's flag and the Pack standard. Each was ceremonially handed to the Pack leader to be stood at either side of the altar. The service followed, with stirring hymns like 'Stand up, stand up for Jesus, ye soldiers of the cross'. The church was full to overflowing and everyone, from tots like me to the oldest adult, was singing their heart out.

The service was followed by the parade around the village. Hundreds of Rovers, Rangers, Scouts, Guides, Cubs and Brownies stood ready to march. I was ecstatic as I listened to the bugles blowing, the kettledrums rat-a-tat-tat and the boom of the big bass drum. Three abreast, the lines of troops in their distinctive uniforms with their brightly coloured kerchiefs and following their standard bearer, stretched as far as the eye could see.

The whole community came out to enjoy the spectacle as we marched past.

Regular Brownie nights were thrilling in a totally different way. I would go out with Dorothy into the pitch-dark night. The hundreds of windows of the tenements were blacked out so that German bombers couldn't tell people were living there. The sky was filled with myriad stars that were so bright it was possible to believe you could reach out and catch one. I never saw such clear skies again until I was in Abu Simbel on Lake Nasser sixty years later. The glimmer of the dipped headlights of the double-decker bus would break through the darkness. We would climb into the muggy heat of the bus and Dorothy would join in the chattering going on all around us. She would be in conversation with someone almost before we sat down. The night world we passed was totally different from the one I knew by day. The factories, the fire station, and the airport tower were shadows outlined against the sky. This was lost after the war when squares of light shone from every window in the fire station and the octagonal airport tower windows shone like jewels.

We walked down silent streets. The church steeple stood out

sharply against the black sky. Entering the church hall I was shaken by the contrast as I was hit by a wall of light and noise. We studied many subjects such as knot making and nature. I enjoyed Brownies but my most lasting memory was being allowed to look into a kaleidoscope. It was passed around the group and I had only one turn but I never forgot those iridescent colours which moved me more than any stained glass window I have seen as an adult. Chartres rose window fell into second place behind that kaleidoscope.

Mam had been brought up in Roman Catholicism but had become cynical about the church by her teens. She was scathing about the celibacy of the clergy. They all had women if and when they wanted them she told us. As a child she had been terrified by mortal sins, which she imagined as scabs all over her body. Her mother, who we called Ma, trembled at the sight of the priest coming along the street knocking on doors, demanding money that took food out of the mouths of her children. If she refused to give him the amount he demanded she would spend eternity in purgatory or in limbo.

My maternal grandfather was of Irish Protestant stock and my mother and many of her siblings married Protestants. Mam told a story of being at a funeral wake on a Friday. Roman Catholics were not allowed to eat meat on Fridays. The plate of ham sandwiches being passed around was refused by the Roman Catholics until it came to Mam. Grandma was shocked when Mam took a sandwich and quickly began to eat before it could be taken from her. 'I've got a Protestant stomach,' Mam told Ma.

When Mam brought the two eldest children to visit, Ma became very agitated when she spotted a priest approaching the house.

'Quick, hide in the back room.'
'Why?'
'He'll say you're not married.'
'Then I will take him to court.'

Mam's antipathy to the church didn't extend to her faith in The Lord. She had a firm faith in The Lord and always attended some small Protestant chapel.

Mam sometimes took us out at night to see Ma, and Mam's sister Aunty Nelly. Both of them lived in The Dingle. Ma lived in a first-floor flat, the only one with its own toilet. The other eleven dwellings shared one toilet between them.

When she was a child Mam heard a neighbour shout, 'Take the salt fish out of the bucket Mam. I want to have a pee.'

Ma was a cheerful woman, with fleshy arms who always made us feel welcome. She had a well-worn chaise longue, table and some upright chairs in the room where she appeared to live and sleep. There was nothing else in the room except a parrot. I never heard it say anything. Dorothy, Freda and Evelyn used to stay there when they had been out dancing in Liverpool city centre if it was too late to go home. Sometimes she wasn't at home when we visited and Mam would tell us to wait on the doorstep while she went to fetch her from the public house.

'She goes there for company,' Mam told us. 'She has a drink of lemonade.'

Dad's grandma was a great friend of Ma. Mam met both of them dancing down Mill Street on one occasion when she had gone to visit. Clearly both of them had been on the lemonade. Mam wasn't allowed to tell this story in Dad's hearing. He idolised his grandma. She didn't take any alcohol, except for medicinal purposes.

Martha's mother, Frances McCarten, with her sister, great-aunt Mary, about 1902

I loved Ma. I didn't see her often once I started school. She disappeared from my life when I was ten.

Seeing the ships on the river in the dark was the only pleasure we had from visiting Aunty Nelly. She spent each visit reciting all the woes of the world to Mam. Uncle Joe, a small, skinny, retired merchant seaman sat sullenly silent. We liked their daughters Josie and Mary and enjoyed their visits to our home but they were never at home when we called. They were about the same age as my three eldest sisters and were very close to them until they married and moved away.

My cousin Johnny Blain lost his mother and two aunts in the pandemic of the winter of 1918/19. He was raised by Ma and shared the family home with my Mam, her sister Lily and brother Richard. Johnny remembered Aunty Nelly with great affection. She was very special to him at a time when he desperately needed comfort and love. In the years when Harry, Dianne and I visited, she must have been going through a low period in her life. To have such pleasant children and grandchildren she must have been a sympathetic and kind person.

Dianne started nursery school at two years old and Harry went to primary school. Mam started working at Speke airport as a lavatory attendant and cleaner. She was always spotlessly clean and wore a white, starched overall. The other attendants wore blue overalls.

If Dad was home after a night shift in the Fire Service or on a late shift, he gave us breakfast and was supposed to dress us for school. It was Evelyn's responsibility when he wasn't there. We had porridge and bread and dripping for breakfast. I was expected to wash and dress myself. Sometimes the results were bizarre. I usually wore a liberty bodice under my frock. If I couldn't find one I wore a jumper instead. Knickers were a real problem. If I found a pair they probably belonged to my older sisters and had to be held up by folding them across my stomach and fastening them with a large safety pin. If I couldn't find either knickers or pin, I went without any until I

Mam's mother as I remember her in the 1940s

Martha's sister, Aunty Nelly, and her children, John, Josie and Mary

Aunty Nelly's husband, Uncle Joe Stockton

Mam's sisters Nell and Frances, about 1902

Mam's sister Nell and her son, Tommy Bell

Martha's sister, Miriam or Ann. Both also died in the pandemic of 1918–19

Aunt Frances Blain, mother of Johnny, aged about 20. Died in the influenza pandemic, 1918–19, aged 22

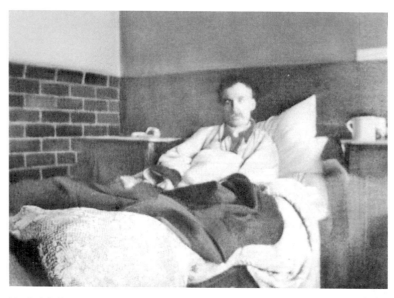

Martha's father, army sergeant Richard McCarten, who died in 1918

Martha's family after the funeral of her three sisters. Centre, grandma Frances McCarten; front left, Martha; back left, Nell; back right, Richard; front right, Lily; c.1918

Johnny Blain, son of Frances Blain, c.1930

was caught bare bottomed one day in school and Evelyn gave me a ticking off for getting her into trouble.

On the rare occasions Dad was responsible for getting Dianne ready for nursery, he didn't know how to do it. She had long, straight hair worn in two plats. Dianne felt quite embarrassed going to school wearing six plats sticking out from her head. After he had given her a bad hair day I asked Evelyn to teach me how to plait hair and I took on the task. Thirty years later she would have been the height of fashion as a Rastafarian.

Evelyn looked after Beaty, Harry and Dianne most of the time during the holidays and stayed off school with us if we were ill as Mam couldn't take time off work. Mam became blind temporarily after Dianne was born so Evelyn stayed off for a few weeks, so the school inspector came knocking.

When our older sisters had left school and started working, there was nobody at home to care for us when Mam was at the airport. We spent our holidays in the airport lounge, which was the height of luxury with honey coloured wood panelling, parquet flooring and thick carpets. As our special treat Mam would buy the *Beano* and *Dandy* from the magazine rack. It was a spacious palace compared to home. We were very well behaved and didn't run about. Eating and drinking were strictly forbidden by Mam as we might spill something. There were very few restrictions imposed by the airport authority. We were able to go to the visitors' balcony and watch the planes take off whenever we wanted a change from the lounge.

Richard took us for a walk to Speke Hall Road when he was nine years old. While he was playing on the wall near the Co-operative milk depot, the wall collapsed and he twisted his ankle and thought he had broken it. He couldn't walk the mile back to the tenements so we had to take Dianne out of the pram and put him in it. I pushed the pram home while four-year-old Harry encouraged the toddler to walk, holding her hand and picking her up each time she fell over and saying 'Upsa daisy'.

Freda spotted us as we arrived outside the tenement block. Richard realised he would be in trouble. On jumping out of the pram he discovered he had suffered little more than a slight strain to his ankle. He ran away before Freda could catch him.

Dad bought a tandem and sidecar when Dianne was a few months old. Harry would sit at the back of the sidecar with the baby between his legs.

Mam and Dad had cycled through the pretty Cheshire village of Frodsham and were heading for Helsby when the tandem parted company with the sidecar. Mounting the pavement, the sidecar disappeared through a gate into a farmer's field. Dropping the tandem, they dashed into the field to find the sidecar stopped beside a caravan. Harry was looking about him with interest, unaware that anything unusual had happened. Dianne was sleeping soundly.

Once Mam and Dad had recovered from the shock, they looked around and realised that they were on a tent and caravan camping site within walking distance of Helsby railway station. The family camped there throughout the school summer holidays for the next four or five years.

We would sit on Allerton station surrounded by packages and parcels containing our home for the next six weeks. There was a marquee, with all of its poles, tent pegs, ropes, groundsheet and flysheet, plus army surplus blankets. Equally important were the Primus stoves for cooking our food and all the attendant pots, pans and cooking utensils. Girls' and boys' bundles of clothes must have been packed separately for easy storage when we arrived. The shoes we were wearing were probably the only ones we possessed but we might have had sandals. A bar of hard soap, about a foot long, and some threadbare towels would have been our toiletries.

I recollect one embarrassing occasion when I was about eight years old. Dad decided to strip me bare in the middle of the camping site field, stand me in a bowl, then lather me all over and wash me. It stands out in my memory so I think it only happened once. There was a stream beside the lane that separated the farm from the campsite. I would sit in it for hours, dreaming while looking at the pebbles, how they changed colour in and out of the water, watching the dragonflies and the tiny flies that skimmed the water. That was my normal bathtub.

I read the advertisements on panels around the station while we waited for the train. On a background of white enamel was a picture of a large pig pulling a string of sausages. The caption read: 'Drawing its own conclusion.'

The luggage was loaded into the luggage compartment. When we arrived at Helsby station we would all be supervised by Dad as we loaded our camping gear on to a handcart. I don't imagine that we were much help. He probably did the bulk of the work himself. Theoretically, we all took a turn at pushing the cart but it wasn't more than token assistance. Tom probably remained around long enough to be useful as he stayed at technical college until he was sixteen. Once the girls were fourteen they left school and went out to work.

'Drawing its own conclusions', a cartoon by Tad Davies (2011), based on a poster Beaty remembers at Allerton railway station

They sometimes came to join us in Frodsham when they had a holiday for a week in the summer.

The compartment on the train had seats for eight or ten adults, and it was the first Saturday of the summer holidays, but I don't remember any other passengers joining the family during the journey. There were six children and two adults. They would look in through the door from the platform or the door onto the corridor and move on.

Each year we looked out from the windows of the train as the tenements, church, gasworks and airport tower disappeared. The Mersey estuary and the Wirral peninsula were bathed in sunlight. The blue mountains of Wales appeared through a heat haze.

I was enchanted by the panoramic sepia photographs on the walls above the seats. They showed holiday destinations at seaside resorts or in the countryside, two different pictures in each compartment. Along the promenade of Victorian hotels, cafés and shops, holidaymakers were busily enjoying themselves. The sun shone down on men in smart white suits and boaters and women in crisp, flowered dresses and broad-brimmed sun hats. Boys wore shorts so smooth and stiff with starch, the cotton could have cut their legs. The girls, in their pretty little hats and dresses, were a smaller version of their mothers.

The sun couldn't have shone for six weeks but I have only fleeting memories of being confined to the tent by the rain, when we would play children's card games, 'happy families' 'Snap' or 'Lexican'. There were always plenty of coloured pencils, colouring books or paper.

We often went on these holidays with the McFetter family. Tom, who was in the Fire Service with dad, his wife, and their son Tommy, a handsome boy a year older than me who I fancied off and on for years. When Harry was about five years old, Mr McFetter showed Harry how to draw a bird sitting on a wall. He drew a large circle, then a small circle above it. I watched as Harry copied him. From that time Harry was rarely seen without a pencil in his hand. He examined the architecture of the farmhouse, the clutter of the animals in their pens around the farmyard, hills, streams, caves and people, and tried to capture them on paper.

American GIs were billeted near Frodsham. On hearing American accents for the first time outside of films, we made a nuisance of ourselves.

'Have you got any gum, chum?' we called after them. We would have been in trouble for being rude if Mam or Dad had heard us.

They were really nice young men and welcomed our advances. They didn't have any gum, or they weren't parting with it. What they did have was watermelon. We were given a quarter of one between us. Mouths watering, we went back to the tent for a knife and cut it into equal slices.

I took one bite and spat it out, describing it as tasting like dirty washing-up water. Not that I had ever tasted dishwater. My palate wasn't ready for a taste so outside my experience.

We children lived a life of almost boundless freedom. Mam would give us sandwiches and shoo us off the campsite as soon as we had eaten breakfast, with an instruction to wave to her from the hills.

Dad and the girls only came to Frodsham on their days off from work or when they had a holiday.

Once Mam had prepared the evening meal and washed our

Camping in the 1940s at Frodsham or Sealand. Mam, Dianne, Dad, Tommy McFetters and his cousin

clothes, she spent the rest of the day with Harry and the baby. As the years passed, Harry joined the older children in their happy wanderings. Eventually, even Dianne wanted to go with them. Mam couldn't bring herself to let the baby go without her so she neglected the cooking and washing to come with us. Mam looked back on those holidays as the happiest of her life.

Meanwhile, in the summer of 1942, I was the youngest of the four intrepid explorers who discovered long-forgotten paths, or forged new ones, on the Helsby hills.

We started from the lane beside the farm and climbed for an hour until we reached a well-worn path above the campsite. We could recognise our tent. We looked for Mam and imagined we saw her as we all waved. She told us she had seen us and had waved back. Tom and Richard became excited by the cars. From that distance they looked like their toy Dinky cars.

On our left we could see the helter-skelter marking the private fairground at the top of Frodsham hill. To reach it we would climb up Jacob's Ladder. At the fairground we would drop down into Frodsham village. On the days we took the right-hand path, an undulating journey lay before us. There was a drop down to the caves and then a steep climb to the jutting-out rock which looked like a man's face. There was an Iron Age hill fort near the summit, but we weren't aware of it at the time. Climbers used to gain experience climbing

Camping at Frodsham or Sealand, with Mam preparing the dinner

the rock which looked like a man's face, with ropes and other equipment. In our early teens we climbed it for fun.

Over the next five years we gained an intimate knowledge of every path and almost every rock and tree on those hills. The sun shone, birds sang and butterflies flew in clouds of colour around us. There was such a wealth of richly coloured butterflies everywhere we turned; the brown ones were dismissed as boring.

Mam came with us to the cave. Taking her hand Harry told her he would look after her when she went inside. He was trembling as he stepped into the darkness, trying to look brave.

All the family, including Dad, were sitting down for breakfast in the tent one day. A tin of condensed milk was being passed from one person to the next as we did every morning. I put a spoonful into my tea and was about to pass the tin and spoon on when the sight of that sweet, sticky delight tempted me. Without thought of the consequences, I took another spoonful and put it into my mouth. There was an intake of breath all around me.

After a stunned silence I was told to leave the breakfast table and the tent and fetch a clean spoon.

'That dirty spoon has been in your mouth. It can't go into the milk now,' Dad said.

I can't remember whether my punishment went further than going without breakfast.

Richard named the private fairground the 'free' fairground. We discovered it on one of our first walks. In addition to the usual swings and climbing frames, there were roundabouts, sea-saws, the longest slides we had ever seen and, best of all, the helter-skelter. We had it all to ourselves and there was no interfering park keeper telling us what we could or couldn't do. Health and safety legislators would have had a field day. Years later we were taken there on a Sunday school trip. We didn't say a word.

Dianne, Harry and I befriended a man who lived in a caravan

Harry making a fire to boil a kettle, wearing his suit from Evelyn's wedding, 1949

all year round. We thought he had a very romantic life and would spend hours in his tiny room, where he ate and slept, enthralled by everything he said or did. The poem 'I wish I lived in a caravan' was a favourite of Mam's. He was the nearest we had come to a gypsy. When we cycled to Frodsham as teenagers we still called in to see him. He was a railway worker.

What could be more joyful than waking up on your birthday morning surrounded by the beautiful Helsby hills and listening to the cows lowing? My prettily wrapped parcel would be waiting for me when I woke. Everybody would share my excitement as I untied the string and took out a book containing a cardboard doll and push-out clothes to dress it in, or a colouring book and a new watercolour set with a paintbrush.

On returning to school all of the class would be asked to write a story about our summer holidays. We wrote about Frogum. Fortunately for us they recognised this as Frodsham, a well-known old Cheshire town of thatched black-and-white houses with an ancient church and hostelry.

In mild weather I loved the walk to school. It was about half a mile along a lane called the Cinder Path. One side of the lane was bordered by the thirty-foot high pebble dashed wall of the gasworks. We used to rub plum stones along the wall to make boats. The yard of the Bryant and May matchworks fenced us in on the other side. Logs were neatly stacked in the yard. We would try to guess how many matches could be made from one log.

Martha and Alf in Frodsham

At the beginning of the lane we crossed a narrow-gauge railway track going through the gasworks to the matchworks. When approaching from one direction a notice proclaimed 'Beware of Waggons'. When coming from the other direction the notice read 'Beware of Wagons'. I never saw any waggons or wagons and my spelling remains idiosyncratic. I lean towards double G because my computer objects to my use of it. I prefer programme to program for the same quirky reason.

There was an open expanse of sky stretching across the yard and the airport. In the summer I would look at the clouds and imagine that it was a different world of hills and lakes. In the winter I cried to myself as the wind bit through my thin clothes. I used to get to school early so that I could sit on the hot water pipes. They were scalding hot but it was preferable to going into the classroom frozen to the marrow.

The matchworks yard ended at the Roman Catholic school and church. My friend Margaret Hicklin was Roman Catholic. When she invited me into the church, I followed her curiously but with great trepidation. The light and beauty of the interior held me enthralled but I was sure I was doing something very wicked. My legs shook and could barely support me. Terrified, I ran outside.

At the end of the first year in the junior school we were given a test. Everyone was excited as we knew it was very important. Miss Rathbone, the teacher of the A stream, had a strawberry birthmark on her face. She also looked very strict. We were afraid of her. To avoid going into her class I decided to write down the first thing that came into my head in response to the questions.

Dad received a letter from a child psychologist. I was to attend his clinic. It didn't occur to me that this was connected to my answers in the test. Mam took the day off work. It was a happy day for me. I had Mam to myself, a rare treat. We went into Liverpool on a tram.

When we were ushered into the consulting room, I thought all my Christmases had come at once. There were brand-new toys. I was hugging myself with delight at the thought of playing with them. The psychologist told me who he was. I wasn't really interested as I wanted to start playing, but I realised the quicker we got over the formalities the sooner I could get to the toys.

'Hello, I'm in the Brownies. Do you like my badge?' I asked showing him the brass elf.

He wasn't the slightest bit impressed. He was very stern and asked me to concentrate and answer the questions he was going to ask me.

Ten minutes later we were outside. The toys were a con. Nobody got to play with them. That was why the stayed looking brand-new.

A week later Dad and the school authorities each received a letter. In essence the psychologist complained that the school had wasted his time. I was a normal eight-year-old child.

I was then put into the special reading class. There were thirty or forty children. The books had thrilling names like *John and Jill play with a ball*. When the teacher called our names we read one or two sentences. This was fine, in theory. On arriving in class the books would be opened and the first child would stumble along to the end of his sentence. I would carry on reading the book to myself while the next child carried out this painful task. By the time my name was called I would be in the world of John and the bouncing ball but had no idea which sentences the child before me had read.

Meanwhile, I had discovered that there was a school library.

I could choose any book I wanted. Every other day I would take a different book out. *Betty's Friend* by Margaret Stuart-Lane fired my imagination. It was a historic novel about the Great Fire of London. There was clearly a breakdown in communications in the school as Miss Leach, the teacher who ran the library, didn't know I was in the special reading class.

Miss Leach was a tall, elegant woman. Ivory or mother of pearl comes into my mind when I picture her. Her translucent white shoes had two- or three-inch stiletto heels. The slim toes tapered to a point. The calf-length A-line skirt in marble or pale cream revealed three inches of silk stocking, while the plain collar of a white blouse accentuated her long neck. If she didn't wear a string of pearls she gave the impression that she did. Glowing straight, blonde hair, held in a bun at the back of her head, was her crowning glory, adding to her classical stature.

My memory of my first library, two shelves of books in a 19th-century classroom full of rows of desks for two, inkwells, scratchy pens and blotting paper, it will always carry the picture of the stylish and beautiful Miss Leach.

The texture and smell of a book would hold me in thrall but words carried me to a land of bliss. One day, after school assembly, the teacher left the big hymn book on her desk. It was a massive tome, almost as big as *Pilgrim's Progress*. Finding myself alone in the classroom with it at the end of the school day, I opened it at random.

In extra-large bold lettering I read:

Immortal, invisible, God only wise.
In light inaccessible hid from our eyes.

I turned a page and found:

Morning has broken, like the first morning.
Blackbird has spoken like the first bird.

I couldn't bear to walk away, leaving it on the desk. Every

page begged to be opened. It must have weighed more than a kilogram but I was barely aware of my burden as I nursed it close to my bosom all the way along the Cinder Path to the tenements. Nobody noticed me leave the school with it and none of my school friends saw it.

'What have you got there?' Dad asked as I came through the door to the apartment. 'A hymn book,' I replied, joyfully. 'Look how big the words are. It's the one we have for assembly.'

He explained to me in a gentle but firm tone that the book belonged to the school. I must never take anything from the school unless it had been given to me and I had definite permission to take it home.

Next day I returned it, carefully wrapped to prevent it being damaged, with a letter of apology to the teacher.

I have often wondered whether my inability to master arithmetic was due to missing vital classes while I was in the reading class. I had never been able to memorise the tables.

As Richard expressed it, 'I know the tune. I just can't remember the words'.

I lived most of my childhood in a dreamy, absent-minded, haze but I began to notice that some children graduated from the special reading class. John and Jill began to bore me, so I made a conscious effort to discover how children achieved this leap forward. The answer was that they observed the order in which children were called and which sentences would be required from them when their time came. Having practised the pronunciation to themselves, they were able to enunciate it clearly and with some sense of the meaning. Once I had grasped the method I spoke out with confidence and was immediately released back into the B stream where I stayed until moving to the secondary modern school, Gilmour, and the D stream.

Daydreaming may have played a major part in my lack of educational achievement but my fear, dislike and anger towards Mr Woolley, the headmaster of the junior school, exacerbated it. He was all-powerful in our small lives and treated my family with contempt. If he had cause to speak to me he was sarcastic

Banks Road County primary School in background. In the foreground Dorothy's children, Michael and Dolly Anne playing in the park, 1960s.

and showed no respect. He called Richard 'The snail'.

When he came into the classroom, looking full of himself, he made jokes that I found stupid like, 'What is better than one Mars bar? Answer: Two Mars bars.'

Dianne and I met him again ten years later, at a Campaign for Nuclear Disarmament meeting in Woolton. He didn't know us. The bile rose up in my mouth at the sight of him. Seeing him put Dianne off joining CND for years.

Mam had been working at the airport for some time when one of the customers reported that she had lost her lipstick. The airport chief executive made an off-hand remark that the cleaner working in the cloakroom had probably taken it. On hearing this Mam put on a clean white overall and marched to the administration building. She flung open the door to the outer office, lined with a dozen desks on either side, and made straight for the boss's door.

'You can't go in there,' they told her.

In full sail, without faltering or knocking, she entered the holy of Holies.

'Do you know who I am?' she demanded of the stunned man sitting behind his massive desk.

'It's Mrs Smith isn't it? What is wrong?' he asked coming around the desk. 'Won't you sit down?'

'I haven't come here to sit down,' she answered, drawing herself up to her full four foot ten. 'You accused me of stealing a lipstick. If I steal, it won't be anything smaller than an aeroplane.' At which she flounced out.

Next day an aeroplane went missing, or so Mam said.

I was asthmatic and had a hacking cough most of the time. Due to a nasal deformity, I had to breathe through my mouth like a goldfish. Having a permanently open mouth made me susceptible to infection and also gave me a vacant look. This nasal problem wasn't diagnosed and operated upon until I was in my twenties. Despite serving no useful purpose, my nose was permanently clogged with two large bogies which I occasionally wiped on my coat or jumper sleeve.

Just after the war Mam took Harry and me to a hall where the government issued us with overcoats. The stamp inside said 'Utility'. Harry's was made from imitation black lambs' wool and was very warm. He looked like a little prince and I was really proud to be walking out of the hall with him. The minute we were outside he took it off. He thought it looked too smart and would cause his school friends to bully him. It was never worn again. The first winter I remember feeling warm was when I invested in a heavy winter coat when I was almost thirty.

On rainy days the infant school children used to dance without their shoes on a big mat in the school hall if they had clean feet. Those with dirty feet put their shoes back on and danced around the outside of the mat. I got to dance on the mat twice. Those two occasions must have been the day after bath night.

One of the infant teachers, Dorothy Banks, was a kind and loving woman. Everyone adored her. Richard had a massive crush on her. She was a Methodist and on one occasion she was at the same chapel function as the Smith family. When Richard saw her his heart started hammering.

Tugging at Mam's hand he whispered in his usual loud voice, 'Mam, Mam, it's Miss Banks.'

'Hello Richard,' she said, giving him a big smile.

He tried to hide behind Mam, so overcome with emotion he could hardly breathe. As Mam was tiny and thin, while he was a little barrel, she didn't hide him very well. He treasured the memory for the rest of his life.

In 1948 she went to India as a missionary. We all missed her greatly.

In the 1930s Mam had been in service to a Mrs Bennett, a doctor's wife, in Aigburth. There was a white apron and headband for Mam to wear if guests were expected. Her employers lived above the surgery. When she saw the guests coming along the street she sent Mam downstairs. She was not to open the door until they rang the bell. Mam had to lead them upstairs and announce them.

'Mr and Mrs Jones have arrived, Ma'am.'

She found it all very silly. Mrs Bennett knew they had arrived. The guests knew that she knew that they had arrived but Mam was being paid to perform this scene. The stiffness of her back as she marched from the room expressed what she thought of this 'stuff and nonsense'.

Mam remained in contact with her. The two women had an arrangement during the war that the doctor's wife bought our clothing coupons. We couldn't afford new clothes. Once a week Richard took most of our eggs and butter to Aigburth. Mam kept six eggs a week and half a pound of butter. Dad had an egg a day because he was working. On Sunday we had a sliced ginger sponge with butter. Our diet was supplemented with dried egg powder which didn't appear to be rationed. This could be used for baking or very strange tasting scrambled eggs. When Richard arrived at Mrs Bennett's house she would interrogate him, including enquiring about our meals. She was of the opinion that we had more to eat than was necessary. That was probably why Tom had a swollen stomach like a Biafran when he was five, during the great depression of the 1930s, and developed cancer of the bowel when he was twenty-seven.

One pleasant summer's day Harry and I were sent to buy fish up the village. On arriving in St Mary's Road we walked for a quarter of a mile past shops but couldn't see anything resembling fish. We knew the butchers, the greengrocers and

Pegram's, where the family was registered for the rations. Every week we went there with Mam. I hadn't thought to ask what a fishmonger's looked like. I considered the buildings with tiny curtained windows and yellow or green tiles, as I had never been into them. I looked in. They were full of men and had a strange, sweet odour. It didn't seem likely. Harry had no suggestions to make so we gave up and decided to return home.

We decided to have a race. He went along Speke Road taking the road over the railway. I took the Willows path along the stream. It was a glorious day. I was singing joyfully as I skipped along. A young man with a bicycle stood near a gate into a field bright with wild flowers. He was a man to me, but was probably no more than a boy of fifteen or sixteen, with sandy hair and freckles. He greeted me with a friendly smile.

'Could you help me?' he asked. 'Part of my pump has fallen into the long grass over there. I have searched but can't find it.'

'Yes, of course I'll help,' I replied.

The race with Harry was forgotten and I climbed over the gate. The man followed me and we searched through the grass together. I chattered away cheerfully as we worked.

'Let's forget about it,' he said after a few minutes. 'I can manage until I get another. Shall we sit here?'

We lay side by side enjoying the sun. He put his arm around me. Gently he stroked my stomach. It was very comforting. He moved his hand down to my private part and I took it away, placing it on my stomach again.

'Don't you like me touching you there,' he asked softly.

'No,' I answered. 'I don't think you should do that.'

It wasn't unpleasant, but I instinctively felt that touching me there would be wrong.

'Fine,' he whispered. 'I won't do it again.'

I lay happily with my eyes closed soaking up the sun. A few minutes later he said mildly, 'Could I show you something?'

When my eyes opened upon to his erect penis I was

dumfounded. I had seen Harry undressed, but his willy bore no relationship to what now stood before me.

'Would you like to touch?' he asked.

I was very tempted. Curiosity was tugging my hand towards it, but I was also experiencing anxiety.

'No,' I said. 'I don't think I'd better do that. I think it's time I went home.' I stood up and walked to the gate.

'Bye,' he said, as I reached the gate. 'Thank you for a nice afternoon.'

I climbed over the gate and waved to him, 'Bye.'

I no longer felt the joy of the day, heard the ripple of the stream, or the song of the birds.

On arriving home I said nothing to anyone about this experience. I was sure I had been involved in something Mam and Dad would disapprove of. I also found the idea of talking about the sexual organs embarrassing.

This was a watershed in my life. Sixty years later I realise how lucky I was in receiving so gentle an initiation into the world of sexual encounters.

Following VE Day (Victory in Europe) the threat of being bombed during a raid on the docks had gone. Dad and Mam started looking immediately for a terraced house to rent 'Under the Bridge'. Trying to keep the peace with neighbours when there were eight, boisterous, noisy children rampaging about the flat, had taken all Mam's diplomatic skills.

There was no lift in the tenements, so the pram and shopping had to be dragged up and down stairs. There was also the ever-present danger of one of the children climbing the landing wall.

Dad was a window cleaner as well as a fireman and would sit on a windowsill to clean the outside of the windows. Beaty thought this was an interesting way to pass the time and when there was nobody about she followed his example. Dad arrived home and came to the room were she was sitting one storey above the ground.

'Beaty,' he said softly so as not to take me by surprise.

I smiled a welcome and waved at him.

He waved back. 'I think you had better come inside now,' he said gently.

'All right,' I answered obediently. I had been enjoying the experience but I didn't mind.

Once I was inside he spoke to me very seriously, told me what I had done was dangerous and I must promise never to do it again. On seeing me on the window ledge a neighbour had come to the house. Mam was cooking in the kitchen and Dad had just arrived home.

VE Day was celebrated by building a bonfire on one of the greens between the tenement blocks. I had never seen a bonfire, not even on Guy Fawkes night because we weren't allowed to light them during the war, so I was very excited. I went alone. Richard was there but he must have gone with Tom. Dolly, Freda and Evelyn met our cousins Mary and Josie in The Dingle and went dancing. The whole community gathered on the green dancing, singing and laughing. With nothing to laugh about and no-one to talk to, I stood watching for a while waiting for some of the magic to rub off on me. After a while I went home.

By the time VJ Day (Victory over Japan) arrived, we had moved to a six-roomed terraced house in Chesterton Street. Red, white and blue buntings made a canopy above the trestle tables down the length of the street, laden with more sugar iced cakes and jellies than we could

Aunt Nell's daughters, Mary and Josie, 1940s

possibly eat. All around me were my family and the children from Bethel, the Methodist chapel, and school. I made a new friend, Maureen Mowatt. We were all chattering and laughing as we wolfed down this feast.

When the tables were cleared away we had three-legged races, sack races and egg and spoon races.

Somebody started 'Hi Hi Conga' and the line wound around us then up and down the street. Next it was 'Knees up Mother Brown', followed by 'The Hokey Cokey'. We were exhausted but exhilarated.

At the close of a momentous day Dad read us the story of the *Land of Eiderdowns* that calmed us and sent us to sleep.

VJ (Victory in Japan) party, Under the bridge, Garston, August / September 1945

2

Under the Bridge, 1945–48

A WEEK OR two after the war ended Dad took us into Liverpool one night to see a parade of the Royal Navy. This was to celebrate the vital part they played during the war. The air was sizzling with excitement. Thousands of people thronged the streets. At last we saw tiny pinpoints of light coming towards us. A wave of cheering and clapping came echoing nearer and nearer as the lights approached. We joined in, although we couldn't see the sailors. At last they were close enough for us to see that the lights were individual rope torches. They were carried by thousands of seamen wearing blue sailor suits with square white-edged collars, bell-bottom trousers and white hats. As they passed, the scent of burning fibres was carried to us on the breeze. The sound of marching feet drumming on the road was ringing in our ears and bouncing off the tall buildings. Everyone clapped and cheered until they were hoarse. All the way home we tingled with the joy of sharing this time with our community.

In the summer of 1945 we discovered that the closed curtains of our bedroom created a camera obscura on the ceiling. We were amazed and delighted to be entertained every evening by our own panoramic film show of the neighbours as they walked about or stopped to chat. Mam and Dad didn't spend time gossiping so we were far better informed than they were about births, marriages and deaths in the community. We had the juiciest bits of scandal on girls who were pregnant out of wedlock and, worse still, those who became pregnant while their husbands were overseas with the army. Occasionally, someone passed on a bicycle. Cars were a very rare sight. Fifteen years later there were still only two or three cars in the street.

During one air raid a bomb landed on one of the gas storage tanks. It rolled off and landed on the road unexploded. The bomb squad dismantled it. Bombs had wiped out a fair amount of the housing stock near the docks. It is surprising that we were able to move back there within months of VE Day. Perhaps no-one else was willing to live next door to our neighbours.

Our clothes were handed down through the family. Constant scrubbing and boiling could not keep them whiter than white. The colours were washed out. They couldn't have passed the Persil test. Compared with our new next door neighbours, however, we were spick and span. They were a family of four children, two boys who I will call Jack and Eric, a girl I will call Jill and a toddler I will call Joe. Both the parents were filthy and smelled of cigarettes, alcohol and body odour, but the man was marginally cleaner than his wife. The children were as grimy as their mother. They had unkempt oily hair. The dresses of the mother and daughter were slimy with dirt. The shirt collars and trousers of the boys shone with grease. The stink that billowed out of the house from the permanently open front door was enough to make me wretch.

Cleanliness came before Godliness on the terraced back streets in Under the Bridge. Neighbours would walk in to your house unannounced at any time. Untidiness and cooking odours might pass without comment but not dust. Any sign or smell of dirt would not be tolerated. We barely scraped by on the acceptability stakes but Mam made every effort to keep up appearances. Each child in the family was delegated to tasks according to their ability.

For many years it was my task each week to wash the window ledge and scrub the front door step. This was an important ritual performed by female members of each household. Women could be seen on their knees all along the street, each with a large scrubbing brush with stiff bristles, a slice of yellow soap cut from a metre-long rectangle, a flour sack cloth, a pumice stone and a galvanised steel bucket of hot water. After the step had been scrubbed, a white line was drawn along the edge with the pumice stone. The white line proclaimed to everyone passing by that the work had been done. When it had been rubbed away the step was due another scrubbing. Those neighbours not engaged in the work made a slow progress from door to door, stopping to gossip.

As a teenager I became embarrassed by this neighbourly activity. Instead of kneeling outside I would lie on my stomach in the hallway leaning out to scrub and hoping nobody would spot me. I didn't realise that I was assigned this task because everyone else in the family was too embarrassed to take it on, including Mam.

My malodorous neighbours never suffered this indignity.

The eldest boy of the family, who was in the same class as Richard, came with us on one of our trips to Frodsham. It was a very hot day. Oil from his hair ran down his face in black rivulets. He was the unfortunate fellow I caused to get stung when we were rock climbing and I put my foot into a wasps' nest.

Despite their unwholesome appearance they were pleasant enough neighbours. None of them ever gave us any problems throughout the years we lived beside each other, apart from Jill, who was about a year younger than Dianne. To my mind she was crazy but Dianne thought she was bored and a bit wild.

I discovered some years later that the parents were related to respectable, educated, working-class members of the community. Some of their relatives attended the Methodist chapel. One of their cousins became a very famous pop singer in the late 1950s.

There was a smartly dressed, well-mannered, young woman who lived at the other end of our street. I was amazed to discover

Alf Smith, with a child scrubbing the
step behind him

Dianne, about three years old

that she was the eldest daughter of the family. She had been
taken away from the parents by one of her grandmothers.

The unhinged younger daughter never attended school. She
would taunt or lash out at children around her own age, but
could be kind and helpful to small children. The education
authority or social services sent her to a residential school in
north Wales. She must have had some kind of intelligence for
she escaped from the residential school and found her way
back home.

Dianne was often the butt of her verbal abuse. She
attempted to physically attack her twice. The first time she
ran towards Dianne with her fists out, Dianne grasped one of
her outstretched wrists, turned her back on her assailant and
threw her over her shoulder. It was a jujutsu move Tom had
taught her.

The girl wasn't hurt, but it gave her a shock. She never
attempted a frontal attack again.

On a day when Jill was particularly bored and had been

hanging around the street for hours with nothing to do, she took an axe and was chopping lumps out of the brown earth on the bomb site next to her house. Seeing Dianne walking home from school inspired her. She ran down the street brandishing the axe. Mam pulled Dianne into the house and shut the door. There was a split in the door where the axe had cut into it. All the years we lived there we were reminded of Dianne's narrow escape each time we looked at the axe mark. When Dianne recalled the incident she said it had planted no dread in her mind. She thought it was funny at the time, and never dwelt on it. The matter was never raised with the girl's parents or the authorities.

Mam and Dad never became involved in arguments regarding their children on principle. They said there was nothing to be gained and it only led to trouble in the future. If children bullied us we were told to stand up to them. The boys claimed Dad had told them that if they came home and complained that they had been hit, he would threaten to beat them again if they didn't go straight back out and hit the bully. He bought them boxing gloves.

Harry and a group of his friends used to meet regularly to learn to box. I went along to their practice once. They accepted me into the gang without question. I wasn't any good and wasn't enthusiastic enough to try to learn the moves so I didn't go again.

Tom was a little bantam and claimed he fought all of Richard's battles for him. He probably did until he went to Toxteth Technical College in about 1945 when he was thirteen.

Richard became a celebrity in his last year at primary school when he made puppets and took a Punch and Judy show around all the classes in the infant and junior school. There were hinged blackboards in each classroom that he used as a stage. It was a truly professional and very funny show. I should have been proud of him and boasted that he was my brother, but I took his ability for granted.

I hero worshiped two ten-year-old girls who were in the

same year as Richard. They were Shirley Fogg and Iris Groves. I knew them from Sunday school in the Methodist church. They were also in the Guides' company. Richard thought Shirley was beautiful. Although she was kind to him she didn't pick him out as special. He wanted to be her boyfriend.

She showed special favours to a good-looking boy in the A stream. Richard thought the boy was a big head. The boy was turning cartwheels in the main hall to impress Shirley. She followed his example and did a handstand against the wall. Her skirt came down over her face. At that moment Mr Woolley, the headmaster, came by. The boy was given a severe telling off for looking at Shirley when she was showing her knickers. Richard had been watching them both, consumed with jealousy. He was delighted when the boy got into trouble.

We suffered from all the usual childhood illnesses like chicken pox and measles. Harry had mumps, which had more serious consequences but nobody appeared to be aware of this at the time. He was left with a low sperm count. It would have been easier for Mam if we had all caught the viruses from each other and been ill at the same time. I don't know how she managed to juggle her work at the airport and nursing us.

I suffered from bronchitis every winter, but I didn't take much time off school. I could usually manage my chest problems without her if I was too ill to attend school. Violent stomach cramps kept me awake at night. She would give me warm milk to drink and a stone hot water bottle to soothe the pain away. The pain was genuine but I enjoyed the time with her. Sometimes I have wondered whether it was psychological, as this was the only time I had her to myself. She must have been weary getting up to go to work next day.

When Dianne was about ten years old she started suffering stomach pains when she was about to leave for school. It was years before she started menstruating. A number of suggestions were put forward including the idea that she wanted to be with Mam or that she was finding her lessons stressful. She has no recollection of either. She interchanged top and next-to-top positions of the A stream with her friend Mary Hughes all the time they were in junior school. There was no rivalry between them.

When I was eight I spent a short time in hospital having surgery to correct a protruding navel. Perhaps it was a small hernia. Generally I found the stay pleasant and enjoyed the company of the other children on the ward and of the nursing staff. If I had an operation I don't remember anything about it. I found one poor little girl hidden behind curtains and went in to chat to her. Her body was covered in small white scabs. I thought them very interesting and she was obviously delighted to have my attention. She was eagerly answering my questions about how long she had had them and such, when the staff came bustling in. They shooed me back to my bed, horrified that I might have become contaminated.

In the summer of 1945 Tom started technical college and Richard moved up to the secondary modern school at Heath Road. He was a gentle boy but big for his age. His size probably protected him from school bullies. His happiest memories were of learning poetry. For the rest of his life he delighted family and friends with his recitals.

Our next door neighbour on the other side from the odorous family was a fisherman. He was a surly man and a strict disciplinarian. His wife and children were terrified of him. They had no life and didn't mix with the rest of the community.

After his funeral his daughter invited me in. I was amazed to find cold rooms with bare floorboards. Everything shone from being scrubbed and the whole house smelled of carbolic soap. Spotless boat parts, fishing implements, and nets hung in an orderly manner from the kitchen walls. It was like a time warp.

The old man died in the mid 1950s. Garston had been a fishing village in the 1850s. This family had been living in the nineteenth century. I doubt he exchanged more than three sentences with Dad or Mam in ten years.

In spite of their strict home life, the son and daughter

emerged from their isolation as very pleasant, companionable people. It appeared that they had managed to have boy and girlfriends in secret, and within a year of him dying they had married. As a teenager I thought they were very old to be getting married, and felt really sad for them. Because people of sixty were clearly old, I had deduced that thirty was middle aged. The daughter was mid-to-late twenties, while the son was at least thirty.

The junior school pupils put on a concert before the summer holiday each year. My class did a play in which we took the roles of fishermen. We were out in a raging storm, trying to keep our footing on the wet, rolling deck.

Wha'll buy my caller herrin'?
They're bonnie fish and halesome farin';
Wha'll buy my caller herrin',
New drawn frae the Forth?

We sang as we hauled in the nets. I imagined our neighbour on a wild winter's morning out on the estuary or on the Irish Sea.

For another concert we learned to dance 'The Sailor's Hornpipe' as we mimed climbing up the rigging and sang songs as we pulled together on the ropes to raise the anchor.

Our lives were constantly touched by the water. All of us had somebody in the family who was a merchant seaman, a crewman on a tug, a docker or, like my neighbour, a fisherman. When we looked from the parish church or out of the bedroom windows at the back of the house, we could see the tall cranes on the docks. Drowning, falls, and accidents were less frequent than they had been at the beginning of the century, but tales of tragedies reached us often enough for us to have a healthy respect for the river. A member of the church, a strong man in his prime, fell thirty feet when working in the docks. He never totally recovered.

Pigeon fancying was very popular in Garston. The man in

the house behind us kept racing pigeons and could be seen in the loft on the roof feeding them, cleaning them, and welcoming them home after a race. Our only contact with him was if our ball went into his yard. Keeping racing pigeons was an expensive hobby, but we weren't aware of that. We thought he was mean spirited and unreasonably angry, along with all adults who complained about our balls going into their territory.

'Please Mr, can we have our ball back?' was our constant cry.

Apart from odd people like the fisherman, the front doors of all the houses were open throughout the summer.

Behind the houses there was a wide cobbled passageway between the houses on our terraced street and the street behind us. A dangerously unstable bombed house, a few houses down from the pigeon fancier, was a favourite venue for playing house. It wasn't demolished for over a decade after the war. The excuse given was that the owner couldn't be traced.

There were no betting shops for working-class people until 1961. Despite all the best efforts of the church and government to prevent gambling amongst the common people, there were illegal bookmakers in every working-class area.

Bombsite in Window Lane, twenty years after the Second World War ended

The bookie's runners could be seen collecting bets from a queue of men on every street corner in Window Lane. The alarm would be raised that the police were coming and everyone would scatter. They would run through any open front door, through the house, down the yard and across the entry into a house in the next street. The police were half-hearted in their pursuit. Nothing they did would stop men from gambling. Trying to stop them was a waste of police time. We found the chase thrilling to watch. The runners didn't come through our house. We were not part of the betting fraternity. Even raffle tickets were not admitted over our doorstep. Money must be earned or no good will come to those who receive it.

I was about eleven when I saw toy musical instruments being raffled in the local newsagents and, succumbing to temptation, I parted with my meagre pocket money. I waited with suppressed anticipation for the day when the ticket was drawn. When the shop owner told me I hadn't won, I didn't understand. I had given him money, therefore he must give me something in return or give me my money back. Once I grasped the point about gambling, that only the person with the winning number received anything, it gave me a salutary lesson. It was better than any lecture Mam or Dad could have given. I was well into adulthood before I bought another raffle ticket or even guessed the weight of a cake at a spring fair. It had nothing to do with religion or morality. If I parted with money, I wanted to be sure I would receive a fair exchange of goods.

Every Saturday we were given pocket money. I was afraid that the coins would burn a hole in my pocket so I had to get rid of them as quickly as possible.

On one of our visits to New Brighton, the nearest seaside resort to Liverpool, we passed a stall selling candyfloss. Mam asked whether we wanted to buy some.

'Will it be out of my pocket money?' asked five-year-old Dianne.

Like Oscar Wilde, I can resist anything except temptation,

so I sampled my first candyfloss. It had the appearance of a soft pink cloud but tasted of burned toffee. I have never repeated the experiment.

We had two ounces of sweets each week out of our pocket money and had to offer them around to Mam and Dad and the rest of the family.

Harry would buy a Mars bar. Taking the sharpest knife, he would slice the thinnest sliver possible for each person present and the scent of vanilla would set his mouth watering. Each week he watched with a jaundiced eye as his precious chocolate bar disappeared. In spite of all his care he was lucky if he had a slice one centimetre thick.

Dianne would buy a bag full of the cheapest and lightest sweets. She had plenty left for herself after passing them around the family.

We were all good at cutting and sharing food. Mam gave us a guide to follow, and we follow it to this day. When dividing a piece of cake in half one person will cut the cake and the other person chooses the first section. We couldn't be more accurate if we measured with a slide rule.

The siren from the bobbin works woke us at 7am every working day followed by the tramp of thousands of boots on the streets leading to the factories at the bottom of Window Lane. At 7.25am, a second siren trumpeted a warning that workers were going to be late and the steady tramp turned into a pounding run. The last siren at 7.30pm told the stragglers that they had been docked a quarter hour from their wages.

The Woodcutters' Club occupied the block from our street to York Street in Window Lane. The kingpin amongst the sawyers in the bobbin works was the turner. The factory supplied precision-made wooden bobbins, about a foot long, to the cotton mills of the north of England and anywhere else in the world where cotton was manufactured.

During the war Dad had built up a window cleaning round in Speke. He left the Fire Service as soon as they would release him, took on a partner, and began window cleaning full time.

Auxiliary Fire Service crew in Garston during the Second World War. Alf Smith is third from the end on the right.

The Fire Service had offered him promotion if he stayed but he hated rules and regulations. He wanted to be his own boss. After a few years, economic necessity forced him to take factory work. Later he became a fitter's mate for Liverpool Transport until he retired. He counted the days until he was sixty-five and was devastated when he discovered that his birth had been registered five days late.

Mam's lack of culinary ability wasn't helped by Dad. He grew all our vegetables on his allotment between Speke airport and Garston shore. Sometimes they were sorry looking specimens but he insisted that Mam had to use them before he picked fresh vegetables. The next produce would go past its best while the previous one was being used. As a child I hated all vegetables apart from potatoes. Now I love them, except for beetroot. If a slice of it has touched my salad I have to leave the meal. Beetroot would be very good for me if I could tolerate it and I have tried to disguise it as jelly or an ice lolly without success. I discovered when we were adults that Harry had the same extreme reaction against beetroot.

If there had been a glut of vegetables, Harry and I were sent around the streets with a handcart knocking on doors and asking people to buy them. Dad probably chose us for the job because he thought we looked angelic. We were a pair of snotty-nosed kids and the vegetables were well past their sell by date. If anyone bought them it must have been out of pity.

The deliveries of bread, milk and coal from the Co-operative Society all came in horse drawn wagons. We kept a bucket and shovel near the front door. The ring of horses' hooves sent me running for the bucket and shovel and I would follow the wagon, waiting for the horse to relieve itself. I breathed in the scent of new mown hay mixed with another pungent scent that made my eyes water. Almost before the horse had finished dropping it on the road I would be shovelling the steaming manure into my bucket. Dad's efforts to teach us gardening failed, but the manure was my contribution.

Cowboy films were our Saturday morning entertainment at the Lyceum Cinema, the local fleapit. There was an often repeated joke that children went in to that cinema wearing sleeveless tops and came out with jumpers. A few doors from the cinema was a shop owned by a Mr Richard Richards. Everyone called him Dicky Twice.

In 1945 *Pathé News* showed the German concentration camps. My stomach turned over as I looked with horror at the piles of ragged, stripped pyjamas and discovered they were bodies. Skeletal, bearded figures, barely alive, peered through the perimeter fence. The distress I experienced when I saw that newsreel stayed with me for the rest of my life.

The royal princesses were pictured in pretty summer dresses while holidaying in bright South African sunlight in the winter of 1946–47. I kept a scrapbook of everything they had ever done since they were little girls. There was great excitement – being stirred up by the papers and magazines – that Princess Elizabeth was going to marry a handsome blond Greek prince.

In one of Mam's magazines there was a picture of the

princesses with their dogs. In the article below it Princess Elizabeth was telling a story of them being caught in a rainstorm.

'When we arrived home,' the princess said 'the dogs were dried by Margaret and me, before we dried ourselves.'

I was nonplussed. Her grammar was clearly wrong. To compound my confusion, the magazine had not corrected her mistake.

When I drew Dad's attention to the 'error', he explained that 'the dogs were dried by me' was not changed by the addition of Margaret. 'Me' remained 'me'. Gems like this have caused me much suffering over the years, as one with perfect pitch is pained by a wrong note.

In an anti-war song that my choir performs I am forced to sing:

> There's a fact that's quite apparent
> Well beknown to you and I.
> No such thing as a deterrent.
> It's a lousy, wicked lie.

I have no wish to offend the lyricist, but I would like to suggest:

> There's a fact that's quite apparent,
> Well beknown to you and me,
> No such thing as a deterrent
> It's a foul duplicity.

Pathé News in 1947 showed India gaining her independence and being divided into India and Pakistan. Ghandi was a revered hero of any northern community connected to the cotton industry. The story of his visit to the mill towns was so familiar that I thought it had happened in my lifetime. It was with great sadness that we watched Indians massacring each other on *Pathé News*. A never ending line of refugees was leaving their homes and everything they possessed;

Muslims heading for Pakistan while Hindus made their way to India.

The fairytale wedding of Princess Elizabeth to prince charming in the late autumn of 1947 delighted all but the most hardened killjoys. It shed light onto our dreary streets.

I was related to the royal family, but I didn't tell anyone. You only had to look at my Dad and then at the king. The resemblance was uncanny.

The assassination of Ghandi at the beginning of 1948 broke our hearts. The boys stared at the screen, trying not to show any feelings but they didn't laugh at the girls, row upon row in the flickering light, with tears streaming down our faces.

After the advertisements, the trailers for future films, the silly B film (I couldn't stand the three stooges) and *Pathé News*, we came at last to the cowboy film.

The Roy Rogers' theme song, about his horse Trigger, had us all singing.

> A four legged friend, a four legged friend
> He'll never let you down
> He's honest and faithful right up to the end
> That wonderful one-two-three-four legged friend.

Roy Rogers would then sing the verses, while we rocked from side to side, waiting to join in again in the chorus. The first verse was about all women being tight-waisted, winky-eyed flirts, while the second told us not to trust even your best man friend, because he would be after your woman.

At the end of the last verse we shouted out 'Whoa Trigger'.

We would come out of the cinema and gallop home slapping our bottoms.

The seats were priced sixpence and nine pence. One morning we arrived to find all the sixpenny seats had been sold. We couldn't think of a way around this problem until I had an idea. I suggested to Harry that he could give me threepence. I would go in and tell him about the films when I came out.

Almost without considering it he turned the idea down. He thought it would be better if he went in and told me about it.

Play centre was held for two hours every evening after school. We were encouraged to indulge in hobbies or games. The big hall with parquet flooring was available to us, plus the classrooms leading off it.

The best part of the night was the film show that was held in a classroom off the balcony above the hall. Upstairs had been the senior school but it was now empty as the seniors had been moved to secondary modern schools in the leafy suburbs on the other side of the bridge. The school for girls was almost in Cressington, while the school for boys was in Allerton. Going upstairs and looking through the balustrades was an adventure in itself. During the shows we saw all the Chaplin films, the Keystone Cops and Buster Keeton.

One evening, when I arrived before any of the other children, a woman teacher gave me a round shortbread four inches in circumference. It was the most delicious food I had ever tasted.

Near the end of the summer holidays in 1945 we were playing in the back yard. It was a glorious day. I was in a swimsuit and Harry in knitted trunks. Mam was dowsing us with the garden hose. Dad's youngest cousin, Ada, came to visit. She was exotic, with long black hair, sallow skin that was scented with cheap flowery perfume, and eyes almost as black as coals. In a fit of spitefulness, a neighbour told me her mother was a gypsy. Certainly she was exuberant. Mam disapproved of her. She didn't say anything. A shrug of her shoulders and the stiffening of her neck spoke volumes. Mam disappeared into the house and we gathered around Ada to listen to her fabulous stories.

Usually her tales were fantastic and funny but this time she looked very serious.

'Have you heard of an atom bomb?' she asked us.

'No,' we answered. 'What's that?'

'It's the most terrible bomb that's ever been invented. Two

of them have been dropped on Japan and wiped out two cities the size of Liverpool.'

Our mouths hung open. My tongue felt dry. We all looked at her in dismay. Tales about the Japanese army had entered folklore. The soldiers were said to be clever and brutal. Kamikaze pilots would fly on suicide missions with no petrol to return home. If they were captured they would kill themselves instead of being taken as prisoners of war. It was regarded as dishonourable to be captured. But for the Americans to wipe out a whole city of men, women and children was astounding. She often invented or exaggerated. Could this be true?

She said the bomb worked like dominoes falling, or like a hundred mousetraps with the one in the centre setting off those next to it and them setting off those near them until all hundred had snapped shut. Then she asked for a pencil and paper. We peered over her shoulder as she drew a small circle in the centre of the page, then a larger one around it. This was continued until the page resembled the ripples from a pebble thrown into a pool. This was what happened when an atomic bomb exploded. She didn't know that babies in the womb, survivors, and the land and sea would have radiation poisoning, but she knew that something momentous had happened and the world would never be the same.

We lived in fear. No matter what occurred in our day-to-day lives after the atom bomb had been dropped, a cloud hung over us.

Everyone in the Methodist church was delighted when the last of our members returned from the war. He had been imprisoned by the Japanese. His transparent skin was stretched over his skull. He couldn't cope with a party where he would be the centre of attention. Everybody nodded to him but we tried not to crowd him or make too much noise around him. His wife and sons appeared cheerful but they were watching over him anxiously.

He was found dead in his armchair a few months later.

There was no longer any pretence on his widow's face. She

had suffered stoically during the years he had been a prisoner, putting the best light on the situation for the sake of her boys. When the war ended she had begun to relax. The news that he was coming home had brought more ease to her step. There was nothing left.

Before another six months had passed she died, leaving boys of about fifteen and ten. They kept the family home and the older boy raised his younger brother. They were attractive young men, well-mannered and smartly dressed. The congregation and their neighbours loved them.

When Tom went to the technical college he had to get up half an hour earlier to start his paper round because it was much further to cycle to school. The older boys supplemented their income at the end of the summer holidays and autumn weekends by pea and potato picking. When we were old enough we followed their example.

The year was marked out for us by the seasons and the Christian festivals. Harvest festival was a joyful occasion. The congregation would bring fruit, vegetables and flowers to the harvest service and they would be arranged below the pulpit. The centrepiece would be bread baked in the shape of a sheath of wheat. Our offerings, whether vegetables or flowers, would be leggy specimens well past their useful life but no comments were made. The church was full of colour, the smell of fresh earth, apples and delicately scented petals.

All good gifts around us
Are sent from Heaven above
Then thank the Lord, thank the Lord for all his love...

After the service the food and flowers were distributed amongst the old and poor.

At Halloween, the night when the ghosts of our ancestors are said to come back to haunt us, Miss Rathbone told us a scary story in school about witches on broomsticks.

'Please Miss, is that a true story?' I asked.

'Yes, of course,' she answered.

I was terrified of going to the toilet. One day I reached the point when I couldn't face the traumatic experience. I had my bowels opened in my pants. Mam was disgusted with me and made me wash them. Meanwhile, whenever Dianne needed to go to the toilet I was instructed to go down the yard with her and wait while she used it.

In the winter of 1946–47 the snowdrifts were up to the top of the street gas lamps and some children had real wooden toboggans for sliding down the embankment between Speke Road and The Willows. We could race just as quickly as they could, although we were using steel dustbin lids. The bedrooms in our house were bitterly cold. We were captivated by the delicate patterns made by Jack Frost on the windows. Dad tried to warm our beds by putting the shelves from the oven next to the kitchen fire into them. It wasn't a great success. They were covered in threadbare cotton sheets that became scorched. We would be burned if we touched them, while the rest of the bed and the air in the room was icy cold.

Dianne slept in her cot in the same room as Mam and Dad. Harry and the other boys had bunk beds. I slept with Freda and Evelyn in a double bed, while Dorothy had the box room. I shivered under a layer of coats and thin army blankets, filtering the chill blast from my asthmatic lungs by burying my head under the covers, until the older girls came to bed. They were cold when they first got into bed, and snuggled up to me for warmth. That was fine until one raw night I must have balked at the thought of going to the bottom of the yard to the toilet. I woke from dreaming I was in a nice warm bath to discover I had peed the bed. My sisters were not pleased.

The toilet in the tenements had been inside the flat. Now we had to go down a dark yard to an outside toilet near the back door where no one would hear if we cried out. I was frightened by the shadows on the toilet walls and couldn't get back into the house quickly enough.

The toilet walls were whitewashed and the toilet had

a wooden seat. Mam scrubbed the seat every day. It was as spotless as the kitchen table. The room smelled of lime and soap. Toilet paper was newspaper cut into squares and hanging from a nail on the door. The first real toilet paper we had was called Izal Medicated. It was shiny and non-absorbent. When it ran out I would attempt to rip a thin triangular layer from the inner cardboard roll. It was probably as useful as the Izal. Mam appeared from nowhere to ensure that we washed our hands with plenty of soap when we came into the house after using the toilet. The galvanized steel bucket we used for cleaning the floors and front door step was not used for scrubbing the toilet. Mam had a bucket specifically for that area. She had the same strict rules for the two enamel bowls in the kitchen. One was for ablutions while the other was for washing crockery, cutlery, pots and pans.

Dad took us to school through the snow that had been churned to slush by the thousands of workers going to the bobbin works, and he carried Dianne across the snowdrift outside the school gates. When I got into school I put my socks on the central heating pipes, where steam rose from them. I towelled my feet dry with the sleeves of my sweater, then rubbed them between my hands to bring back the circulation. Itching painful chilblains would develop if I didn't dry them, and I could burn myself if I put my cold, wet feet onto the pipes.

The spring of 1947 didn't bring good news for the farmers. With the thaw came devastating floods. Tens of thousands of cattle drowned.

Every Christmas Mam and Dad took us to a pantomime at the Liverpool Empire. Riding from Garston to Liverpool city centre on the 33 tram at night was a magical experience. We joined the queue opposite the tram sheds and watched the flashes of electricity from the overhead cables. There were dozens of conversations going on at once and the shelter smelled of steaming bodies and cigarette smoke. As we climbed aboard the tram the queue divided and the smokers went upstairs while we went on the lower deck. If there were any empty seats we would sit down, but usually we stood for the whole journey. If the tram filled up then we stood up for adults. Men stood up and gave their seats to women.

'Madam, would you like this seat?' Harry said, offering his seat to Mam with a bow and a flourish when he was eight years old. She flushed with pride. She tried to hide her feelings for him, but he was her favourite.

When the tram went through the posh areas, Cressington and Aigburth, they were as dark and quiet as they had been during the blackout. The middle-class people, it would be misnomer to describe them as a community, hid behind their hedges from their neighbours and the common horde. Gradually, through the darkness, we saw lights twinkling. They came from the main road just past the Victorian entrance to Sefton Park.

Soon we were in the built-up area of small shops and rows of terraced houses where lights blazed from every window. The windows of each shop were dressed with cotton wool snow scenes. Strung along the road were snowmen and Christmas trees made from cardboard, paper and tinfoil bunting and strings of multicoloured electric bulbs. Lark Lane, Toxteth, and The Dingle were glittering in a kaleidoscope of light. Each city centre shop window took up splendid themes of Christmas in the snow, with reindeer, Father Christmas, fairies and parcels.

Almost unable to breathe with excitement we entered the theatre. There the resplendent chandeliers sparkled on the rich red curtains with their golden tassels. We watched, enchanted, as the patrons in the dress circle, stalls and boxes were shown to their seats. The women were attired in fashionable evening dresses while the men wore smartly tailored suits.

Mam would pass a bag of sweets along the row. When we had unwrapped it we would keep the sweet paper in a pocket until the interval when she would collect them.

At last the curtain went up. The pantomime began. Buttons,

the page boy, would be a pretty woman. The dame, who was a baddy, would be a big, ugly man with large bosoms who wore a turban and a flowered pinafore. He would chase Buttons around the stage and tell jokes with double meanings.

'He's behind you,' we yelled.

Dad was a total innocent throughout his life. He never understood double entendre and couldn't comprehend why the audience laughed so heartily. Forty years later, at the Sherman Theatre in Cardiff, we were watching *Princess Ida* by Gilbert and Sullivan.

'I'm half a fairy,' said the leading man.

The audience erupted into hysterics when his future father-in-law asked, 'Which half?'

Dad looked totally bemused.

'I don't see what was so funny,' he said to me, while everyone else was still howling with laughter.

'I think the audience is in that kind of mood,' I replied. 'They are ready to laugh at anything.'

Back at the pantomime we followed Mam and Dad to a corner of the noisy bar during the interval. Whenever we went out Mam was always loaded down with shopping bags of food and drinks. These were handed out to us and we were watched carefully to ensure we didn't spill or drop anything. Some years, when our parents had money to spare, we would be treated to ice cream.

We trouped back to our seats surrounded by the deafening chatter of hundreds of happy families. The curtain went up and we were transported to a wonderland of slapstick and beauty.

For three hours we laughed and shouted. Tears ran down our faces, our jaws ached and voices were hoarse from shouting and singing.

In the last dazzling scene the princess married her prince and the whole cast came on to the stage two by two in their fairy-tale costumes of satins and silks, to thunderous applause, and the music reached a crescendo.

We were in a dream as we followed Mam and Dad out of

the theatre and onto the tram. Staring out of the window at the street decorations, our minds were filled with the spectacle we had been immersed in all evening.

At the beginning of the school holiday Mam took us into Liverpool city centre to see the decorated windows in the big stores and to visit Father Christmas. Each of the stores would have a Christmas scene in the window. While busy shoppers crowded the pavements, weaving past each other in every direction, we stood with our noses against the glass and looked in wonderment at the displays. Many windows would take a theme from popular fairy tales *Snow White and the Seven Dwarfs*, *Cinderella* or *Babes in the Woods*. Most had snow scenes with snowmen, sleighs, reindeer and Father Christmas. There was usually some animation. The dwarfs would nod their heads, sleighs would rock, Father Christmas climbed into a chimney carrying his sack of toys. It was a world of sheer magic.

When we had seen the windows of five or six stores, we would go to Blackler's. Santa's grotto was the length of the toy department. Tiny lights sparkled from the ceiling. Reindeer stood in snow. Fairies or angels flew above us. Trees were hung with icicles. Bells tinkled. Christmas carols played. My heart was ready to burst by the time I reached the cave, filled with light, where Father Christmas sat waiting for me. Beside the cave was the sleigh, overflowing with parcels. Father Christmas wouldn't be giving me a present. I would tell him what I wanted and he would bring it on Christmas Day. At last it was my turn. He took my hands and invited me to sit on his knee. Then he asked me my name. I could hardly speak for excitement when I told him what I wanted as a present. Did I ever receive the requested gift? I honestly can't remember. When Christmas Day arrived I was delighted with the gifts I received.

A Christmas fair was held in the main Sunday school room on the last Saturday before Christmas. The women's sewing group would have made a whole variety of handicrafts, from crocheted doilies to protect polished surfaces, to padded coat hangers covered in frilly taffeta. Delicious home-made cakes were for sale on another stall. The back of the room had tables and chairs near the hatch to the spacious kitchen where toothsome treats were being served with cups of weak, milky tea or mineral water.

In the evening there was a Nativity play on the big stage at the other end of the room.

There were plays and pantomimes performed throughout the winter months. The actors were usually members of the congregation but travelling amateur dramatic groups visited occasionally.

In Bethel there were variety concerts with boys doing solo tap dances, troops of girls dancing ballet, instrumental quartets, piano accordionists, singers, choirs, piano soloist and duets.

One year the Methodist congregation put on *Robinson Crusoe*. Dorothy played a black woman in a straw skirt. Her hair made a great impression. She spent most of her life trying to get it to lie down. For this play she rubbed in cocoa and brushed it up until it stood around her head like a halo. Her performance brought the house down but the audience couldn't believe she wasn't wearing a wig.

Pantomime at Banks Road Methodist Church. Dorothy is on the far right, next to the blacked-up man.

Uncle Tom, Aunt Mamie and baby Elaine visited once or twice a year until he was posted to Germany in 1946. Mamie was making a name for herself on the stage before Tom came home from the war. She gave it all up to marry Tom. I knew nothing of Mamie's past fame but found her large, stately and bosomy. She was full of airs and graces and talked down to me. Uncle Tom had dark, Mediterranean, good looks. I was fascinated by him.

It would be difficult to find two brothers more diametrically different than Alf and Tom Smith. Dad was open to new ideas throughout his life, an artist and a hedonist. With his abundant blond hair and pale blue eyes he could have been Scandinavian, or one of Hitler's master race. He had no dress sense and took no interest in his appearance but he was proud of his hair. In accordance with the fashion he had a short back and sides and a straight parting. Uncle Tom was a bigot from the time I met him, when he was in his twenties, until the day he died. His serge uniform was smooth and every lapel pressed flat. The crease down the centre of his trouser legs was razor sharp. Many years later, when my brother Tom was in the RAF, he told us some of the tricks service men use to achieve that result. Some stitched lapels and leg creases while others used soap to hold them in place, or so our Tom said. Uncle Tom's shoes shone like twin mirrors. His straight, black hair also shone as it was slicked down with oil.

Drawn by its strange texture, I stood behind his chair and, reaching out, began to stroke it. Totally absorbed, I caressed it from parting, across the top then down to the shaved area at the nape of his neck.

A howl of laughter, from brother Tom, woke me from my reverie. I looked up to find the whole family grinning at me. We never touched each other. Their laughter was to cover their embarrassment. I felt myself blushing to my roots.

In the back kitchen of our house we had a wooden table that Mam scrubbed white and there were benches on both sides. A few weeks before Christmas, Mam bought centimetre-wide spools of pastel coloured paper, pale green, yellow, blue and pink, for making decorations. There were one or two rolls of silver foil too. We spent the dark, cold evenings cutting the paper and making paper chains. The paper would be stuck with paste made from flour and water. Silver foil had to be handled with extreme care. It ripped easily and could cut your fingers. Commercial gum was needed to form the foil strip into a chain.

Then came the special day when Dad hung the decorations in the living room, which we called the kitchen. This was his favourite part of Christmas. He started by attaching a string of paper chains or a paper streamer to the ceiling in one corner and taking it ninety degrees to the opposite corner. This would be repeated with the next corner, taking the next streamer ninety degrees. Then he would cross and re-cross the room from every angle, taking care not to break the delicate gas mantle that hung from a tube in the centre of the room. After this he would wind streamers in and out of the ones crossing the room until the ceiling disappeared under a spider's web of coloured paper.

On the weekend before Christmas we would go for a walk and find holly with berries to surround the picture frames and sprigs of mistletoe to hang above the front door and the kitchen door. If we couldn't find any mistletoe we would buy it. If we failed to find holly with berries we made them with paper and glued them to the holly twig.

One evening the congregation of the Methodist chapel would meet carrying lanterns and collecting boxes to go carol singing around the streets. We would knock at the doors of a dozen houses, then stand in a circle in the centre of the road and the people would come out to enjoy two or three carols, often joining in with the singing. This was repeated at intervals. Sometimes the neighbours stayed out to listen as we moved further along the street and took the opportunity to chat to each other. Our fingers, toes and noses tingled in the cold night air. As I took a breath in to sing the sub zero air hit my lungs.

We filled the air with steam when we exhaled. I soon learned to cover my mouth with a scarf to keep out the worst of the chill. Woollen fibres in my mouth muffled the words and had a detrimental effect on the quality and power of my singing.

Freda and Evelyn often took me with them to see a film at the Garston Empire Cinema. One of the films was *My Uncle Silas*. It was a horror film with an eye on the screen but no body. It terrified me and gave me nightmares for weeks.

The fear I had from Uncle Silas was nothing compared with the terror of *Pinocchio*. The journey to the cinema with Mam, Dad, Harry and Dianne had been full of joy and excitement. Tickets for the Plaza in Allerton must have cost Dad a week's wages. Entering through a tall doorway we found ourselves in a palatial foyer ablaze with white light. The floor was tiled in cool, pale marble. The centrepiece was a ceramic bowl, two metres in diameter, containing goldfish. My senses were exploding.

Enraptured, we went into the cinema and took our seats. I was captivated by the big screen, the colour, the magic of the story unfolding. It was good for the woodcarver to have a son. I started worrying when he was persuaded not to go to school. After that my anxiety level rose higher and higher. My stomach muscles were clenched tight. I don't know which was most terrifying, the boys developing the ears of donkeys, or Pinocchio's nose growing each time he told a lie until it became a branch. Identifying with a fictional character like Dick Barton Special Agent and enjoying their thrills and spills didn't cause any lasting damage. The scrapes the hero found himself in were not caused by lying or disobedience and I knew he would escape in the next episode. *Pinocchio* is a Victorian morality tale that should have had an X certificate. It disturbed my sleep in the weeks following the film and returned to haunt me day and night for years to come. It probably marked me for life.

One night Freda and Evelyn took me with them to New Brighton. I was hugging myself with delight as we rode to

Liverpool on the tram and waited for the ferry across the Mersey. Lights from Cammell Laird's shipyard and Birkenhead docks lit up the river opposite Liverpool Pierhead. I had never been on the ferry at night and had never crossed directly to New Brighton. Whenever we went with Mam we crossed to Wallasey and walked along the shore. The Wallasey crossing was much cheaper. The men leaning on the rails of the ferry wore heavy overcoats over their uniforms or demob suits. Most of these National Service men were in the Army but there were a few RAF and Royal Navy. They smoked woodbines and whistled at the girls who were parading the decks and pretending to ignore them. Occasionally, one of the women would stop.

'Who y whistling at fella? I'm norra dog.'

These were the early moves in the flirting game. Some of the women had found a man for the evening by the time we disembarked. RAF men were regarded as a better catch than Army, while Royal Navy men were definitely a few notches up from merchant seamen.

The Figure of Eight could be seen for miles around. As we walked towards the fairground, I could barely contain my ecstasy. I had never been on any of the rides. Now we were going to go on everything. I was convinced we were. I followed them around with bated breath. After walking around for half an hour or more we left the fairground and crossed the road to the pier. It began to dawn upon me that we wouldn't be going on anything. Hiding my disappointment, I tried to take an interest in the sideshows. One of them was a tank with half crown coins at the bottom. If you could get a penny to land on a half crown you would win it. I couldn't see how you could lose. Maybe I had a penny or Freda took pity on me and gave me one. In my daydream I had already won my prize and was on my way to take a ride on the Figure of Eight. Back in the real world I dropped the penny into the water directly above the half crown. I couldn't believe my eyes when my penny went nowhere near the coveted prize.

Once Dad started working as a fitter's mate on Liverpool

Transport, we joined the children of the transport workers for the annual pantomime at the John Lewis Theatre. These outings were memorable. But I would be happy to forget them.

We would board a cavalcade of buses at Garston bus sheds for the twenty-minute journey. If there were adult stewards travelling with us they kept their heads down. Everyone shouted at full volume while throwing anything that wasn't tied down. Thankfully, it was before the days when hooligans started ripping out seats. The missiles were hats or caps or sweets given to us by naïve adults as we boarded the bus. The bags the sweets came in became paper aeroplanes.

The production was amateur, but I didn't realise it at the time. I was aware that it didn't measure up to the pantomimes at the Empire. There was no luxury, no romance and the jokes weren't funny the first time. We couldn't believe our eyes and ears when we found it was exactly the same performance year after year. We were very obedient and uncomplaining children but we begged to be excused when it came around for the next year. The day after going through this tedious experience for the third time, we took our courage in both hands and told Dad we hated the bus ride and the show had been the same as the previous years. He listened, and we never went again.

Freda was a trainee confectioner at Wallers. Dad wouldn't allow her to work in an office, because she might get ideas above her station, but he didn't want her working in a factory and mixing with common girls. She made the Christmas cake every year, and still does.

We used to sing to the tune of 'Colonel Bogey':

Wallers, they make the best mince pies.
Wallers, they make the best mince pies.
Wallers, I tell you, Wallers, bla bla bla, etc.

A few days before Christmas we all helped Mam make the Christmas pudding. In the kitchen Dad was battening down the hatches. He shut us into the back kitchen with Mam and closed the door to the front passage. After putting more coal on the fire and pulling out the damper, he climbed on a chair to close the curtains. Curtains were one of Mam's few indulgences. The kitchen window was barely one and a half metres wide by two metres high but the heavy, pleated chintz curtains were three metres wide and three metres high with a matching pelmet along the top to hide the curtain fittings.

In the draughty back kitchen we gathered around the table to take in the aroma of nutmeg, ginger and allspice as Mam added them to the massive mixing bowl of flour, lard and cheap margarine. The nutmeg was scraped on the cheese grater, scratching Mam's fingers. We only ever saw spices at Christmas. They must have been carefully stored for this annual event of making the Christmas pudding, for they retained some of their distinctive bouquet over the years. I can't remember whether dehydrated egg powder was used. Fresh eggs might have replaced the powdered variety now that we were living Under the Bridge. We had hens in the back yard once more. Before the mixed peel and raisins were added, the mixture was carried into the kitchen.

'Shut the damned door,' Dad would shout.

We all crowded into the room as fast as we could. We didn't want him spoiling the ceremony by getting in a rage.

From September to April he would bawl at us to shut the door. We would just be getting used to closing it when May arrived and he would yell at us to 'Leave the damn doors open. You are all going to suffocate.'

At last Mam was going to allow us to stir the pudding. Dad was sitting in his chair, the only armchair in the room. We sat in straight backed dining chairs facing the fire waiting for our turn, brim full with excitement. At last the bowl would be between my knees and, as I beat the mixture, I closed my eyes and made a secret wish. The longer we whipped the pudding the more possibility there was of our wish being granted. With the best will in the world I couldn't manage more than five minutes, though it seemed much longer. The ache in my arm forced me to pass the bowl on.

I would sit staring into the fire, seeing fiery caverns, yellow waterfalls, castles, mountains and fairy glens, knowing that my wish would be granted.

From the age of two until I was eight years old I had lived in the tenements. Harry and Dianne had never lived anywhere else. The only animal we had through those five years was Mary the cat.

It was a novelty for us when a dog and hens joined the household. In later years rabbits and ducklings were added to the menagerie that was kept in our air-raid shelter. They also had the run of the back yard. Neighbours were always bringing hens back after they made a bid for freedom over the yard wall. Throughout the year the hens supplied us with eggs. We would hunt for the eggs each day among Dad's tools, bits of rusting bike parts, broken furniture, and all the other stored treasures that might be needed one day. The hens were very good at ferreting them away. Sometimes we found none for days and thought they had stopped laying, then we would uncover half a dozen.

The day before Christmas we found Mam in the back kitchen plucking feathers from two dead hens that lay on the kitchen table. I retched at the sight. Harry and Dianne were chalk white. No-one else in the family found the killing of the hens remarkable. Normal life had resumed. Before the war it had been traditional for Dad to kill hens for Christmas dinner.

When Mam called us to the table to eat our tea, the chickens lay pink, pimply, and bare. She was absorbed in the task of disembowelling them. We looked in amazement at the soft eggs without shells. I can't remember whether they had a use, but nothing was ever wasted, so they must have done. The offal became soup.

For the few years, while we couldn't keep animals and meat was rationed, Dad would bring home rabbit and joke that we were having four legged chicken.

We were sent to bed early on Christmas Eve. 'Father Christmas can't come until you're fast asleep,' Mam told us. We didn't seem to doze at all but we must have slept for our stockings were filled and tied to the bottom of the bed.

'Is it morning yet?' we would call downstairs to Mam.

She would stay up all night, dozing in Dad's chair, guarding the presents Father Christmas had brought for us.

'It's too early,' she replied for the umpteenth time between 2am and 7am.

One unforgettable Christmas when, at last, we were allowed to come down to the kitchen, she pushed back the chair to reveal a cradle draped in pale blue taffeta. I stood looking at it. The shimmering of the beautiful silken folds in the dim gaslight left me speechless. At last I knelt beside the cradle but I didn't want to disturb the fall of the curtains to open them and look at the doll within. I was mesmerized by the play of light on the fabric.

There was always one special present and the Christmas stocking.

During the war lots of fathers who were serving in the forces made pedal cars in the form of tanks for their sons. Dad made a wonderful fire engine for Richard with all the pumps, lengths of hose, and lots of meters, nuts and bolts. There was a photograph of Tom aged about five sitting on a toy steam engine. I expect that was his pedal car. Harry's was a straightforward open-topped car. Unfortunately his knees hit the bonnet when he was pedalling.

While the boys received pedal cars, the girls were presented with a doll's house. The entire front of my house was hinged so that I could re-arrange the furniture upstairs and down. Each of the rooms in the house was wallpapered in a different pattern and colour. That is surprising, as I remember all the walls in our home being painted, including the passageway to the front door which had a chocolate brown embossed dado to a height of four feet. With the front of the doll's house open, I saw similarities to the half-bombed houses. This didn't carry any frightening undertones for me. I knew nobody who had been bombed and my memories of the air-raid shelter were full of jollity.

The ground floor had been furnished as a sitting room and living room with the wall-to-ceiling curtains favoured by Mam. In the kitchen there was a plain table, a cooking stove, a mangle and a big sink containing a scrubbing board and a wooden dolly for swishing and twirling the clothes in the water. In the bedrooms there were beautiful curtains again. Each bed was covered in a pretty counterpane.

Fashionable Miss Leach, the keeper of the school library, was my form teacher in my last year in junior school. When she asked whether any of us had a doll's house I jumped up and down with excitement waving my hand in the air. She invited those who had them to bring them in.

I searched all over the house and eventually found it in the air-raid shelter where it had lain neglected for years amongst the coal dust and hens droppings. There was little left of the furniture. The wallpaper was stained. The front had gone. The house had been made of plywood that had separated into curled strips of wood that hardly held together. It didn't occur to me not to take it in to school. I was sad to see my glorious toy reduced to this sorry state, but I had promised I would bring it. For a day this dirty collection of plywood lay in the corner of the classroom, the odour of chicken dung mixing with the bouquet of unwashed bodies. Nobody asked me what it was or why I had brought it. By the next day it had disappeared.

A favourite toy Dad used to make for us was a scooter. That was made from two pieces of wood at right angles to each other and two small wheels. This gave us hours of fun, scooting and racing along the street, and the materials cost barely anything.

We had clogs one year. Where he bought them I can't imagine. We wore them for a short time as a novelty but they weren't practical when strapping on roller skates or using the scooter. We couldn't be persuaded to wear them for school. He

101

had hoped they would save on new shoes or on shoe leather. He always repaired our shoes. Every effort was made to get us to clean and polish shoes as he said they would stay weatherproof longer. We rarely remembered. Life was too short and we had so much to fit in.

Dad bought a piano for Freda for five pounds, half a week's wages in 1945. She was eighteen and boys, clothes, make up and dancing took precedence. However somebody else was making use of the piano. Sunday school songs and nursery rhymes were being picked out tentatively with the right hand. It was Harry. At seven he was sent off to take lessons with the two maiden ladies who ran the drapery shop in Window Lane.

He loved singing. Freda sat to listen when he was singing 'Christopher Robin'. She didn't want to correct him but at seven he was too old for baby talk.

When he sang, 'Hush, hush, whisper who dares. Christopher Robin is saying his prayers,' she said, 'It's whisper who's there.'

Decades later I was singing a lullaby to one of the grandchildren and sang 'Hush, hush, whisper who dares.'

Freda had an eureka moment and went into a fit of giggling.

'I thought Harry was talking Liverpudlian. Who dat down der in the dark,' she laughed.

Once Dad was up, at about 8am on Christmas morning, we could look inside our Christmas stockings. We each had one of his socks. Inside there would be small presents to unwrap, for example cheap sweets that took few ration coupons, coloured chalks, and a pencil sharpener. At the bottom would be an apple and an orange, or in later years a tangerine. Tiny cracks in my thumb tip would smart as I dug my nail into the tough orange skin to reveal the white pith. Droplets of sharp, mouth-watering juice would shoot out to spill over my hands as I pulled the segments apart and the scent would fill the room. There were no oranges or bananas during the war.

Dianne took half an hour or longer to peel and eat an orange.

She couldn't start eating it until every speck of pith had been removed from the outside, then each white strand had to be taken from a segment before she could put it into her mouth.

There was a family tradition that once we had taken all of our presents out of our stocking Dad would put a hand into his. After fighting to free himself from the contents, he would pull out a sprouting onion, an ugly misshapen carrot, a potato full of eyes and an ill-assortment of other amorphous vegetables. We would watch him with tears running down our faces every year.

Christmas was Sunday writ large. Everyone was at home and falling over each other. The nerves of our older siblings and the adults were jangling as they tried to prepare the vast array of vegetables, stuffing, gravy and other ingredients necessary for a traditional Christmas dinner.

We three little ones sat on the floor near the kitchen fire, engrossed in our games while mayhem reigned around us. It didn't occur to anyone to light a fire in the empty sitting room and send us to play in there. The bedrooms, like the sitting room, were freezing cold. There was no heating anywhere in the house except the fire in the kitchen and the gas cooker in the back kitchen.

We were fortunate in having an oven and hob beside the coal fire and the gas oven in the back kitchen. The kitchen oven was no use for cooking where the heat had to be controlled, as with the roast chicken, but it was handy for warming plates, keeping cooked food warm or heating mince pies. It was perfect for roasting chestnuts on Christmas evening. The Christmas puddings were so enormous they had to steam for hours. They bubbled away merrily on the hob. The kettle stood next to the steamer to refill the water and make endless pots of tea.

At ten minutes to eleven Mam was left amongst the vegetable peelings, watching the ovens. The rest of the family, each dressed in the one good outfit kept for wearing on Sundays, piled out of the house to go to Christmas morning service in the Methodist chapel. Mam would have been worried sick with the responsibility of seeing to the food but the quiet and space must have been a great relief.

Although providing meals on a day-by-day basis was a constant trial for Mam, at Christmas, when she had to produce the most challenging meals for the largest number of people, she came into her own. Christmas dinner was always a triumph. Four hours later a scrumptious tea of sandwiches, trifle, Christmas cake, and mince pies would excite our eyes and taste buds. Paper lace doilies decorated the sandwich and cake plates.

The tantalizing smell of ham boiling filled the house on Boxing Day. Dinner would start with lentil soup made with the stock from the vegetables, offal and a leg of ham. This was followed by piping hot ham with vegetables and a dessert of rice pudding that was light brown and creamy from being in the oven for hours, or an apple pie of short crust pastry and custard. For tea we would have cold meats with bread and butter, to finish the chicken and ham, followed by hot mince pies.

Our footsteps and chatter echoed in the crisp winter air as we made our way to chapel. There were very few people about and there was no traffic. The tuneless bell of St Michael's church called the congregation to the Church of England. Churchgoers were the only ones about.

The joyous organ music greeted us as we opened the inner door of the Methodist chapel and felt the warmth and light envelop us. Our chapel community was packed into the pews, whispering their Christmas greetings to each other. The organ and people fell silent and the minister rose to his feet to announce the first carol.

Hark the herald angels sing
Glory to the new born king.

The singing raised the roof. We savoured the perfect harmonies, the graceful poetry of the words and treasured these precious moments when we were lifted above worldly knowledge.

After an hour in the realms of heaven the service was over and we were disgorged onto the cold, mean streets once more. Christmas would have lacked its essence without this transcending hour.

We returned to our games beside the kitchen fire, oblivious to the chaos around us, until we were called to join the crush of bodies around the table. Dianne sat on Dorothy's knee. There was barely room for Harry and me even though we were standing. The table was weighed down with food. Beside each plate was a Christmas cracker. Inside each cracker there would be a crown made from pastel coloured tissue paper to be worn for the meal, a cheap gift and a joke.

On my plate was a piece of dead hen. I gulped, feeling horrified and nauseated. Looking up I caught Harry's eye. All colour had drained from his face. Dianne was quietly declining a morsel offered to her by Dorothy. I began working my way around the plate, eating the crisp, golden roast potatoes, the mashed carrots and turnips, firm emerald sprouts, delicious herbal stuffing and plump pork sausages, carefully circumnavigating the dead pet.

Normally Dad would have punished us for leaving food, but we discovered that the rules were different at Christmas. The most likely explanation was that our rebellion went unnoticed because there was satiety of food. Maybe he wanted to keep the atmosphere jolly. Recognition of, or empathy with, our feelings was the least probable answer, but perhaps my low opinion of his insight and sensitivity was misplaced. Almost two decades later, when an emotional entanglement was tying me in knots, I was surprised and grateful for his understanding.

After dinner it was the task of Harry, Dianne and me to wash and dry the crockery and cutlery. The older children would deal with the more difficult work of cleaning pans and bowls.

We would have liked to return to playing with our toys after our work was done but it was traditional to go for a walk once all the cooking implements had been returned to their place. This gave Mam and Dad a few hours of peace. The teenage girls were glad to be out, flirting with the boys they had been making eyes at in chapel during the morning service, while the boys chased each other and fought.

We usually walked around the perimeter of the airport. In front of us and behind us walked other family groups, gangs of giggling teenage girls or youths, squabbling boys, and doe-eyed couples. It was the nearest open aspect, with grass and an unbroken view of the sky as far as Speke church, Speke Hall and the river Mersey. Across the river was the Wirral peninsula. Far away, on a clear day, the hills of Wales could be seen beyond the flat landscape. At the tenements, where we had lived during the war, we crossed the road. We walked down Meredith Street, then along Vineyard Street beside the stream that ran from Garston village, through The Willows and under a culvert to the ditch where we used to make mud pies when we lived there.

Surprisingly, a man called Meredith once owned a vineyard in Garston.

We turned right, away from The Willows, under the railway bridge and along The Avenue to Allerton. Apart from walking along the Mersey, this was the nearest open space where we could take a walk. Between the gasworks and the airport, then along a railway siding, could hardly be described as a stroll in the country. There were parks. The nearest was Garston Park, flat and uninteresting. Further afield were Calderstones Park, Sefton Park and Woolton Woods a joy of hillocks, greenhouses, statues, landscape and flora. Unfortunately, they were all beyond our childhood strength and horizons. We needed somewhere within a two-mile radius that we could reach without transport.

When the three babies had washed up the crockery and cutlery after tea on Christmas evening, we joined the rest of the family in the crowded kitchen. We squeezed into a space on the floor with Tom and Richard. They were in front of the fire between the four dining room chairs that were occupied by Mam and the three older girls, Dad in his armchair, and the Singer sewing machine. The sideboard took up the whole of the wall opposite the fireplace, between the two doors.

Every evening we would be sitting like this in the kitchen, knitting, sewing, darning socks, drawing or writing as we talked.

My job for many years was darning socks for the family. Dad had learned when he was at sea and taught me the craft. By the age of ten I was proud of my prowess. Imagine my distress when Tom caught sight of the sock I was darning for him, and laughed. My weaving was a work of art.

'They are my grey school socks,' Tom chortled.

'Yes,' I responded. There was nothing wrong with my eyes. I could see they were grey socks.

'You're darning them with black wool.'

Each time Dad had illustrated the craft of darning to me he had used the first wool he found in the wool box irrespective of the colour of the sock. I dutifully followed his example.

Dad was colour-blind.

There could be three or four different discussions in progress in the kitchen and we were able to dip in and out of other arguments while continuing our own discourse. If we were reading we could switch off totally from the hubbub around us.

On the evenings of Christmas and Boxing Day, Mam and Dad organised games for us to play like: I spy, Pass the Parcel, Simon Says, word games or starting a story.

Simon Says was one of my favourite games. Dorothy was usually the leader. The rule was that everyone had to do what 'Simon Says'. It could be: Simon says touch your knees with your nose; Simon says put your right elbow on your head or put your thumbs in your ears and wiggle your fingers. If you did the last one, thumbs in ears and wiggle your fingers, you would be out, because Dorothy hadn't said 'Simon says' before the action. The winner was the person who stayed in the game the longest.

After the games Mam would bring out well-thumbed books of community songs.

In Dublin's fair city,
Where the girls are so pretty,
I first set my eyes on sweet Molly Malone,
She wheels her wheelbarrow,
Through the streets broad and narrow,
Crying, 'Cockles and mussels, alive, alive oh.'

We loved the descant in the last chorus, and sang with gusto.

Alive, alive oh!
Alive, alive oh!
Crying, 'Cockles and mussels, alive, alive oh.'

Clementine would follow, 'Blowing bubbles mighty fine.' Then there were love songs from the 1920s such as: 'If you were the only girl in the world'. Mam would become nostalgic and starry-eyed.

We would be carried to bed at 7.30. If we were awake we would say our prayers, then Mam or Dad would tell us a story.

Next morning the siren would blow from the bobbin works and the holiday was over for the adults, except for New Year's Eve.

Banks Road Methodist chapel held a social in the big Sunday school hall on New Year's Eve. There was a barn dance with a caller. I always dreaded the moment when my partner and I were the first in a set in the folk dance, as I could never remember which way to go. In the other folk dances I would change partners at the wrong time and bump into people or lose my next partner completely. I didn't improve with age.

It was more like bumper cars on a collision course than a dance.

This was followed by a service in the chapel that ended at midnight. While everyone else was wishing each other happy new year, we were wishing Mam happy birthday. It was a magical experience to be in the brightly lit chapel in the middle of the night. Outside, under the lamplight, we joined hands in a circle with the congregation to sing 'Auld Lang Syne'. All along the streets people called out 'Happy New Year' to us as we passed. There was singing and dancing everywhere we looked along side streets. Ships on the river hooted their foghorns and the bells rang from St Michael's church.

We arrived home to find the table set for a party to celebrate Mam's birthday. She loved her lace paper doilies and decorated all the side plates and cake plates with them.

The adrenaline kept us going for another hour as we demolished plates full of sandwiches, cakes, and jelly with evaporated milk.

At 1am our Mam and Dad would take us up to bed, for we were tired little teddy bears.

Downstairs the family was singing old favourites from the community songbook to the clatter of crockery being washed and dried.

They crawled bleary-eyed from their beds as the siren blew next morning. The winter festival was over for the adults for another year.

We still had one week to play with our friends in the street. The possibilities were endless. At the end of each block of houses there was a playground. Besides swings ours had metal bars for tossing over or balancing on. It also had monkey bars and a ladder laid across two steel upright supports two metres from the ground. We would swing hand over hand from one end to the other, a distance of six or seven metres.

Two or three years after the Second World War, we were still calling 'Bombs over Berlin' and making Tommy gun sounds as we flew through the sky on our swings.

At the beginning of the 1960s the smaller swing parks disappeared. The reason given was that they were unsafe. Council houses were built on the vacant plots.

There was a tiny leisure area next to the school that had a bowling green, a grassed area for walking a dog, and a well-endowed playground that had every kind of swing, climbing frame and roundabout imaginable.

The playground on the other side of Window Lane was outside of our territory, although it was geographically nearer than the one by the school. It was a known fact, amongst the children on our side of Window Lane, that the children who lived in the terraced streets near that playground went to the tiny Church of England school. They were the sworn enemies of the children in the county school. The Roman Catholics were reputed to live in the tiny two-up, two-down back-to-back houses that bordered the dock wall. If any of these groups ever crossed paths, it was their duty to call each other names.

It is unlikely that the community Under the Bridge was cleanly divided. Residents took houses to rent as they became available, but they would naturally gravitate towards people of like mind. Mam had grown up in a home divided by religion. She tried to discourage all forms of discrimination. One of her stories was that the local dressmaker, a Roman Catholic, made the dresses for the children for the Orange Parade on the twelfth of July. Inter-religious rivalry and violence were rife when Dad arrived in Garston in 1912. 'A plague on both your houses' was his attitude when I was growing up. Nevertheless, he lived with his Uncle Harry and Aunt Jane on the Church of England side of Window Lane and attended the Church of England school as he had done in Ainsdale. Dorothy and Freda started their education in the Church of England but by the time Evelyn was ready to start school he had changed his allegiance to the county school.

Once Harry, Dianne and I discovered one special pleasure in the playground on the Church of England side, we were prepared to cross into an alien land and face unknown children to play on it. This tempting piece of equipment was a gigantic swing that looked like a battering ram. It took fifteen or more children. The group at one end faced the group at the other end. From a very slow start the two groups pushed back and forth on the ground until the battering ram rose up, heavily and stolidly at first, then, as we all leaned in the direction of its backward or forward motion, it was carried higher and faster until we were flying.

Hidden away in his shed was the park keeper. His word was law, but he didn't bother us if we didn't bother him.

Dad made a swing for us in the back yard. One winter, after a heavy snowfall, I wiped the crunchy snow from the seat and kicked off from the enclosed yard to be carried above the wall. Virgin snow covered the rooftops, air-raid shelters and pigeon coops. Along the yard walls it stood, like icing on slices of Christmas cake. The stark, empty perfection moved me to ecstasy. I sang joyfully as I pumped the air.

Suddenly I felt intense loneliness. 'What is the point of this?' I asked myself, possibly for the first time. Many times in the future I would pose the same question.

I had been delighted when Dad put up our own swing. In the swing park we had to wait in a queue for our turn and the time we could spend on the swing was limited as others were waiting. Part of the pleasure of playing on the swings, I realised, was chatting with other children in the queue, or competing with those on the other swings to see who could rise highest or stay up longest.

The Methodist Sunday school filled the three church halls and vestry every Sunday. At the back of the church the young people were in the vestry while the seniors occupied the main hall. Across the road in the church hall, infants were in the small room and juniors filled the big activities room that housed the stage, kitchen and toilets.

Once a year we were taken to Woolton Woods in a convoy of buses for the Sunday school treat. The sun always shone. We ran races with egg and spoon, in sacks, or three-legged. Trees were climbed and grass banks were rolled down.

Happily exhausted, we would form a crocodile to cross the road to Woolton Methodist church hall. Trestle tables were weighed down with sandwiches and fairy cakes of all shapes and sizes, iced in dozens of pastel shades.

There was none of the anarchy on these trips that we experienced on the visits to the pantomime organised by Liverpool Transport employees. Each Sunday school teacher kept a friendly watchful eye on her charges on the bus, on the field, and at the party. If we took a sandwich or cake we knew we would be expected to finish it. Food was scarce and couldn't be wasted. We were well mannered and well behaved and having the time of our lives.

My best friend Maureen Mowatt and I spent every evening and all day during the holidays playing in the street or exchanging books. We would sit on the front doorstep reading them.

She loaned me her copy of the Greek myths. The binding had gone long before and the pages were ragged from much turning. Perhaps it had belonged to her mother or father, or maybe it had been bought second hand at a jumble sale.

In the evening when the family was gathered in the living room I would be oblivious to whatever activities or conversation were taking place while I was reading. Dad used to become very angry when he addressed me and received no response.

In the winter I strained my eyes as I read by the dim gaslight. At bedtime I secreted a bicycle lamp under my jumper. After Mam and Dad had told us a story, said prayers with us, and gone downstairs, I switched on the torch under the blankets and continued reading.

The Greek myths terrified and enthralled me. I picked the book up as soon as we finished washing up the dishes after breakfast every morning and had my nose back in it until I fell asleep at night. If there was shopping or cleaning to be done, which wasn't very often, I had to be shaken before Mam had a response from me. When I came to the end of the book I went back to my favourite parts. With great reluctance I returned it to Maureen after devouring it for two weeks.

We spent hours every day honing our acrobatic and ball game skills. Tucking our skirts into our knickers we did handstands against the wall of the house, tossed right over and walked like crabs or did cartwheels along the street. Ball games were accompanied by songs.

> One-two-three alera
> Four-five-six alera
> Seven-eight-nine alera
> Ten alera, post the ball.

The ball was bounced against the wall. Each time you said 'alera' you stood on the left leg and bounced the ball under the right leg and onto the wall. To post the ball you turned your back to the wall, bounced the ball between your legs then turned round to catch it. We started with one ball. As our co-ordination improved we juggled with two balls and then three.

All the children in the street joined together for 'Truth, Dare or Promise', singing games and skipping games.

Maureen and I hated Truth, Dare or Promise. You could be dared to do something frightening, dangerous, or very naughty. Promise was just as bad. It was like playing Chicken. We could have refused to play but they would have laughed at us. The children who thought up the penalties must have had twisted minds. I went for Truth, as the safest option.

The only question I can remember was, 'What is your mother's first name?'

The answer was Martha but I was trembling as I whispered it. I was sure I wasn't supposed to know.

'Orange and Lemons say the bells of St Clement's' we sang as we all skipped in pairs under the arched arms of two of friends. We giggled with feigned fear as we approached the arch at the end of the song.

'Chop off your little, wooden head.'

The arched arms would fall on the pair passing under, grabbing them as they tried to run out.

> The big ship sails through the Alley, Alley O,
> Alley, Alley O, Alley, Alley O,
> The big ship sails through the Alley, Alley O,
> On the twenty-first of August.

We sang as we skipped in a line under an arch formed by one person standing against the wall. As we came through the arch we faced the line going in. Our arms were crossed as they would be for 'Auld Lang Syne'. By the time the whole line was through we were standing in a circle facing outwards.

> Now we've sunk to the bottom of the sea,
> The bottom of the sea, the bottom of the sea,
> Now we've sunk to the bottom of the sea,
> On the twenty-first of August.

We collapsed onto the street in a giggling mass.

Children sang versions of this song in playgrounds and streets throughout Britain and Ireland. The most popular date was 'The last day of September'. It is said to refer an event that happened in North America either during the War of Independence or the Civil War.

Skipping rope games and songs were prolific. The ropes for communal skipping were washing lines. Most of the games used one line but some of the really difficult games had two ropes being turned in opposite directions to each other.

> Once you get in
> You can't get out
> Unless you touch the ground,
> Turn around
> And shout ralevo.

Roller skating in our street was very tame. There were no slopes and we soon ran out of ideas for playing on them. At the bottom of the next street was the lane leading down to the river. The street dropped to river level where a brook ran under the road through a culvert and then rose at the other side of the lane.

There was a new council housing estate on the other side of the brook called Hollywood. The estate was between the brook and Speke airport. Tom was born in Hollywood. The house had a garden at the front and back and was Mam's favourite house. She was very reluctant to leave. Dad insisted on returning to a terraced house in The Dingle, three or four miles away, because it was nearer to his ice cream business. The family moved six or seven times in the first twenty years of the marriage, with the children changing schools each time.

The move to Under the Bridge in 1945 was the last one until Mam and Dad moved to a pensioner's flat thirty years later. Was Dad still paying for his faux pas when Mam overheard him giving advice to Dorothy when she was sixteen?

I went with one of my friends to roller skate on the slope near Hollywood. Dad's best friend, Charlie Winkles and his wife, lived on the corner of the estate and we called to see them.

At the end of the war his daughter, Nancy, married a GI and went to America. At the time we all thought it was very romantic. She was a beauty, with dark, wavy hair. Her American GI was bound to be rich and live on a ranch like the cowboys we saw in the films every week.

Charlie had been best man at Dad's wedding. He was a staunch member of the Orange Lodge. Dad had no tolerance for The Lodge or Roman Catholicism, so the subject was avoided. Meanwhile, Charlie and Mam would look on as his wife and Dad had wide ranging discussions late into the night on everything from current affairs to the meaning of life. Sparks flew as they scored points in their arguments. Mam felt sidelined by their relationship. She resented their bond and was extremely jealous.

Dad had arrived in Garston from Birkdale near Southport in 1912, four or five weeks before the Glorious Twelfth of July, as the Orange Lodge called it, and he had strayed onto a Roman Catholic patch. A street gang cornered him to question where he stood on Irish politics and religion.

'Are you Accra or Demo?' He learned later this meant Unionist or Republican.

He replied in a broad Lancashire dialect that he didn't understand the question.

'He's a bl**** foreigner,' one of them said, and they let him go.

Amongst the family reference books, *My Brief Against Rome* had pride of place between the Holy Bible and the English dictionary.

When Harry was about ten the sound of him practising 'Ave Maria' on the piano brought Dad storming into the living room.

'You will not play music supporting that Roman heterodoxy in this house,' he yelled.

There was no one at home in the Winkles' house when we called after skating.

'Let's go and see Tommy Mac,' I said.

They lived in a pretty house on one of the side roads on the estate. Mr McFetter had been in the Fire Service with Dad and we went on holiday with them every year. I thought of them as part of my extended family. Tommy was a handsome blond boy a year older than me.

I knocked. Getting no answer we went through the gate to the back garden. I stood in delighted amazement. It was a blaze of colour and patterns. In total joy I danced along the footpaths that wound their way around the flower displays.

'What are you doing in my garden?' Mrs McFetter stood in the gateway. Her face was white, her eyes shining with rage and her mouth and jaw twisted and venomous.

'Get out,' she shrieked. Before I could recover from the shock and answer her.

'Get out and don't ever come here again.'

Nobody had ever treated me in that way. I was bemused. We returned to the skating slope near the river.

A brook ran beside Bankfield House and continued towards the river between the Welsh cottages on our side and Hollywood council estate on the other. Bankfield House was built for the manager of the copper works, while the cottages had been built for the Welsh-speaking tradesmen who had moved from Swansea to Garston with the works. The bobbin works backed onto the terraced houses on our side of the brook. The bottle works and a number of other factories faced the bobbin works and were sandwiched between the bobbin works and the river. The allotments where Dad grew our vegetables and blackcurrants were on the opposite side of the brook between Hollywood, the airport, and the grassy headland overlooking the river.

Discarded or broken bottles were piled against the factory wall and spilled down to litter the muddy estuary. Wrecks had been towed along the river and left to rust and rot.

Throughout the summer the children thronged there to paddle in the mud. Strong swimmers like Tom would board the submerged wrecks, dive down and swim in and out of the cabins.

I imagined that the boats had been scuttled by pirates. I was convinced that the walls of the cabins would be panelled in oak. There would be brass fittings and velvet covered chairs. Somewhere there must be trunks filled with gold or silver. If Tom discovered treasure, he never brought any home. Being a poor swimmer I never climbed aboard.

There was a sex fiend on the headland. All of the children were talking excitedly about him.

'Let's go and find him,' they cried.

Everyone went down on their hands and knees in the long grass and began to search for him. I didn't know what a sex

Welsh cottages built by the copperworks for their tradesmen from Swansea

fiend was or how I would recognise him when I found him. After a short time we tired of the game and looked for another distraction. It didn't occur to any of us to tell our parents about him.

I borrowed Harry's home-knitted swimming trunks as I had arrived without my swimsuit. He hadn't brought his sleeveless pullover that I usually wore with the trunks. I wasn't bothered.

One of the boys laughed and pointed at me as I walked into the water.

'What's wrong with that daft idiot?' I thought

In no time, all the children were laughing hysterically.

'You've got a pair of golf balls on you're chest,' one of them shouted, setting them all off chortling and rolling around in glee.

My boobs had just begun to develop. I hadn't noticed.

'So what?' I asked, paddling through the mud to the water.

When we weren't on Garston shore we were following the headland path. The family, with all Garstonians, knew every step of the footpath from Garston shore to the next village, Oglet, two miles along the Mersey estuary. The sea wall, thirty feet above the shore, was on one side of the narrow path while we were hemmed in on the other side by the airport fence. After a hundred yards or so, the headland opened out again into an open grassy area with a few trees. Out in the estuary

Smith and McFetters, Garston shore, 1948

were two iron posts, about a mile apart, which we used as markers to tell us how far we had come. We called them umbrellas. There was a wooded area with a stream running through a deep gully. A thick rope hung from a stout tree. All the boys from the village used to swing on it. Apart from showing their acrobatic skills, they would use it to save the long walk down the slope and up the other side.

I was often tempted to try it but didn't want to do it while they were there in case I fumbled it, and was too scared when I was alone in case I hurt myself. The stream was the one the family camped beside.

Speke Hall, an Elizabethan stately home owned by the National Trust, could be seen through rusty wrought iron gates a quarter of a mile from the river. We imagined ladies and gentlemen in silks and satins embarking on ferries to be rowed across the Mersey, or Cavaliers arriving during the English Civil War. Did contraband come to the hall? If there was once a landing stage it had rotted away. The gates were never open. This didn't stop regular passage in and out. There were deep holes under the fence where the children had burrowed their way through. Sometimes we dropped by to admire the colour and order of the garden beds and topiary before returning to the headland and continuing the walk. On other occasions we used it as a short cut through to the main Speke to Garston road. We had to avoid the janitors as we were covered in mud and clearly hadn't paid to enter by the official gateway.

Next to Speke Hall was Home Farm. The fields of corn

weren't fenced off from the path along the promontory. At harvest time we picked a scratchy golden corn head, rubbing it between our hands as we walked, then chewing the kernel. We debated whether this was stealing. We knew scrumping for apples was. Scrumping was a bit like foraging or scrounging.

We never scrumped and it was awkward for us if our companions did. We would wander off, pretending that we weren't with them. When they offered us their ill-gained goods, we pretended we didn't fancy them, even when our stomachs were rumbling. If they were close friends we would tell them not to do it, but we had to judge the situation.

On the matter of picking corn, we were faced with an added problem on Sundays. If picking corn could be described as working, that would make it a double sin as you mustn't work on Sunday unless it was life-saving work like fighting fires or nursing.

The stream in the gully was the only fresh water between Garston and Oglet. Dianne, Harry and I often had a raging thirst before reaching the stream. We were delighted to discover clear water being carried to the river in open concrete shoots. Each time we came to one we took our fill. Years later, I discovered they were conduits for gutter water or, possibly, sewers.

The walk ended in the little hamlet of Oglet and the wood of rhododendrons called the Dam Woods.

When Dianne was five, Harry was seven, and I was nine, Richard took us on an outing that started as a ride to Liverpool Pierhead on a tram. He must have earned quite a bit on the pea picking harvest. On arriving at the Mersey he decided we would take the ferry across to Wallasey. We walked for mile upon mile until we arrived at a beach. Many years later Richard claimed we had walked to West Kirby, then back to Birkenhead. He had an excellent memory and grasp of geography. It was five or six miles each way. On arriving in Birkenhead he asked for directions to the boats. Footsore, hungry and weary, we found ourselves at the docks, miles from the passenger ferry. A bus conductor took pity on us, for all Richard's money was gone.

The bus dropped us at the ferry. Mam was frantic with worry when we stumbled into the house at midnight.

It was impossible to keep Garston's children away from the water. Despite all the efforts of parents and teachers to warn us of the danger children still drowned. A policeman came to speak to us at school assembly about some pits connected to the railway sidings close to Vineyard Street. Three boys had dived in for a swim and drowned because it wasn't possible to climb out.

That evening Dad called Dianne, Harry and me in from playing in the street. We were all worried as he looked very serious. He repeated the story we had heard in school about the boys drowning.

'These are not ponds,' he told us. 'They are very deep and dangerous.'

Every effort was made to instil into us the dangers and to teach us to swim. Each class in junior school was taken to the swimming baths once a week. We would line up two-by-two in a crocodile to walk half a mile along the wall of the gasworks, past St Michael's parish church and across the road at the bottom of the village. The village policeman would stop the traffic while we crossed.

Many children became swimming champions. In 1920 four women from Garston represented Britain in the freestyle relay team in the Olympic Games and won a silver medal.

A carnival was organised in the village every summer to raise money for a Church of England games and social clubhouse for the young people of Garston.

Each street would hire a lorry and decorate it according to a theme, for example a nursery rhyme, or representing a particular country. On the day of the carnival, the lorries would be driven around the streets in procession. They would be led by the men from the woodcutters' club, who would be dressed as women in pinafores, showing their hairy legs and wearing hairnets, headscarves or wigs. They would be playing bazookas.

Garston carnival in St Mary's Road, The Village

The Scouts met in the scout hut before the procession. Their job was to collect money from the crowd. They wore fancy dress of their own choosing. Many of them were pirates. Being short on money and ideas, Tom borrowed one of Evelyn's dresses, her socks and shoes. He covered the back of his short back and sides with a girl's hat and put a slide in the front of his red curly hair.

'No girls,' he was told, as he walked into the scout hut.

'I'm a Scout,' he replied, blushing.

'What are you supposed to be?'

'He's his sister,' the scoutmaster said.

Everyone laughed. He looked the image of Evelyn.

From the time she left school Dorothy was employed as a domestic in Speke church vicarage. She was an untrained but highly gifted needlewoman. Hand-me-downs would be altered to fit the younger brothers and sisters. The more pleasurable working of her craft went into making a sailor suit for Tom and toddlers' clothes for Dianne. Row upon row of tiny stitches were pulled to gather the material across the baby's chest and allow it to fall in soft folds to the knees.

When she was twenty-one she became a factory hand at the Dunlop rubber factory and then in the bobbin works. Dad was sick at heart. She had so much talent he couldn't bear to see it wasted but, more than that, he didn't like the thought of the type of people she would be mixing with.

Soon after this she started bringing home a man who worked with her. I thought he was slow witted and that she was looking after him because she felt sorry for him. He was neither handsome nor intelligent and had nothing in common with Dorothy or anyone else in our family.

When he had been spending evenings at our house for some months, his mother threw a party and we were all invited. Freda didn't want to go. We hadn't met his mother but with Bill as her ambassador I wasn't surprised Freda didn't want to meet her. I found him repugnant and wanted nothing to do with him but nobody asked my opinion. Dad persuaded Freda to come with us, much against her will.

His mother was a fat, motherly soul who loved company. She could play all the old songs on the piano. Harry stood beside the piano watching and listening with shining eyes. He fell madly in love with her.

'Will you marry me?' he begged

She promised to consider his proposal when he was a few years older.

Freda had been standing near the stairs when a vision in army uniform appeared before her eyes. They were both infatuated with each other immediately.

Day after day throughout his leave they met. They couldn't see enough of each other. Whether they were dancing at the cinema or just walking, they had to be together. Everywhere they went they talked and talked and kissed urgently and joyfully, as if it all had to be said now. His name was music. It was Les.

After a whirlwind romance Freda ended her relationship with Les, the great love of her life. Neither she nor Les ever understood why. They were both heartbroken.

She left home with Evelyn to work in The Blossoms hotel in Chester.

Dad was upset that they both had left reliable trades for unqualified work and very worried because he couldn't keep an eye on them. Unfortunately he didn't handle the situation very well.

'You'll be back in a fortnight,' he told them.

It was the first time they had been away from the family. They were very lonely. Many decisions had to be taken and they had no-one to turn to. The first week seemed endless. They would have been glad to come home. But Dad had thrown down a challenge and Freda was determined to prove him wrong.

They stayed in Chester until they found work for the summer season at Butlin's holiday camp in Pwllheli in 1948. It was there that Evelyn met Elwyn, her future husband.

When the family was at the party where Freda met Les, I was thankful that Dorothy's boyfriend stayed away from me in his mother's house.

Soon after he had met Dorothy he joined my family in our crowded kitchen. He invited me to sit on his knee. I had no wish to sit there as I regarded him as pretty thick but there was very little room to sit on the floor. At the time I had no strong objection. Of course, within no time he had his hand inside my knickers.

Dad made a garden on top of the air-raid shelter where Harry, Dianne and I used to play and sunbathe. One beautiful summer afternoon, Mam had just called us down for tea when my abuser appeared in the yard. I was already down before he reached the ladder. He lifted Dianne down. I felt sick.

One night, soon after that first time he sexually abused me, he was in the living room and asked me to sit on his knee. The family were gathered together, including my Dad.

Summoning up all my courage, I stood up and said clearly and loudly, 'I don't want to sit on his knee.'

My Dad chastised me for being rude to a guest. I was too embarrassed to tell Dad and the family that he was abusing me. On the very evening that I had tried to tell the family, he abused me again.

His behaviour was outside of the experience of my family so they didn't hear what I was telling them. Mam was more worldly-wise, and might have picked up what I was trying to tell everyone, but she wasn't present when I spoke out. I never dared say anything again.

From that time on I disappeared upstairs, into the cold and dark, whenever he came to the house. At first there was nothing to do in the bedroom. I wrapped myself in blankets but I couldn't read, knit, sew or play games. I found a bicycle lamp and then I was able to lie down in bed and read under the blankets.

***

We were always surrounded by animals. Beside the hens we had Bonzo the dog who was beige with one or two dark brown spots, Mary the black cat with a white underside, and a few rabbits. When Dad brought home half a dozen yellow ducklings, we were delighted. Unfortunately, all but one died within a month. We named the tough little survivor Marmaduke.

Freda came home on a visit a month later. She went down the yard to the toilet. On returning to the kitchen she couldn't get the back door to shut. After banging it a few times without success she looked to see what was stopping it closing. Marmaduke's head hung down inside while his body was out in the yard.

She screamed and opened the door. We all rushed out to see what had happened.

Marmaduke was running around the yard with his head hanging down. Dad caught and killed him.

Animals had to be tough to survive in our household. Tom was chopping firewood in the yard one day when Bonzo ran in front of the log being chopped. Amazingly he recovered within a week and lived to a ripe old doggy age with a scar in his skull

125

as deep as the one in the front door that had been left by our crazy neighbour.

***

The first election I was ever aware of was the local election in May 1948, two months before my eleventh birthday. The name Billy Sefton was painted in letters two metres high right across the King Street and Dale Street junction, between the redbrick Victorian Jubilee Institute and the highly ornamental public toilets. Councillor Joe Cleary claimed to have been instrumental in having the toilets built. Garston community called the toilets Joe Cleary's palace.

For weeks before the election all the children were dancing through the streets singing:

Vote, vote, vote for Billy Sefton
Here come Tories at the door.
Now the Tories had their run
And they had a bit of fun
But we won't vote for Tories any more.

Billy Sefton addressed the crowd here in the council election campaign of 1948, at the corner of King Street, dale Street, Church Road and Banks Road. Billy Sefton's name was painted in two-foot letters across the road.

He was the local hero. Imagine our excitement when we heard he was speaking in public. Crowds of children were running along all the streets, overtaking the adults, singing with gusto as we went.

There was a blond, fresh-faced young man, speaking from the back of a lorry that was parked next to Joe Cleary's palace, the public toilets. People were coming from every direction. The crowd that filled the area from the Jubilee Hall to the Cock and Trumpet cheered each time he stopped for breath.

The name Billy Sefton could be clearly read on the road for a decade after the election. It was obvious that St Mary's ward, Garston, would be represented by the Labour party. I was totally confident that he had won.

Fifty years later he told me he had lost to the Tories by a handful of votes.

This rundown working-class area elected a Tory councillor until 1954. It remained a marginal seat until I left Liverpool in 1962.

The division between Labour and Tory supporters was bitter and had existed since the bobbin works strike in 1912 that lasted for three months. Labour voters had been trade unionists during the strike, while the Tories had been scabs (workers who didn't join the union and continued to work during the strike) or non-manual employees. The story of the 1912 strike was never told in our school history lessons.

Although Dad had arrived right in the middle of a vicious strike, when residents had battled with mounted police, suffered injuries, and been hauled before the courts, it had all washed over him. He had been preoccupied with the move from a quiet rural backwater to a noisy, dirty factory area where he had to settle into the home of his newly-married uncle and aunt and start a new school. Personal confrontation from a gang of Catholic youths had shaken him so much that he remembered it for the rest of his life. He was unaware of the strike that was to divide the community for more than half a century.

Tom left Toxteth Technical College in the summer of 1948,

127

the first in the family to remain in school until he was sixteen years old. Dad was proud of his firstborn son. He was going to be a tradesman. Once he had served his time as an apprentice, he would be a qualified electrician.

Before starting his apprenticeship in Preston he went on a cycling holiday in the Wye Valley with Richard. They stayed at YHA hostels. Dianne, Harry and I were as excited as they were, although we had no idea where the Wye Valley was. It was a wonderful adventure.

Everyone in the street came out to watch them set off. As they turned the corner into Window Lane, I couldn't contain my enthusiasm. Mounting Dianne's medium-sized bike, I pedalled madly after them, needing to hold onto the pleasure of the moment. I reached the crossroads at the bottom of the village, but they were well gone. Smiling to myself I turned for home.

In the summer of 1948 Dorothy and the other Guide officers were taking the Girl Guides from the three local packs to summer camp. She persuaded her colleagues to let me come, although I hadn't moved up from Brownies. I would have my eleventh birthday that summer.

It was very kind of her but I'm sure she regretted it. I had become quite nasty to her in Sunday school and Brownies, making jokes in front of the other children about her growing a beard and shaving. She never responded to my goading. Despite my being a little horror, she took me again the following year.

Beaty, aged ten

We were taken to the camp in a lorry with a canvas cover. The only view we had on the twenty- or thirty-mile journey was out of the rear if the curtains were tied back. All the way there we sang songs from the First World War and the 1920s and 1930s.

Pack up your troubles in your old kit bag
And smile, smile, smile.

We didn't bother to ask why soldiers in the British Army had girlfriends in Tipperary, or why the soldiers were in London. It was great to sing: 'It's a long way to go without your mother.'

The naughtiest song was 'She'll be coming round the mountain', especially 'She'll be wearing captain's knickers'. We would all giggle and nudge each other and blush. I was too embarrassed to join in.

We slept eight to each bell tent. They were large marquees shaped like a bell, with the main supporting pole in the centre. Our beds were placed around the pole like spokes around a wheel.

Toilets were privy middens, tin huts at the far end of the field, each with a wooden seat inside over a hole. They stunk from the day we arrived.

We washed in cold water, so our bodies rarely saw water for the week we were there, unless we went paddling in the local stream. Hands and face were the limit of our ablutions.

In the camp most of the day was spent preparing food. We would all be set tasks: fetching buckets or massive jugs of water; peeling mounds of potatoes, carrots and swedes; frying sausage, bacon and eggs, or stirring great cauldrons of porridge for breakfast or, for supper, a stew. After the meal there was the mammoth operation of washing crockery, cutlery and the large cooking pots.

I suspect that the older Guides and the officers did most of the work, particularly the dangerous tasks near the fire.

Prayers and hymns were sung before meals and before we went to bed.

Once breakfast was over and our beds were made, we were free to explore the local countryside and the nearby village. Before reaching the village I spotted a confectioner's that was also a café. I had made a new friend who belonged to the Guide pack that met at Gilmour Secondary Modern School for Girls. We went into the café and ordered tea and doughnuts. They were straight from the oven and the first doughnuts I had ever tasted. Afterwards that café was our first port of call every morning. I have never tasted doughnuts to equal the ones we had in that café. When I think of them I taste again that light hot sponge cake dripping in sugar and fat.

In the evening, after supper, we would gather around the camp fire and Dorothy and the other Guide officers would tell ghost stories or other weird and wonderful tales. The evening would end with us singing the old songs again.

My new best friend was asthmatic. A few days after we arrived she had a severe attack. The Guide officers handled the situation professionally, some caring for her while the others continued to run the camp with a semblance of normality. They didn't try to hide that her illness was a serious matter but they had it in hand. We had total confidence in them.

I was sad to see her go home as we had grown very close. A few weeks later I met here again in secondary school. Meanwhile, I introduced some of my other new friends to the doughnut café.

Many of the Guides had letters from home waiting for them at the farm when they arrived at the camp. Each morning Guides collected parcels of cakes and other goodies that had been sent to them by their families.

We were encouraged to write letters home. I wanted the other Guides to see me receiving gifts from my family that I could share among my friends. It was important that they knew I had parents who were missing me.

When nothing had come for me after three days, I wrote a

letter to break the heart of any parent who read it. Here I was, alone amongst strangers, living on bread and water, longing to receive the smallest gift from them so that I didn't die of starvation.

I put it in the box with all the letters to be posted.

Dorothy came to see me in the tent next morning. Her eyes were laughing. Out of her pocket came my letter. I felt acutely embarrassed. She was her usual calm, cheerful self as she asked me why I had written it.

'Are you hungry?'

I looked at the ground as I shook my head.

'Lonely?'

Again I shook my head.

'Well then? What is this about?'

'I wanted to get a tuck box from home so that I could show off and the other Guides would see how special I am to Mam and Dad.'

'You are special. That is why I want you here with me. None of the other Guides have a big sister who wants to be with them.'

I would still have given the earth to have the postman arrive with a bigger parcel than anyone else had received.

'You're right,' I said. 'I'm very lucky.'

'Mam and Dad are probably missing you. Do you still want to send the letter?'

'No, I've bought a postcard. Will you wait while I write it?'

I sent the usual message. 'Wish you were here.'

3

Across the Boundary, 1948–52

It was the first day of the autumn term at Gilmour Secondary Modern School. One hundred excited eleven year olds were sitting at our desks in four classrooms. The groups had been divided alphabetically. We were all taking the same examination. The stream we would be placed in was to be decided by this test.

In junior school there were A and B streams. I was in the B stream. That could be forgotten. In this school we were starting with a clean slate. The teachers would be amazed to discover they had a child genius in their midst. I was bound to be top of the first-year intake for 1948. Perhaps, on realizing their mistake, the school would send me to grammar school immediately. Maybe I would have to stay in the top class until I passed the Thirteen Plus examination.

'Turn the paper over now,' said the teacher.

I found myself looking at symbols, squares, triangles and circles. I read the instructions but they meant little or nothing to me. Moving on I tried to find questions I could answer, but they were few and far between. This wasn't the level playing field I had been promised. The middle-class girls who lived in the gated estates of Cressington and Grassendale might have been familiar with tests like this one. The A stream in Banks Road County Primary might have been taught how to answer these questions. I had never seen anything like them before. My optimism was shaken but I ploughed on, determined to make some sense of this gobbledegook. I knew that I was as bright or possibly brighter than the girls I had met that first day. The examiners must be able to recognize it too.

Class 1D met in a broom cupboard. To be more precise, it was a room intended for staff meetings. Our twelve desks were crammed next to each other. We would enter and exit in the same order and once in we couldn't leave until everyone else was leaving.

School leaving age had gone up to fifteen in 1947. The school was so overcrowded that many of our lessons were held in the Congregational church hall next to Garston Park. Art was taught at Springwood Infants' School while the domestic science room was over a mile away in our old primary school, Banks Road.

Once I recovered from the initial shock of finding myself in the bottom class, I decided that the problem was arithmetic. Because I had been in the special class for slow readers, I had missed learning decimals and fractions. I decided to approach my form teacher. When I realized who she was I knew I was wasting my time. Miss Elkinton was a poor wizened old soul who looked about eighty. My three older sisters had talked about her when they were in senior school at Banks Road. Everyone had teased her and made fun of her because she was a useless teacher. She hadn't improved with time. I was amazed to discover, when doing research for this book, that she had a BA, no mean feat for a woman at that time. Sadly, the council education department didn't appear to have given her any teacher training. She was just childminding.

We were given a stack of Enid Blyton's *Sunny Stories* to read every day. I was delighted with my first taste of secondary modern schooling. The books in the primary school library had been far more challenging and we had no easy books like these at home. I soon became bored with them.

One lunchtime, a short while after this, I discovered the local library. It was located less than five minutes from the school. In my memory it was a beautiful half-timbered mock Elizabethan

Gilmour Secondary Modern School for girls, on the edge of the leafy suburbs of Liverpool, opened c.1945/6. Banks Road Senior School closed.

Springwood Infants School. Overflow classes from Gilmour were held in Springwood, the Congregational chapel, and the domestic science room in the defunct Banks Road Senior School. It must have been a logistical nightmare.

building surrounded by a small garden. Inside I found a wood-panelled room with parquet flooring. Everywhere gleamed. It smelled of furniture polish. There were rooms upon rooms full of books from floor to ceiling. The first time I went in I wanted to cry, I was so overcome.

The librarian gave me a card for my Dad to sign, so that I could join.

I couldn't wait to get my hands on these treasures. I filled the form in and signed it myself.

As soon as school finished I rushed back to the library and handed over the card. I was in. That evening I cradled my first public library book in my arms. From that day on I read one book a day most days throughout my four years at secondary school. Challenging books like Dickens and the Brontes took a day or two longer, even when I skipped the boring descriptive sections. Boarding school adventures and popular tales like *Anne of Green Gables* and *Black Beauty* were devoured in great hungry gulps.

When the family was packed into the living room in the evenings, sitting on straight backed wooden dining room chairs and following three or four conversations at once, I would be totally absorbed in a book, unaware of the hubbub around me. Often my world would be shattered by Dad booming at me to answer him when he spoke to me. When I looked at him in total bewilderment, he refused to accept that I hadn't heard him.

After he had said 'Good night and gob less,' we were alone for the night. I listened to him descend the stairs and close the living room door, then I switched on the bicycle lamp to continue reading my novel. Mam caught me one night and told me I would ruin my eyesight with all this reading, particularly reading in semi-darkness.

I usually went to the library at lunchtime. The first time I finished reading my book by 4pm I tried to change it after school and learned that we were only allowed to take out one book per day.

Garston library

Dad loved *Lorna Doone*. He wanted me to share his delight in it. I tried a few times but couldn't get into it. Milton's *Paradise Lost* also failed to grab me. As an adult I attempted to read them again with the same lack of success.

Once or twice each day we escaped from Miss Elkinton for specialist subjects. Most of the teachers treated us with respect and recognized that we were keen to learn. The science teacher opened my eyes to new horizons. I was thrilled to learn about the single-celled amoeba in the first week and waited with anticipation for the next lesson.

Harry was the artist in the family. He had always drawn. In our art class I discovered I could draw too. In the playground of Springwood Infant School we looked at a tree, really observed it for the first time, and drew it with charcoal.

The art teacher asked us to bring something from our gardens for the next lesson. We didn't have a garden and it was a long way to the allotment on the shore of the Mersey. The first spring I cycled to Gilmour I gasped when I saw the white blossom. I was so heavy that the branches were weighed down.

That evening I asked Dad, 'Who do the trees and blossoms in the park belong to?'

'They belong to all of us,' he replied.

Next day I set off early for school. My heart was overflowing with joy as I climbed a tree and chose an exquisite branch full of blossoms and began to gather them. Every blossom on every tree was so wonderful I would have loved to collect them all in my arms. But I knew I had to be sensible and be satisfied with half a dozen.

A bellow from below shook me from my daydream.

'You little vandal! Get down from that tree. Leave the blossom alone,' the man shouted.

He ruined a delightful morning.

'The blossoms are mine,' I told him, near to tears. 'I can take them if I want to.'

'Get down this instant or I will call the police.'

I was used to men and their bad tempers. I climbed down and rode, empty-handed, to school.

Geography was amazing. On a map of the world there were great red areas that belonged to the British Empire. Africa, India, Australia, Canada all belonged to us. It was the same with religion. We were shown a great cake divided into sections. The biggest slice was Christianity, the best religion, while all of the other world religions were smaller. Some were a tiny fraction of the size of Christianity. They were all heathens and needed to be converted by our missionaries.

> The sun that bids us rest is waking
> Our brethren 'neath the western sky,
> And hour by hour fresh lips are making
> Thy wondrous doings heard on high.

Miss Bowyer had taught us to knit in junior school. At seven years old I would get the wool and the square of plain knitting into a tangle. The teacher thought I might be left handed because I was so uncoordinated. The idea appealed to me as it meant I was different and might, therefore, get more attention. She persevered. Due to her patience most of us were such accomplished knitters by the time we moved to senior school that we could produce a pair of baby boots or mittens in knit one pearl one pattern in an evening.

There was nothing remarkable about Miss Bowyer's appearance apart from her hair. She was of average height and build and she dressed neatly. Plenty of the teachers came from Wales or were the first generation born in Liverpool. We would hear them talking Welsh to each other. The peaches and cream tone of her skin and her raven-black hair marked her out as a Celt. She had the same distinctive hairstyle throughout the thirty-seven years she taught at the school. The sleek hair was parted down the middle from forehead to the hollow at the back of her neck then worn in plaits, like earmuffs, on either side of her head.

Needlework took on a whole knew meaning at Gilmour. There was a room set aside for the subject with tables ten foot square for spreading out our work or cutting out garments from templates or from tissue paper patterns.

The tutor was an expert at her craft and a gifted teacher. Here we absorbed every type of embroidery stitch, cross stitch, and smocking, with a multicoloured array of silks. Samplers were produced and patchwork cut and sewn.

Step by step we mastered skills for creating objects of beauty and practical necessity, from making stuffed toys to producing our own clothes, from making the template or pattern to producing the finished article.

On our first day the teacher instructed us to put our hands on the desk. She was going to come around and inspect them. I was proud of my hands. They had been washed immediately before coming into the sewing room. The teacher spoke to most of them about biting their nails and making their hands look ugly. They were given a lecture on something distasteful they could apply to the nail to help them to break the habit. I was hugging myself with self congratulation. My nails were long and strong.

'Your nails are black,' she said, in horror.

Yes, my nails were black. They had always been black. I wasn't aware that they were supposed to be any other colour.

Fortunately, that was before my first domestic science lesson. A stiff-haired little brush had always stood beside the block of carbolic soap on the big ceramic kitchen sink the family used for their daily ablutions. Luckily, I discovered its use before kneading the dough for my first loaf of bread.

There was a fully-fitted domestic science laboratory in the now-defunct senior school at Banks Road, while the one at Gilmour had been converted into a classroom. We spent a whole day once a week in my old junior school. Coming Under the Bridge and walking between the gasworks and the smelting foundry must have been a whole new experience for my classmates from Cressington and Grassendale.

The playground at Gilmour was marked out as a netball court. We also played rounders there in our sports period. I loved all sport, despite reacting too slowly for the rest of my team. The two team leaders would toss a coin to decide who would start first to pick their players. I knew I would be the last to be picked in the team that lost the toss.

On sports day we were taken by coach to a field near Otterspool, on the Mersey. Everyone had an opportunity to win an event. I entered the slow cycling race. I was a

This domestic science room became another classroom. Previously the domestic science room, this was the classroom in Gilmour where I took the entrance examination on my first day. In my fourth year I wrote and read poetry in this room.

proficient cyclist and speed wasn't required. Fully confident, I mounted my bike convinced I would take the prize. The other contestants balanced on one spot while I had cycled a yard ahead. Once more I took the booby prize.

In our final year we went to the boys' school, Gilmour Heath Road, about a mile away, to use their playing field for hockey. The boarding school girls I read about played hockey and I cherished the idea of moving into their world. Each time I played I was euphoric, although I was no better as a hockey player than I was at any other competitive game. I was so proud that I was dressed in school uniform and playing hockey and I wanted everyone to see me carrying the hockey stick as I returned to the girls' school.

I won a swimming race once. It was at a school swimming gala. Proud parents filled the viewing area to watch dazzling acrobatic diving from the top board, amazing feats of underwater swimming for the whole length of the baths, life saving exhibitions and relay races. I swam a whole width of the baths, and won. Mam and Dad were not there to cheer me on or to congratulate me when I won. This wasn't out of indifference. It was a major event on the school calendar, but I have no recollection of telling them about it before or afterwards. I sang in the choir at the nativity tableau and appeared in the summer concerts. I didn't expect my parents to attend. School had no connection with life in the family home.

If respect and pride in ones self and your school can be provided by a school ethos, then Gilmour would have raised us all onto a higher plain. Apart from two nasty teachers, the staff – and the ideal they aspired to – were exemplary. The only failure I can recognize with hindsight was an absence of communication between parents and school. If there was a parent teacher association I wasn't aware of it. Even had there been one, it would have been attended only by the middle-class parents. If the school had specifically invited Mam or Dad to an event or instructed them to come to a meeting, they would have complied, otherwise education and school matters were the business of the school. They would have lacked the self-confidence to talk to teachers or join gatherings of parents. In addition to all of this, they had a home to run. Caring for the spiritual and physical needs of their large family left very little time for any other activities.

If Dad had been interested in swimming, as many Garston parents were, Mam might have gone with him and enjoyed the conviviality of the swimming gala, but that wasn't his sport. He loved football. As a young man he played in the copper works team and possibly in St Michael's Church of England team. His spitting image is on a photograph of the 1916/17 team. He supported Everton through hail, rain and sunshine, and would have loved to have taken his sons with him, but none of them were interested.

Gilmour was divided into four houses as in the fictional boarding school novels I immersed myself in. Each form was divided between the four houses. When sports days, gala days and quizzes were held, houses competed against each other. I was in Marie Curie House with members in A stream fourth year, B stream third year and C stream second year. On a week by week basis school monitors, elected by their classmates, kept a tally of marks pupils had received for good or bad behaviour. These were called stars and stripes. Each week the best behaved stood on the platform to be praised, while the worst stood with bowed head in front of the platform to be admonished. The marks may have been added up at the end of each term for each house.

I usually aimed for getting the most stars, as I was a goody two shoes by nature but, as the end of the week approached, if I could see I was not going to win I would go out of my way to clown around and be disruptive. Whether I was noticed for being best behaved or worst was immaterial. I had to be noticed by the whole school. These were the days of corporal punishment. I would take my place with pride in the queue outside the head mistress' study for her to cane me. The pain was worth suffering for the glory. By my second year the canings appeared to stop. I don't know whether I had changed or if there was a change in school policy. Caning pupils hurt Miss Baldwin, the headmistress, as much as it hurt me but unlike me she got no reward.

The houses were named after female heroines. Once more we were being presented with mentors. The message we were given was that you didn't have to be a man to acquire greatness. Votes for women had been won, after a long struggle, only twenty years earlier. The beginning of the campaign for equal rights for women, called Women's Liberation, was treated with derision even in the 1970s. In 1948, at Gilmour, we were encouraged to believe that women can achieve any goals that men can reach.

Marie Curie, the namesake of my house, received the Nobel Prize for science twice, first with her husband and next in her own right. Women have proved they can be great scientists.

Elizabeth Fry House was named after a noted prison reformer who also started a training school for nurses at Guy's Hospital.

Florence Nightingale, whose name was given to the next house, was famous for her work in the military hospitals during the Crimean War. Many of the nurses she took with her had been trained at the nursing school established by Elizabeth Fry. Florence wrote to Elizabeth Fry giving her credit for many of the nursing practices that she adopted. Florence was nicknamed the lady with the lamp.

Nineteen-year-old Grace Darling was the renowned heroine of the fourth house. She lived with her father, a lighthouse keeper. A ship was wrecked. She rowed out with her father in a violent storm to rescue the survivors.

Each morning began with assembly in the main hall. Apart from about twenty pupils who were excused on religious grounds, the school of about five hundred, plus the teachers, met for a short Protestant religious service and notice of events.

Now here hath been dawning
Another blue Day:
Think wilt thou let it
Slip useless away.

Out of Eternity
Each new Day is born;
Into Eternity,
At night will return.

Long live the Protestant ethic. There isn't a word about God in this song...

In the Methodist church and at school assemblies I came to savour beautiful words, from Charles Wesley, John Greenleaf Whittier and a whole galaxy of poets and hymn writers going back to the fifteenth century and beyond.

O brother man, fold to thy heart thy brother;
Where pity dwells, the peace of God is there;
To worship rightly is to love each other.
Each smile a hymn, each kindly deed a prayer.

Pleasant sentiments, but it was the final verse that truly moved me.

Then shall all shackles fall; the stormy clangour
Of wild war music o'er the earth shall cease;
Love shall tread out the baleful fire of anger,
And in its ashes plant the tree of peace.

Before our first assembly at Gilmour, class 1D was instructed to stand in line, with the smallest child at one end and the tallest at the other. At eleven years old I was third from tallest. Each class entered the hall in line, with the tallest girls at the back. For the next four years we retained that position in our line. I am sure that pupils nearer the front soon outgrew me.

Assembly was followed each day by religious education or instruction. We must have touched on world religions because

I was aware of Islam and Hinduism but the hour was spent mainly on the background of Judaism and Christianity. It didn't stray from the accepted Protestant position.

On my first day I met the friend I had made at Guides' camp, the one who had returned home after suffering a severe asthma attack. I thought she was very well off. Her school uniform was always clean and pressed. After school I often went home with her. She lived over a shop in St Mary's Road, the road known locally as The Village.

Her mother fed me jam sandwiches. They were delicious. I would demolish half a loaf each time I visited.

There was a tiger rug in the living room. Her mother was amused by my fascination with it. On one occasion when left in the room on my own, I examined the animal from nose to tail. I could imagine it flashing through the green undergrowth of the jungle. She returned to find that I had become so excited that I was dancing and twirling around as I circled it.

After school and at weekends we had our designated tasks at home according to age and ability. In addition to scrubbing the front step and window ledge once a week, I took up the horsehair doormat and scoured the linoleum in the front passage and wiped the dark brown embossed dido. When we first moved to the, house the thinnest, cheapest linoleum covered all the floors. It had probably been left behind by the previous tenants.

After a few years Dad painted the walls of the living room with shiny green paint that remained wet for months, and painted the woodwork dark brown, including the doors. All of our clothes had green and brown paint on them. He made amazingly intricate Christmas presents for us, and ruined them because he never learned to clean surfaces before painting.

We went around for weeks singing:

Ma was stuck to the ceiling
The kids were stuck to the floor.
Did you ever see such a blinking family
So stuck up before.

But we didn't sing it when he was around.

House decorating completed to his satisfaction, he went off with Mam to buy new linoleum. He was delighted with his purchase. It was the most expensive, but it wasn't bought for its aesthetic attraction. This dark brown, inch-thick floor covering with its matting base and heavy rubberized surface was made to last throughout his lifetime and mine. Twenty-five years later, when they moved to a pensioner's flat, he left it behind with great reluctance. Mam insisted on wall-to-wall carpet. Dreadfully unhygienic flooring, he complained. It encouraged fleas and house bugs.

Food was rationed and we were registered at Pegram's, the grocers in the village. When we lived in the tenements during the war it was probably the nearest shop. The Co-operative store and Jimmy Lunt's in Window Lane were two minutes from home. I had to walk three quarters of a mile from Pegram's each week, weighed down by two heavy canvas shopping bags.

The assistant confused me on one occasion when I went for 'The Rations', the only name children knew for groceries.

'Would you like a box of cereals?' she asked me.

I didn't understand the question. In the first place, I had never been required to make any decisions. Mam gave me the family ration books and a shopping list and I simply handed them to the assistant with the bags. In the second place, it was the middle of June so nobody was having a birthday and it wasn't Christmas. Why would I want cereals? We had porridge and bread with dripping every morning, except for very special occasions. I shook my head, dumbfounded by her stupid question.

Carrying eggs was a major cause of worry. They were handed to me in a brown paper bag. This was before the days of egg boxes. The assistant would place them at the top of the shopping bag. I was very conscious of them as I struggled down the slope towards the bridge. My back ached and I felt as though my arms stretched to the length of a gorilla's. Every fifty yards the strain became intolerable and I put the bags down. No matter how carefully I did this the eggs were crushed by other items in the bag. At least one egg would be broken by the time I arrived home. Usually all of them were cracked.

I wasn't criticized for smashing the eggs every week. It was a constant source of worry to me but no suggestion was made for avoiding this problem. Why wasn't half the shopping done on a different day to make it easier to carry? Dad couldn't have known. He would have given me something padded to carry them in. I expect Mam scrambled the eggs for tea that night or baked with them. We didn't have a refrigerator.

Mam wasn't particularly shy. Surrounded by her friends in the chapel she was gregarious. For many years she was the sick visitor for the women's group, but she found the camaraderie in the local shops embarrassing. While everyone else was on first name terms, she was always Mrs Smith. Over the years she became more and more reluctant to go into the grocers or butchers, where neighbours shared the local gossip as they waited in the queue to be served. In old age she would have starved if the family hadn't restocked her refrigerator and kitchen cupboards regularly. Perhaps she chose Pegram's for her rations during the war because it wasn't within the immediate community.

Every Monday throughout the summer, Mam heaved a massive galvanized steel tub onto the gas stove were it frothed with soap suds as it boiled. White cotton clothes went in the first wash, including Mam's overall coats for the airport and Tom's school uniform shirts. After being boiled they were transferred to the big white ceramic sink to be twirled with the three legged dolly pegs and scrubbed against the scrubbing board before being rinsed and put back into the wash tub for another boil, then rinsed again. The same process was followed with coloured clothes that didn't have dyes that ran. Any clothes that looked likely to run, particularly reds and black, were washed separately in tepid water. Woollens were handled with special care, washed in lukewarm water, and item by item if the colours were likely to run. Sheets were boiled, dollied, scrubbed and boiled again.

Robin's Starch was in powder form in a cardboard box. It was made up by mixing starch powder to a paste with cold water, then boiling water was poured on. I was always fascinated to watch it change from white paste to clear jelly. A Rickett's blue bag was added, and the sheets and white clothes, except the knickers and vests, were immersed in the mixture. Coloured clothes were also starched but without the blue bag.

Mam added extra starch for her white overalls. After they were ironed they were so stiff they could have stood up like mannequins.

As each washing cycle was completed and clothes were placed in baskets or the small galvanized tin bath, we carried them out to the wringing machine in the yard where Dad heaved the unwieldy handle that turned the rollers. The older children of twelve years or more fed the clothes into the rollers at one side under the eagle eye of Dad, while the little ones collected them into a tub at the other. He told us how dangerous it would be if our fingers went between the rollers, but he watched and shouted anxiously all the time he was turning the handle. Finally, they were pegged out on two washing lines and hoisted up to billow in the smoky, smut-filled air.

During the winter Mam piled the dirty washing into Dianne's old pram and trundled it to the washhouse next to the swimming pool at the bottom of the village. She hated going there as the male attendants were over familiar. Their chumminess would have been met with a haughty stare as she held her head high and pushed out her bottom lip. There was a lot of gossiping, and jokes were being told that she preferred not to hear. Unlike Dad, who remained naïve throughout his life, she understood double meanings. She didn't want to listen to the coarse chatter but had no choice. In the washhouse, in the local shops, and in her workplace as a toilet cleaner at the airport, she was always addressed as Mrs Smith.

Ironing the clothes for the family became one of my tasks.

This was done in the living room with a flat iron that I heated on the hob by the fire or on the kitchen stove. To check whether it was warm enough I had to spit on a finger and drip it on the iron and see it sizzle. Shirts were the most difficult in every way. I don't remember being shown how, but I must have received instruction as I knew the end I was trying to achieve. There had to be a crease along each sleeve and the rest had to be smooth, including the oddly-shaped area across the shoulders. It was probably taught in domestic science. Unfortunately I didn't know what to do with the shirt to prevent it from crushing once it was ironed. I realize now that it should have been hung on a coat hanger in a wardrobe, but Tom kept his shirts in a drawer. By the time I had folded the shirt, my beautiful smooth ironing was ruined. If I wasn't feeling frustrated enough, Tom was always annoyed with me. Neither he nor anyone else put forward any suggestions.

The doormat from the front passage and the rag mats from the living room were hung on the line to be whacked with the cane carpet beater. Straight backed wooden dining room chairs were taken from the living room and stacked in the passage. Dad's armchair was pushed into a corner. The boys must have done those jobs. Meanwhile, I scrubbed the room from end to end as quickly as I could. The sooner it was done the sooner I could be off to the Lyceum to see my cowboy film.

One Saturday morning Dad came in waving his leather belt at me, as I cowered on my knees, scrubbing brush in hand. I can't recall what misdemeanour I was alleged to have committed. Perhaps the water had gone cold or it was dirty and needed changing. There was no hot water on tap. It had to be boiled in large pans or kettles. Near to tears for fear of anger and frustration, I complied with whatever he was complaining about. He went off to vent his anger on someone else while I returned to scrubbing the floor. This must have been after 1948 because Evelyn had left in 1946 and she was now married and living in the front room. She came to ask me what the fuss was about.

'I'm going to report him to the NSPCC,' I told her through gritted teeth.

'Please don't,' she pleaded with me.

'Why shouldn't I? I didn't do anything to deserve that. I'm doing my best.'

'Yes, I know you are,' she answered, trying to console me. 'But it will bring trouble to the family.'

I continued to fume and make threats, but I had no idea how to contact the NSPCC even if I really wanted to.

He was always threatening us with the belt that he used for sharpening his razor. I have no recollection of him ever striking any of us, either in anger or to discipline us, unless we were near enough for a quick swipe of his hand. His booming voice was enough to frighten us.

On one occasion, fifteen-year-old Richard was being attention seeking as usual. Having riled Dad, he then asked for a battery for his bicycle. Dad threw it to him. He didn't catch it and it struck him on the forehead causing him to bleed. Dad ran to him immediately, full of remorse and concern.

Ada, Dad's sultry cousin, gave birth to her illegitimate son Eric when I was about eleven. I didn't know where babies came from. Having babies without being married was talked about in hushed tones. When we were lying in bed we would hear the neighbours gossiping. They would make jokes about unmarried women becoming pregnant because they had eaten too much porridge or finding babies under gooseberry bushes.

We learned a song from the Boy Scouts that included two verses that questioned the virginity of Pharaoh's daughter. The song was bordering on blasphemy in the days when the majority of British people paid lip service to Christianity. We delighted in being allowed to sing naughty words about bible stories:

Black folk, white folk, everybody come
To join the darkie Sunday school
And make yourself at home.

Bring your sticks of chewing gum
And sit upon the floor.
And we'll tell you bible stories that you've never heard before.

Now Pharaoh had a daughter with a most enchanting smile.
She found the baby Moses in the waters of the Nile.
She took him to her father who said,
'That's a likely tale.
It's just about as probable as Jonah and the Whale.'

Another version of the third, fourth, and fifth lines of this verse is:

She took him to her father,
Said, 'I found him on the shore.'
And Pharaoh winked his eye and said,
'I've heard that tale before.'

A very pretty woman who lived a few doors from us became pregnant while her husband was abroad on National Service in the Army. It was the scandal of the year and the end of her marriage. Most of the neighbours were critical but Mam felt sorry for her.

She wouldn't join in the gossiping, but she must have been so irritated by the hypocrisy of the neighbours that she spoke her mind. She didn't know that I was eavesdropping.

'Her husband had been away a long time. At her age, after you have married and been with a man,' Mam said, putting it very delicately, 'You have these feelings and it's hard to control them.'

I had no idea what she was talking about.

Her sympathy for fallen girls didn't stretch to that hussy Ada. Whenever Ada visited with her son Eric, Mam didn't make any comment but the straight back, stiff neck and jutting bottom lip spoke volumes.

I always loved singing and was delighted to pass the audition for the school choir. The best soloist in the school entered regional and national singing competitions. Much as I admired her singing, I was convinced I was equally talented. Between lessons I would walk about, singing my best pieces, in the hope that one of the teachers would notice my ability but they never did. I remained in the alto section and sometimes struggled there as I was happier singing an octave lower than anyone else. Instead of choirs taking advantage of my exceptionally low voice, I had to ignore my bottom range. It was thirty-five years later before I came into my own, singing tenor solo in a Welsh choir.

At Christmas each year the nativity story was performed in a series of tableau on stage, while I sat below them at the front of the hall singing carols in the alto section of the choir.

Carol singing around the streets in Garston was a way of making money for Christmas presents. Dianne, Harry and I, with scrubbed faces, combed hair and polished shoes, would don our smartest clothes and, carrying a carol sheet with us, knock at doors and politely ask if the occupant would like us to sing a carol or two. We were excessively polite, no matter what response we received. All the verses would be sung and when they paid us we thanked them and asked would they like us to sing another carol. If they had a front gate we made sure we shut it after us.

In January and February we made money by clearing snow from the drives of the lower middle-class houses in Allerton. We asked for half crown per house. This is the price an adult would have paid to visit a castle or a stately home.

Tom wasn't happy with his electrical apprenticeship in Liverpool. He found a new placement in Preston. He had contributed to the family budget with his paper round since he was nine or ten years old. He continued to send money home during the five years he was learning his trade. On visits home he would tell funny tales about landladies.

'Always choose a landlady that is fat when looking for lodgings,' he told us. 'If they don't eat much themselves they won't feed you.'

It caused Dad great heartache when Freda and Evelyn left home but Tom appears to have gone without any censure from Dad or any parental support. Did Dad go with him to help him settle in? I doubt it. Was Tom was an adult in Dad's eyes? How did he pay rent out of his paltry wage and send money home? Mam and Dad seemed to have taken it for granted and we were too young to realise how difficult it must have been for a boy of seventeen.

Richard suffered from dyspepsia throughout his life. He taught himself to make cake mixture and used up the fat ration for the week for the whole family on one batch of cakes that he made and ate himself.

He started work on the horse drawn Co-operative bread van when he left school at fifteen. He always wanted to work with food as he hoped he would be allowed to eat some of it.

He was a slow worker but conscientious and observant. Once he had learned a skill he never forgot it. From the age of eight, when we spent the long summer holidays in Frodsham, he spent many hours on the farmyard. I enjoyed going there and stroking the lambs or feeding the hens. He was watching how the animals were cared for and how the cows and sheep were taken to and from the pasture. Harvest time, when we were pea or potato picking, Richard was taking in how the horses were harnessed and how the farm machinery worked. When he applied to work on the bread van he was already comfortable with horses, which probably helped him get the job.

He was never satisfied with his lot and came home every evening whining about the miserable day he had suffered.

'Here he comes, the voice of spring,' Dorothy would comment as he walked through the door.

He could always laugh at himself. 'It's only my cheerfulness keeps me going,' he moaned, using the byline of a depressing character on the radio.

Evelyn was the first of my siblings to marry. She met Elwyn, her husband, at Butlin's holiday camp in Pwllheli.

A girl in our street, who had never been particularly friendly towards me before, invited me to go to the cinema with her. On our way home she asked me whether Evelyn was pregnant. That would have created a real scandal, particularly as we were a chapel-going family. I thought she was quite insane.

'Of course not,' I replied. 'She isn't married yet.'

Evelyn, in her beautiful white dress with copper curly hair, was the prettiest of brides.

Somebody told me the dress was made from a parachute. I imagined my three older sisters sitting in some secret room with the voluminous silk all around them as they unpicked the seams. Evelyn's measurements would have been taken. It would have been quite a challenge, laying out the pattern on these oddly-shaped pieces of silk and chalking around it. Dad would have sharpened the scissors on the back doorstep but it must have been nerve-racking cutting the slippery fabric. When all was prepared and Dorothy had tacked it together, she would have had the boring task of treadling away on the sewing machine, hour after hour, every day for months.

The wedding dress probably was made from parachute silk, as textiles from other sources were in short supply, but it is unlikely that Dorothy produced it. Most likely, it was hired, along with the turquoise bridesmaid dresses worn by Dorothy and Freda. Where the money came from I can't imagine, but I had a smart woollen skirt and jacket and Harry had his first suit. Richard isn't in the photograph. He missed the wedding ceremony because he couldn't find his trousers.

On the other hand, his namesake, Mam's brother Dick, was very much in evidence. It was probably the first wedding he had been to where there was no alcohol at the celebration, but he didn't allow that to kerb his exuberance.

We were all packed into the living room and spilling out into the back kitchen and front passage and stairway. Someone was accompanying the community singing on the piano and Uncle Dick joined in playing the comb and paper. The paper he had wrapped around the comb was a ten shilling

Wedding of Evelyn and Elwyn, 1948.
L–R front row: Tommy McFetters, Beaty Smith, Mair Roberts, Freda Smith, Elwyn Roberts, Evelyn Roberts (nee Smith), Best Man, Dorothy Smith, Martha Smith, Suzanne Smith (Alf's mam), Dianne and Harry Smith, Aunt Nell Stockton (Martha's sister), unknown.
Back row: Nell and Richard McCarten (Martha's brother), Tom McFetters Snr, unknown, unknown, unknown, unknown, Tom Smith, Alf Smith, Charley Winkles (Alf's best friend), unknown, Nell Winkles, Mrs McFetters.

Harry and Dianne at Evelyn and
Elwyn's wedding, 1948

note, enough to pay the rent for our three bedroom house for a week.

Richard McCarten, called Uncle Dick, was one of a long line of Richard McCartens going back generation after generation. His eldest son Richard was known as Richie. Rumour had it that there was a Richard McCarten who was a minister or vicar in London.

The day after the wedding, Prince Charles was born and I pasted his first pictures in my royal scrapbook.

After the honeymoon Evelyn and Elwyn went to the home of his family in Anglesey. She was barely there for two weeks. Desperately unhappy, she returned with him to Garston. She was isolated in a Welsh-speaking community and probably very lonely. They lived in the front room of our house for the next four years.

Elwyn had lived away from home before. He had been

conscripted into the Army for National Service. It must have been a traumatic experience for him and other boys from the Welsh-speaking community.

Employment at the holiday camp was seasonal work so he would have been unemployed when he arrived in Garston that winter. He found work almost immediately and I can't remember him ever being unemployed from then on, but it didn't strike me as remarkable at the time. I was shocked to discover that many of the boys who left school at the same time as me were unemployed five years later and had never worked. After a few temporary jobs, Elwyn found work as a store man in Lewis's department store where he was the union rep. He remained there until he retired at sixty-five.

I had been attending Gilmour for three months when Elwyn and Evelyn married. Pupils were expected to wear school uniform. The minimum nod to this requirement was a white blouse and black skirt. By the end of the first week in the school, I had found a large black skirt, crushed up in the back of a drawer, and one of Tom's cast-off white shirts, not only cast-off but off-white, frayed at the collar and cuffs. The size of the waistband of the skirt was reduced by folding it and securing it with a large pin. My idea of 'uniform' and the opinion of the school were not running along parallel lines. The teachers probably dropped hints but I didn't get the message. Exasperated, somebody in authority in the school sent me home and told me I was not to return until I was wearing school uniform.

Mam always ensured she wore a starched white overall for her work. She had been too busy to notice my clothes, while it wasn't a matter I had concerned myself with. When she looked at me she blushed with embarrassment at the realisation that I had been going to school in dirty, shabby clothes. She tried to hold back the tears, but they ran down her face. She was a very proud woman. The shame of me being sent home from school was almost unbearable. I couldn't see what all the fuss was about.

She boiled a kettle of water and told me to strip off, wash all over and change my underwear and brush my hair. Then, wonder of wonders, she told me to wear my best suit, the one I had for Evelyn's wedding. When I was ready she gave me a note to take to the school. She promised that she would buy me a school uniform at the weekend. I walked into the classroom proud as any panjandrum.

On Saturday Mam took me to Sturler's department store in The Dingle. Clothes could be bought there and paid for by weekly instalments or 'on the never, never' to use the colloquial expression. Dad would have been furious if he found out Mam had been buying there. In his book if you didn't have the money to pay for something, you couldn't have it. Eight years later Harry, at seventeen, was head boy at Liverpool School of Art. Being six foot tall he needed a man-size blazer. Dad's wages for a week would have almost covered the cost. There was no acknowledged conspiracy of silence between us. We knew this was something that was better forgotten.

The unique scent of new clothes enveloped me and Mam as we entered the department store. My first impression was of polished wooden counters, polished wooden floors and, overlooking the whole store, the cashier's office, a raised area like a little wooden cabin with windows. At arm's height above each counter was a line to the cashier's office. When the customer handed cash to the shop assistant she put it into a small tin attached to the wire. The tin went zinging along the wire and returned a few minutes later with change and a receipt. Every minute a little tin went zinging over your head from every direction. Behind the counters were shining wooden shelves piled high with woollen goods, cardigans, pullovers, and jumpers. Below these were glowing wooden doors with brass handles for drawers containing secret items like brassieres, corsets and underpants. The floor space was filled with rack upon rack of new, pressed garments.

Apart from the suit I wore for Evelyn's wedding, I don't remember having any new clothes. Shoes were always new and for me alone. Socks were new, but shared. Mam had two obsessions. One concerned lavatory hygiene and the other was about foot infections. My clothes were passed down from the older girls. Dorothy occasionally altered them to fit me but it was all hit-and-miss. Aunt Mamie, Dad's sister-in-law, made two dresses for me for my thirteenth birthday. She hadn't realised I was developing large breasts, so I had a struggle getting into them but once over that hurdle they fitted fine and I was very grateful. In the sewing class I made a dirndl skirt.

In the school uniform department of Sturler's store I was measured and fitted out with a black uniform dress, two white blouses, a black cardigan, a black blazer, two pairs of white socks, a black gabardine raincoat and a black beret. I already had black shoes. The dress had box pleats. It was hard work, as I had to stitch the pleats into place each week before I washed it. Then I had to iron the pleats in before the dress was too dry and unpick the stitches. When Mam bought me a new one about two years later I had one without pleats.

Tom and Richard had an amazing holiday in 1948 cycling around the Wye Valley and staying at youth hostels.

Dad persuaded his friend Tommy McFetter to join the Youth Hostel Association in 1949 and he planned a holiday around Glastonbury for the two couples. This was the beginning of his love affair with the YHA that lasted over thirty years.

All dental care became free on the National Health Service in 1949. When the NHS was established in 1948, Dad was convinced that the government would never be able to sustain all these free hospitals, prescriptions, and doctors' consultations. Now free dentistry was added to the list. He decided that he and Mam had to have all their teeth out immediately. Mam protested in vain. Dad booked their appointments; perfectly good teeth were removed at one sitting and two weeks later they were wearing dentures. The operation was a severe shock to her system. She was only forty-three and he was forty-seven.

Leaving Chesterton Street for the first YHA holiday in Glastonbury, 1949. L–R: Martha, Alf, Tommy Mac, Mrs Mac.

Alf and Martha, Glastonbury, 1949

He was quite right, of course. Free dental care didn't last forever. It ended about fifty years later.

Public transport was easily affordable, even from our meagre pocket money. At holiday time and on Bank Holidays, Harry, Dianne and I would be off to explore our world.

The sixty-six bus started from the bottom of Window Lane, near the Tanyard, and took us all the way to Woolton Woods, the same park we went to on the Sunday school treat every summer. We would build a den in the bushes and play house, climb the trees, and roll down the grassy embankment. The old village, with its small shops and sandstone houses, would draw us from the park when we started feeling peckish. A banana from the greengrocer squashed inside a barm cake from the baker would satisfy our hunger.

Sefton Park was a favourite destination. It was entered through tall Victorian ornamental gates with a marble drinking fountain. A sandy bridle path ran around the periphery.

We would make straight for the boathouse by the lake to book our rowing boat. From the first time we took a boat out, nobody questioned our age or our ability to row. Harry was ten, Dianne seven or eight, and I was twelve. There were no life jackets. We had been in boats with Tom and Richard and had no doubt about our ability to master the skill. After pushing off from the landing stage, Harry and I took an oar each and went round in circles for a time, making very little progress. After a few minutes we got the hang of it and moved off towards the centre of the lake. On our first few attempts we occasionally lost an oar. One of the other boats would pick it up for us. Soon we learned how to manoeuvre with one oar and retrieve it ourselves. By the end of that holiday we were proficient rowers. Fortunately, there were no health and safety fanatics at that time.

After boating we wandered through flower gardens looking at statues and the exotic greenhouse made of wrought iron and glass. There was a water fountain that worked, unlike the one at the park entrance.

We were tempted by Wall's ice cream on one occasion and bought a box between us. It was the most creamy, scrumptious ice cream I have ever tasted. Unfortunately, we used our bus fare to buy it and we were three miles from home. Drivers didn't collect the fares in those days. We probably got on and travelled a few stops before the conductor came for our fares and ejected us. Sometimes they let us get away with it.

If we went to Pierhead we could listen to the public speakers on their soapboxes spouting about religion or politics. Hecklers went there to make jokes at the expense of the speakers. The crowd enjoyed the banter.

'Do you save fallen women?' one of them shouted to the preacher.

'Save me one for Saturday night.'

After listening to this we would go down to the landing stage. There we could watch the ferries come in from Birkenhead, Wallasey, or New Brighton. The men on the boats would throw thick ropes to the ferrymen on shore. We would watch them catch the ropes and wind them around the bollards to secure the ferry to the landing stage.

Fares were collected on the Wirral side. We could take a ride to the port of our choice, step off at the other side without going through the ticket barrier, then return to the ferry with the passengers going to Liverpool. We loved being on the river, watching the waves in the wake of the boat, the sunlight dancing on the water, the distinctive skyline of the Pierhead buildings or the seashore and funfair with the Figure of Eight at New Brighton.

Charlie, a friend of Harry's, came with us along the shore to Oglet and the Damwoods near Speke. It had been a glorious summer's day but by now it was seven or eight in the evening. We had made a den in the woods and decided to camp over night. Charlie was going home so we asked him to tell Mam and Dad where we were. It was a balmy summer's night and we had a wonderful adventure.

The following morning, when we were playing on the shore, a man in his twenties came up and started talking to Dianne. I was too far away to stop her talking to him and she started walking with him along the shore. I was terrified and called to her not to leave with him. She came back but it ruined our lovely adventure. I was responsible for her and was sure he had molested her. Years later I spoke to her about the occasion. She assured me that she didn't go out of sight. She could tell I was worried and came back to us. On arriving home she told Mam about the man, and that he hadn't touched her.

Charlie, Harry's friend, hadn't given Mam and Dad the message that we were camping out.

I always loved walking. One day I had walked all the way to Speke Hall along the headland. It was a beautiful evening as I made my way back home. I had swung across the brook on the rope we always played with and had almost reached the path between the sea wall and the airport when I saw the man who had sexually abused me in my living room coming towards me. After he molested me I ran home feeling sick and angry. I didn't realise how lucky I was that he didn't know what his penis was for.

On recalling that encounter on the headland I remembered the game the children had played, hunting for the sex fiend on the shore, on the day my boobs started to show. It occurred to me that I was unlikely to have been my tormentor's only victim. He was probably the sex fiend we were searching for.

By the time I started at Gilmour the financial position of the family must have improved. We no longer had free school dinners. Dorothy came home and made a meal for us. One day she brought my sexual abuser home with her. Dianne and Harry returned to school and she left with him for the factory. I was washing up when he re-appeared at the kitchen door. There was no way to escape.

From that day on I made sandwiches and took them to school for lunch until Dorothy left home and he disappeared from our lives.

I had to pass his home going to and from school and had a dread of meeting him but I never did.

Dorothy left home to train as a State Enrolled Assistant Nurse in Ormskirk in 1949. She often spent her days off visiting Freda, who was working a few miles away in Southport.

If Dorothy knew she was coming home she would send a letter to Mam and Dad but didn't normally have advance notice of when she was off duty. When she arrived home during the night there wasn't a bed for her. She would be found sleeping in the most unexpected places. Dad was always first up. He found her early one morning sleeping on the big wooden table in the back kitchen, fully dressed and covered in the few overcoats she had found hanging in the hall. There was never any heating in the house until the fire was lit in the living room. The chill in the back kitchen was barely affected by weekday cooking but could become quite hot when cakes were being baked or the Sunday roast was in the oven. She was fortunate that it wasn't winter, when Jack Frost created his feathery patterns on the windows.

The school was taken to concerts in the Liverpool Philharmonic Hall. I loved the cathedral-like atmosphere; the darkness of the audience chamber contrasted against the sparkling brass instruments reflecting back the light from the brightly-lit stage. I had decided that, as I considered myself a cut above the girls in my form, I should prefer classical music to pop. When the orchestra was tuning up I didn't join in the whispered murmur of conversation of my schoolfellows but sat serious and attentive, partly because I wasn't sure whether the music had started. We listened every week with Dad to *Friday Night is Music Night* with the Palm Court Orchestra. I knew that the audience didn't applaud each time the orchestra stopped playing. While girls around me found themselves in the embarrassing situation of clapping on their own, I would wait until one or two of the teachers started clapping before I joined in.

We had music appreciation classes on alternate Wednesday mornings. The teacher loved music and we were caught up in her enthusiasm. Before we went to a concert she would play the music on a gramophone and encourage us to imagine what was happening. I particularly remember *The Carnival of Animals* and *Bolero*.

The headmistress, Miss Baldwin, took choir practice. She was very critical of crooners, the pop idols of the day. They wobbled all over the place and slid from note to note. If we wanted to be good singers we shouldn't follow their lazy habits.

At the beginning of the autumn term, when I was twelve years old, a new music teacher was engaged. The school offered violin lessons for seven shillings and sixpence a term. I imagined myself as another Yehudi Menuhin and raced home to beg to be allowed to join the class. When Dad said yes I was in heaven.

We were a small class of about ten pupils. The other girls were from the lower middle class and already had a grounding in music. They read music and played recorder and piano. It was a totally new experience for me and my first lesson was sheer ecstasy. Walking home carrying the violin in its case, I was puffed up with joyful pride.

It was all downhill from then. The new teacher found me too slow. She made fun of me and had the other pupils laughing at my expense.

We were to perform at the end of term concert a year later, before the summer holidays. I was in a quartet. On the day I had a severe migraine and couldn't stop vomiting. I didn't go to school. I hadn't told Mam or Dad about the way the teacher bullied me. They didn't know I should have been playing in a concert. Perhaps they would have written to apologise.

For years I worried about having let the other members of the quartet down but I realise now that it was such a simple piece one of the other pupils or the teacher probably took my place.

While we were practising for the concert, Mrs Bath, the deputy head, came into one of the lessons. I was frightened of her before I started at Gilmour. She was always having rows with Dorothy when she had been in the senior school at Banks Road. She was Miss Stewart at that time. I was the image of Dorothy, so she started picking on me as soon as she met me.

Dorothy had always been spotlessly clean and kept her clothes ironed and shoes polished. When she started senior school at eleven we had moved to the tenements. We had a bathroom and she bathed every day.

This was a typical dialogue between them.

'Have you had a wash today, Dolly?'

'No, Miss.'

'Why not?'

'Not my week for washing, Miss.'

Or the dialogue might be:

'Dolly, when did you last wash your hair?'

'Never wash it miss.'

'Wash it tonight.'

'Can't Miss, we're keeping fish in the sink.'

Dorothy knew how to deal with bullies. I didn't, and tried to keep my head down, but it didn't work. Freda was only two years behind Dorothy, but she didn't look like her. When Miss Stewart was around she managed to make herself invisible.

The term after Dorothy had started nursing was quite eventful. That was the term that the man I feared and hated stopped coming to our house, Mrs Bath upset me in front of the violin class, I missed the concert, and violin lessons became free of charge. Any pupil could join. When I arrived for my lesson the music teacher told me the class was full and took my violin from me.

I was distraught. The shame of being put out of the class was so embarrassing I couldn't tell any of my friends. I marched up and down the paths in Garston Park, in a highly agitated state not knowing how to cope. My throat hurt. Slowly the tears leaked out and began to course down my cheeks.

Lunchtime over, I returned to school. Nobody noticed that I had been crying.

When I arrived home I said nothing to anyone. I dreaded the day Dad would offer me the money for my lessons for the term, but he didn't remember. As the weeks went by, I began to relax, thinking he had totally forgotten I had ever played the violin.

One evening, six months after the classes ended, Dad asked, 'How is my little violinist doing?'

He was sitting reading and just looked up carelessly from his book.

I stood by the open door, resting my head against the edge.

'Isn't,' I muttered, swinging the door back and forth.

'What do you mean?'

There was a smile in his eyes. I decided it would be safe to tell him. Frankly, I didn't have any choice.

Falteringly, swallowing after each syllable, I told him what had happened. The tears I had been holding back for six months began to run down my face again.

Sitting me down, he assured me that I hadn't done anything wrong. He wasn't angry with me.

'Let me read a poem to you,' he said.

My fairest child, I have no song to give you;
No lark could pipe in skies so dull and grey;
Yet, if you will, one quiet hint I'll leave you,
For every day.

I'll tell you how to sing a clearer carol
Than lark who hails the dawn or breezy down;
To earn yourself a purer poet's laurel
Than Shakespeare's crown.

Be good, sweet maid, and let who can be clever;
Do lovely things, not dream them, all day long:
And so make Life, and Death, and that Forever,
One grand sweet song.

Meryl, Evelyn's daughter, was born in September 1949. Evelyn, Elwyn and Meryl lived in the front room of Chesterton Street until Meryl was four. It couldn't have been easy for them. There was only a tiny kitchen that Evelyn had to share with Mam. It was still home to the other seven children in 1949, if and when they returned home.

165

Early in 1950 Richard applied to train as a cook in the merchant navy. He was looking for a job with food, as usual. Dad wouldn't sign the papers for him to go. Dad was fourteen when he first went to sea but he thought Richard, at sixteen, was too young to leave home.

The first general election I remember was February 1950. Our form teacher announced that we were going to have a debate. Three of our classmates would represent the views of the three political parties. We were to prepare for the debate by reading a national newspaper and writing notes in an exercise book.

I made a cover for the book with pink embossed wallpaper and traced a picture of Churchill onto the front. He was a national hero and was bound to win. I had never heard of Clement Atlee and had no idea that Labour had been in government since 1945. Mam and Dad never voted Conservative in their lives. In my late teens and early twenties, I learned about Socialist theories. Dad's views didn't fit the Socialist pattern and I thought he lacked clarity in his thinking. I was middle-aged before I realised he was an old-fashioned radical Liberal and only voted Labour when there was no Liberal candidate. Mam never told anyone which party she voted for. She said it was a secret ballot and no business of anyone else but herself. My parents never objected to using our front room as a Labour party committee room. To prepare for the debate about the 1950 election, I read the *News Chronicle*, a Liberal paper, in the library when I went to change my novel each day. Dad took the *Liverpool Echo*, so I read that, although it wasn't a national paper and, when we went to the cowboy films on Saturday morning, I gleaned everything I could from *Pathé News*. I was shocked when Labour won.

When Dorothy left there was no-one to run the Guides' pack at Banks Road Methodist chapel. My friend from Guides' camp went to the pack that met at Gilmour. I joined her there but found the bike ride home for tea and back to the school too much of an effort and gave up after a year.

Dorothy came home from Ormskirk with a black boyfriend. In theory Mam believed in being tolerant. She said nothing but found it difficult. She kept a strict, respectable home and didn't like attention being drawn to the family. Dorothy was always causing her embarrassment. Dad also tried to raise us to be tolerant but he was convinced that the black would come off on the sheets. He thought that black people were lesser beings but we should be kind to them. We were brought up on 'Little Black Sambo' and the need to give money in the Sunday school collection to send out missionaries and governors to those lacking our enlightenment and intelligence.

The tall, blond, Russian sailor Dorothy brought home next took our breath away. A pale blue cable knit sweater added to the width of his broad shoulders. Everything about him looked clean, handsome and totally charming. Dianne and I fell for him in a big way. We would sit gazing at him, hanging on to every word. He was the first major crush of my life.

Everyone came home for a big family party on the 6th June 1950. It was Mam and Dad's twenty-fifth wedding anniversary.

Mam's pièce de résistance at parties was a trifle made with tinned mandarins, orange jelly made from gelatine squares, the mandarin juice, white bread cut into fingers and the bowl topped off with custard when the jelly had set. I couldn't bear the sensation of wet bread in my mouth. It made me retch. I was well into adulthood before I conquered my aversion to trifle. Today I love food in all its rich variety from every corner of the globe. Beetroot is the only blot on my gastronomic copybook. It is said to have many health-giving properties, so I have tried disguising it in cakes, drinks and jellies, to no avail. If a salad has been touched by a slice of one, the plate has to be given to someone else. Harry had the same violent reaction to it. Dad grew them, but he grew all of our vegetables so that couldn't be the reason why we couldn't tolerate them. So long as vegetables are not drowned in saltwater and overcooked, they are delightful.

Freda had made a spectacular anniversary cake decorated with royal icing. Our mouths were watering at the sight of it. I particularly craved for the marzipan, though it was many years before I tasted the genuine article made from almonds. During the Second World War soya with almond flavouring was used. The party came and went, while the cake remained in all of its pristine glory.

Four days later, on the 10th June, Dad's Mam, Susannah, and her twin brother Harry, celebrated their 70th birthday. The 25th wedding anniversary cake was still uncut.

We were now into the pea and potato picking season. I can't remember which crop came first but it was all back-breaking work. We would rush to the farms after school and on Saturdays to raise spending money for our holidays. We were out in all weathers, covered in mud, with our hands too cold to pick anything, or baking and sweating, desperate for a drink and the chance to straighten our backs. Warm days were pleasanter, with the country smells and birdsong, but it was one long slog with no respite. We were all going along our own furrows and even if there was anyone near enough to talk to, we didn't talk because talking slowed you down. At the end of the session, whether after school or all day, I would drag my harvest to the wagon to be weighed and was always bitterly disappointed

with the pittance I received. Everyone was paid more than me. With the best will in the world, I was always a dreamer and a slowcoach.

Dad had two weeks' annual leave in June. He

Seventieth birthday celebration, 10th June 1950. Great-uncle Harry, Martha and Grandma.

168

applied to our schools and they granted us a fortnight's holiday to go away with him. Our first youth hostelling adventure was in 1950. We cycled through Wales to Bath.

Dad, Mam and Dianne were riding a working-class version of the people carrier, similar to a tandem, but for three. I was at the front of a tandem with Harry at the back. Smelting iron, gas and petrol filled my mouth, nose and lungs as we cycled around the church wall. My ears rang as a train rumbled over the bridge that separated our part of Garston from the village.

Now we were on the main road to Liverpool city centre. Lorries thundered past. The vacuum pulled the bike towards them. Riding in the gutter was safest, except that there was a danger of hitting grids. Villagers swarmed along the narrow pavements as they moved from shop to shop. Tramlines were a constant worry. The bike wheel could get caught. Added to all of these problems, we were cycling uphill.

After a quarter of an hour we passed the half-timbered library and the road to my school. Once out of Garston the road became flat and widened. Above a tall wall we glimpsed the stand in the cricket ground and La Sagesse, the imposing grammar school for girls. Stone pillars and wrought iron gates guarded the entrances to the two grand Victorian housing estates of Grassendale and Cressington, where the middle classes hid themselves away while enjoying views of the river. In Aigburth there were grass verges and trees. Neatly trimmed privet hedges boxed in houses with gardens. Tall trees in Otterspool Park spread their branches towards the road. Then, the imposing Victorian gateway of Sefton Park, with its highly ornate stone drinking water fountain, came into view on the other side of the road, bringing memories of boating on the lake, the Peter Pan statue, and glasshouses of tropical plants. Above the sound of traffic I could hear birds singing. Then we were plunged back into the noise, smell and grime of Toxteth and The Dingle.

At Liverpool Pierhead we were taking the ferry over to Birkenhead on the Wirral peninsula. Ferries ran half-hourly and were always crowded. An hour later public speakers would be on their soapboxes, with crowds gathered around to listen to the fun as hecklers crossed verbal swords with them.

The politicians would be lambasted with gossip about their family life.

'Take your mother out of the old folks hospital, you hypocrite.'

Dad was kicking his heels as I wound my way on the tandem between the fifteen or so double-decked green buses arriving or leaving the bus station. We were more than a quarter of an hour behind him. He had fumed as he watched one boat leave while he waited, but his anger evaporated as quickly as it came.

We followed the queue onto the boat. As we leaned over the rails, watching the ferrymen untie the ropes holding the ferry to the landing stage, we could barely contain our excitement. He jumped aboard and we were off on a great adventure. The prison doors opened and we escaped from all those endless ugly buildings walling us in. Now there was nothing but the waves, the broad expanse of sky, and the distant hills of Cheshire. Dad had crossed the ocean on the banana boats to the West Indies when he was only a year or two older than I was when I crossed the Mersey that day. We imagined the ferry carrying us off to the open sea. The image of the neo-classical buildings that define the skyline of Liverpool Pierhead was the one sailors and emigrants took with them to distant lands. I always felt a surge of pride as I looked at this inspiring vista. This was my city. Too soon the ferrymen were tying up and we were disembarking to be entombed in the clatter and filth of industrial Birkenhead.

But that short river crossing had given me a taste of freedom. I flew along the road in a dream, oblivious to the honking and screeching of traffic, the claustrophobic pressure of the terraced streets, brick factory walls, warehouses and cranes.

...mid the din
Of towns and cities, I have owed to them,
In hours of weariness, sensations sweet,
Felt in the blood, and felt along the heart,
And passing even into my purer mind,
With tranquil restoration...

In no time we left Birkenhead and Ellesmere Port behind us. We were in the gentle Cheshire countryside heading towards Sealand, where we had spent our summer holidays for a couple of years. Crossing the river Dee to Queensferry, we headed for Mold where Ma, Mam's mother, had been born.

Our maternal great-grandparents were Irish. Great-grandfather Upton was a stonemason. There was a great demand for houses during the industrial revolution. His work had taken him and his family to Mold. The local women taught Welsh nursery rhymes and cradle songs to great-grandma and she sat on the doorstep rocking the cradle and singing happily. When she learned the language she discovered that she had been singing crude songs with every swear word imaginable.

When great-granddad retired, the family settled in The Dingle in Liverpool and he bought or rented a grocery shop.

Mam remembered him as a lazy old man who never moved from his armchair at the back of the shop. He would sit there all day puffing away on his pipe. I had the impression that great-grandmother was serving. Her granddad must have been mid-to-late fifties when Mam was eight, which was very old for a man in 1914. Perhaps he served in the shop when he was starting the business a few years earlier. Mam worked in a grocery store from the time she left school until she married. It was probably in the family shop.

Mam's father never spoke to Mam if he passed her in the street. One day, when she was about eight years old, she had been on an errand to the shop when two boys barred her way. Suddenly her father appeared. He was a tall man of smart, military bearing. The boys ran off immediately. He asked her whether they had harmed her. She was so shy in his presence she could barely answer him. That incident was treasured all her life.

From Mold we took the Horseshoe Pass to Llangollen, a quaint old town on the river Dee. The tandem Harry and I were riding was a solid, sturdy piece of engineering built of heavy steel and intended to withstand being run over by a tank. We pushed down hard on the pedals, determined not to be defeated by the steep slope winding ever upward for a mile before us. We stood up and zigzagged across the road barely making any progress while holding up all the traffic behind us. It didn't occur to us that it would have been quicker to dismount and walk. I was in my forties before I realised I didn't have to face every challenge head-on.

We arrived in Llangollen soon after three in the afternoon. We couldn't get into the hostel until five so, after a cup of tea at one of the pretty teashops beside the river Dee, we remounted and climbed the steep road to Plas Newydd, the home of the Ladies of Llangollen.

The Ladies of Llangollen, Eleanor Butler and Sarah

Plas Newydd, Llangollen, 1950; Dianne, Harry, Mam and Beaty

Beaty, Harry and Dianne

Ponsonby, ran away from their families in Ireland. They had tried to escape once before but were caught and taken back home. On their second attempt they succeeded in reaching Wales where they bought Plas Newydd.

Young women made a habit of escaping from domineering parents in the 19th century. My favourite runaway was the poetess Elizabeth Barrett Browning who eloped with her poet lover Robert Browning. This was later brought to the silver screen in *The Barretts of Wimpole Street*.

Escaping lovers didn't need an explanation. Why two rich young women would run off from their luxurious homes in Ireland was a goldmine for my fertile imagination. Had Lady Butler been left the family fortune by her grandparents, leaving her parents penniless? Did she have a wicked stepmother who kept her locked up in a dungeon or made her work as a servant? Did they sail to England under a tarpaulin in a fishing boat? Was her money in gold coins sewn inside her cloak? Did she buy the house with the gold coins?

There must have been something very special about these women and the manner of their escape because many poets and artists and other important people came to visit them, even the Duke of Wellington and Wordsworth himself.

When we descended into the town the postcard shops were still open and I bought one for every girl in my class. I was bursting with excitement that evening at the hostel as I told different aspects of the story of our journey to Llangollen and addressed the cards. I don't remember writing down their addresses before going on holiday or where I put the list for safekeeping in all the rush and bustle of packing. I always carried a book for writing poetry. The names were probably written in it. Why did I send those cards? Was it an open generous wish to share my good fortune with my schoolfellows? Or was I saying, look at me, I'm seeing places you will never have the good fortune to see, while you are sitting behind a desk in school? I think it was a little of both.

The hostels occupied an amazing assortment of buildings. I can no longer remember which specific hostel was a water mill, a chapel or a barn. I can see the courtyard of a half-timbered house and hear Harry playing Chopin on the tinny piano. It was a hostel in Wales in 1950.

Next day we cycled through the pretty little village of Betws y Coed, known by my father as Betsy Code, and visited the Swallow Falls, the first waterfall I had ever seen. There were many 'first' experiences on that holiday. Days filled with joy and wonderment that kept my pulse racing.

On we rode between mile after mile of wild green hills as the road cut its way along the Vale of Conwy to the Irish Sea.

We hardly gave second glance to the medieval town of Conwy with Elizabethan, Jacobean, Georgian and Victorian houses. The town walls with their battlements, the narrow gateways, but most of all the imposing castle, held us spellbound.

We knew nothing of the battles of Edward I against the Welsh. If Dad tried to tell us, I have no recollection of Welsh history. I doubt he knew any history apart from the accepted

English version. He was unswervingly for king, country and the British Empire.

Our heroes were King Arthur and the Knights of the Round Table. We were seeing the Arthurian legends with new eyes since Bing Crosby had gone back in time in the film *A Connecticut Yankee in King Arthur's Court*.

'We're whizzing down the Horseshoe Pass on the tandem when we hit a hole in the road and go flying off and bang our heads,' I said, copying the story of the Yankee knocking himself out and waking in King Arthur's court.

'As you fly over the three-seater, Harry catches his foot in the shoulder straps of my skirt and carries me with him,' Dianne chimes in, afraid that she is going to be left out of the game.

'There's a loud roar, like Dad shouting at us. We all wake up to find the tandem lying over a tree trunk close by, and a big knight in armour above us brandishing his sword.'

'He is about to strike me. Quickly I reach over the handlebars and switch on the front light.'

'A tin monster,' he screams, backing away.

'We're surrounded by knights on horseback who poke us with their javelins and make us walk in front of them to the castle.'

'Make them lead the fire breathing monster,' says the first knight. So we pushed the tandem along beside us.

And so the game progressed. We proved we were brave warriors when Harry showed the brightly coloured glass marbles he had in his pocket. They were the eyes of dangerous animals that we had killed. The knights began to lose their fear of our tandem, and came closer to us. They laughed at the idea of it being a monster. I raised the back wheel onto my shoulder and patted it to try to stop it being angry and Harry turned the pedals quickly. The dynamo shone out from its backside. They were convinced and gave us a wide berth while we had our monster to protect us. We won jousting tournaments riding the tandem, competed against Merlin by making fire with a Primus stove, and killed a tin animal with a tin opener. The meat inside was ready to eat. The tin opener also came in handy when a visor became jammed.

We heard Dad calling and realised we were hungry. It was time for lunch. Soon we were on the coast road and on our way to Bangor.

After cycling through Upper Bangor, we came to the top of a steep tree-lined lane. Taking our feet off the pedals, we hurtled down the hill, leaning to the left or right as we took the turns on the winding path. A man shouted a warning but we took it as a greeting and waved to him. Further down an old woman cried out to us. We thought the locals very friendly. Our velocity carried us ever faster down the plunging slope. Bang! Without warning our journey ended on a shale beach. The front wheel stuck in the pebbles. As with our game at Conwy castle, Harry flew over my head. Fortunately, he didn't knock himself out or disappear into Arthurian legend. I was filled with guilt at my irresponsibility. He stood up to find he had come to little harm, only a few scratches. Mam cleaned them with TCP when we arrived at the hostel. It was less than fifty yards away along the shore.

Next day we left the coast road and took narrow winding

Top of Upper Lane, Bangor

Lane from Upper Bangor

roads through tiny villages comprising of little more than a chapel, a post office, half a dozen houses, and a couple of sheep farms. We were enchanted by the foreign names we didn't understand: Glasinfryn, Rhyd-y-groes, Pentir, Llanddeiniolen and Rhiwlas. Now as I look at them on a map I try to comprehend the meaning of the names, Blue slope, the Cross by the Ford, Hilltop, St Deiniolen and the green hillside shimmering in the sunshine on a beautiful summer day.

Harry and I forgot our tumble of the night before. We were tearing along the road, leaning to the left as we swerved around left curves, over to the right for right bends.

We heard Dad shouting and slowed down to find out what he wanted. Overtaking us, he stopped and walked back. It was obvious that he was very worked up over something. We knew we were in for a telling off.

'Didn't you learn your lesson yesterday?' he demanded, in a great state of agitation. 'You are going to get yourselves killed or cause a serious accident.'

'Sorry Dad,' we chorused.

'Right. When you see a sign for bends it is to warn you that you can't see what is coming. So you're going to ride slowly and carefully.'

177

'Yes, Dad.'

But the adrenalin was racing and we were in a silly, giggling mood. We tried to see how slowly we could ride without losing our balance, as we would in a slow cycling competition. The pedal of the wobbling tandem caught on a stone on the verge, throwing me forward against the handlebars.

Blood poured from my chin. Dad tried to staunch it by pressing with a handkerchief. He was sick with worry as he knocked on the door of the first house we came to. They directed us to the home of the district nurse, two miles away.

How we got there I can't remember. Perhaps we hitched a lift in a lorry. When the nurse saw the cut she thought it was going to need stitches. Whatever she did the bleeding stopped and I escaped with an Elastoplast, a shock and a scar on my chin for life.

After this detour we returned to the road for Llanberis, the village at the foot of Snowdon. Because of the delay we didn't have time to climb the mountain. We continued on our way to Caernarfon.

Caernarfon castle was our final destination that day and the main attraction. Our former high spirits returned as it came into view. Dumping the tandem against a wall, we rushed to peer through the wrought iron gates. As we gazed with wonder at the towers and turrets on the high walls we could barely contain our joy at the thought of the games we would play.

'Half a crown!' we heard Dad explode. 'Half a crown. I'm not paying half a crown.'

Thirty years later I visited the Albert Dock in Lverpool with my brothers and sisters. The man at the ticket office informed us that there was an extra charge for watching the exhibition of barrel making.

'Half a crown,' Harry cried. 'I'm not paying half a crown!'

The cashier sat looking totally bemused as we all collapsed in uncontrollable laughter.

'No,' he said, 'it's five pounds.'

That set us all off again.

We had cycled all day to get to Caernarfon. Now we stared through the railings, knowing that this was the most we were going to see of Caernarfon castle. After a few minutes we went to the sweet shop. Harry bought a Rollo instead of his usual Mars bar because he didn't have a knife sharp enough to cut it into slivers. I bought liquorish torpedoes, while Di surprisingly settled for a chocolate bar. Having dutifully given one of our sweets to Mam, Dad and each other, we sat on a grass verge in front of the castle to munch the rest.

We awoke next morning to bird song and a dozen shades of green under an almost cloudless sky. Only the distinctive peak of Snowdon rising up on our left and the twin peaks of Yr Eifl ahead of us on the Llŷn peninsula, were wreathed in early morning mist.

At Beddgelert we stopped at the tomb of Gelert. Dad told us the story of how Llywelyn left Gelert, his faithful hound, to look after his baby son when he went to a battle. A wolf tried to kill the child but Gelert fought and killed it. When Llywelyn returned he saw his tent destroyed and the dog, covered in blood, sitting beside it. Heartbroken that his child had been eaten by Gelert, Llywelyn shouted out loud and lunged his spear into the dog. The noise woke the baby who began to cry. Llywelyn found him under the canvas with the dead wolf nearby. Returning to the dog, Llywelyn held him as he took his last breath. Before he died he licked the hand of his master. Llywelyn built a tomb and buried his faithful hound.

As midday approached, my heart leapt as we left the valley, and the turquoise sea met the brilliant blue sky. In the distance I saw another castle but I didn't dare hope that we would go inside.

Dad knew how disappointed we had been at Caernarfon. He didn't want that to happen today so he said nothing about us seeing a Harlech castle until we arrived.

As usual we went to the gates and took in all that we could see from there.

Perhaps this castle was cheaper or he calculated that he

could afford it. Whatever the reason, this time he paid for us to go in. I have no recollection of Mam and Dad coming in with us.

The protagonists in our battles, as we chased along the walls of Harlech castle, were Robin Hood, hero of the poor, the wicked Sheriff of Nottingham, bad King John who was forced to sign Magna Carta to give us our rights, and his handsome, dashing brother, Richard the Lionheart, who had had to leave England to lead the crusade in Jerusalem to save the Holy Land from the Arabs.

After lunch we made our way in a fairly leisurely manner to Barmouth. We were worn out and happy to spend a quiet evening on the beach.

Next day we left the coast to head south through mid Wales. There was no stop at Machynlleth, as nothing of major historical significance happened there, just a small matter of an internationally recognised parliament and one Owain Glyndŵr, mentioned in passing by Shakespeare, but not by my Dad.

We rode for over fifty miles through the Cambrian mountain

Alf, Martha and Dianne at Caersws

range to spend the night in a hostel converted from a chapel or a farmhouse somewhere between Caersws and Llangurig.

By the following day we had cycled along country roads in the gentle undulating countryside of the heart of Wales, sped through the Victorian splendour of the spa town of Llandrindod Wells, passed the livestock pens of the cattle and sheep markets of Builth Wells and on through Brecon, the military town at the foot of the Brecon Beacons. The name Sennybridge has lodged in my mind as the nearest village to the youth hostel.

We were overwhelmed by the beauty that surrounded us every day but once again history was shouting to us from every road and every farmhouse, even the ones we stayed in, but our ears weren't tuned to the voices around us. I think there was a café we stopped at in Builth called The Drovers. In all probability we had been following the drovers' road from the north coast to south Wales. It is more than likely that Dad would have known about drovers but we didn't ask and he didn't think to tell us. As for the 'daughters of Rebecca', the only Rebecca we knew of was the one weeping for her daughters in the Bible. We learned about her in Sunday school. They had nothing to do with the injustices of the tollgates and the struggles of a downtrodden people.

The fields and hills around us were bathed in sunshine when we woke next morning. It couldn't have been bright and warm every day but I remember nothing but unbroken sunlight.

As we set off for Merthyr Tydfil along a quiet country road, a wispy cloud of mist circled the mountain. The rest of the sky was unbroken blue. We joined the main road and continued to climb.

'We are in the clouds,' Dad called to us.

Suddenly we were damp and cold, but the idea of being in the clouds was thrilling. As we continued upwards the cloud was left below us, hanging above the valley while the sun shining on the mountain peaks dried the mist from our clothes. It was a moment of sheer magic.

A warm wind blew through hair and clothes as we

freewheeled down the mountain road into Merthyr Tydfil. We had been spoiled by day after day of the unbroken prettiness of the villages and chocolate box splendour of the landscapes. The poverty of the town hit me like a blow to the stomach. The countryside of south Wales, with its green country lanes and hillsides, was as picturesque as any in the north, if we could close our eyes to the slag heaps, but the villages, the towns and the people were down at heel and shabby. Blackwood, Crumlin and Pontypool we put behind us as speedily as possible. It was a relief to surface in the pretty little town of Usk and breathe in the pure air beside the river.

In Chepstow, another border town and another castle, we allowed our imaginations free reign as we climbed and ran and jumped on castle walls that had once intimidated the people of Wales. The best was yet to come but Dad was keeping that a secret.

Now is the time for a confession. My memory is letting me down. Mam, Dad, Beaty, Harry and Dianne were on this holiday in Wales in 1950. I know this because we have photographs to

Chepstow castle. Back: Alf and Martha; centre: Beaty; front: Harry and Dianne. Beaty is holding a notebook for writing poems.

prove it. In 1951 Mam, Dad, Beaty and Harry went to the Festival of Britain. Dianne went to the festival with Evelyn, Elwyn and Meryl. Dianne told me about the experience and there is a photo of her with them in Trafalgar Square. She was very disappointed to have missed our first visit to London. Richard went to the festival with Mam and Dad before he set off for Australia. I'm running ahead of myself.

The first point I wanted to make was that I don't know where we went on holiday in 1952, but I think we toured Wales again. Those who know the geography of Wales may have found our 1950 tour contorted. If there were two holidays in Wales they have become one tour in my mind. The same has happened with the Festival of Britain 1951 and the Coronation in 1953. As I will be devoting the whole of chapter four to the Coronation, I will probably skip lightly over the route we took to the Festival of Britain and visits we made to museums etc. in London.

The second blank in my memory concerns the McFetter family. We took our camping holidays with them in Frodsham and Sealand for many years. The tour of 1950 ended in Bath, Somerset, and they were on a photograph with us in Bath beside a drinking fountain. I have no recollection of them being with us during the tour of Wales or when we went into the Roman Baths. This is particularly odd because I had a mile-high crush on young Tommy, who was a handsome blond. If he was there why wasn't I ogling him instead of playing cowboys and Indians and writing poems about castles?

'Once more into the breach.'

We were on our way to Monmouth, birthplace of Henry V of Shakespearian fame. Prince Henry honed his battle skills while fighting the Welsh army led by Owain Glyndŵr before going off to Agincourt to fight the French. If Shakespeare is to be believed, while Henry IV was dying, young Henry picked up his father's crown to see whether it fitted him, but you can't believe everything Shakespeare wrote.

The 1944 film, with Laurence Olivier as Henry V, was

soul-stirring stuff. The British galloped to victory in WWII, burning with confidence after that glorious production.

Dad said he had heard on good authority that Monmouth was still at war with Germany. According to many local people, when war was declared in 1939 Monmouth was officially informed because it was part of England. At the end of the war there was confusion about whether it was in England or Wales so nobody officially informed Monmouth council that the war had ended.

Many Elizabethan and Georgian houses and shops lined the main street of this small market town. The street was much wider than I had expected it to be. Some of the roofs were sagging, and looked as though they could collapse at any minute. There were a number of coaching inns, with arches for the coaches to go into the courtyard. At one end of the street was the imposing Georgian pile, the Shire Hall, while at the other end there was an ancient bridge across the river with an unusual old stone tower on it.

Whether by accident or intent, we didn't discover that there was a castle in Monmouth.

Although Dad told us with his usual enthusiasm about the buildings we were passing– who had lived in the tall Georgian house with wrought iron gates or the tiny narrow one squeezed between two others on the High Street, he could barely hide his wish to set off on the last part of our journey. It was to the YHA at St Briavels in the Forest of Dean.

As we cycled along a country road a castle came into view.

'Dad, Dad,' I called to him. 'Can we go there?'

He stopped riding and waited for us to catch up.

'Well,' he said seriously, 'You've already been to Chepstow castle. It's getting late.'

'Please Dad,' we begged.

'Oh all right, but we can't stay long.'

At last we reached the castle and saw the imposing doorway in the castle wall.

I could hardly breathe. 'Was it closed?' I asked myself. 'Would Dad be willing to pay for us to go in?'

Harry, Dianne and I were watching him, looking for a clue as to his intentions.

'Here is an interesting wall,' he said.

'Wall,' I thought, 'Who wants to look at a wall?'

I was near to bursting.

Obedient as ever, we looked at the low stone wall at the side of the path leading to the door.

Attached to the wall was a large triangular YHA sign. For some time we stared at the notice trying to marshal our thoughts. Harry was so overcome with ecstasy he couldn't say a word. I was no better.

'Dad, are we staying here?' Dianne asked breathlessly.

Hugging himself with delight, he remembered the joy he felt when he read about St Briavels Castle.

We slept that night in a stone cell in a real castle. I wrote poems about our experience, Dianne soaked it in, while Harry filled his sketchbook with tracery, bosses and cornices.

I would say more, but the story of our visit to St Briavels is told in chapter four.

St Briavels Castle YHA, Forest of Dean

Drawings by Harry Smith

Pulteney Bridge,
Bath

BATH : Pulteney Bridge,
inspired by the Ponte Vecchio (Florence)

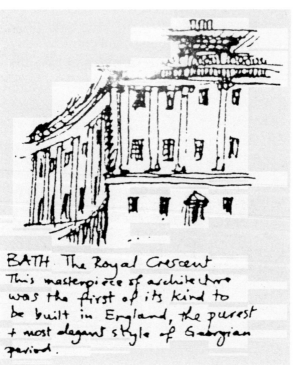

The Royal
Crescent, Bath

BATH The Royal Crescent
This masterpiece of architecture
was the first of its kind to
be built in England, the purest
+ most elegant style of Georgian
period.

N: Tower Bridge with us in front of the Tower of London

Tower Bridge, London

Merton College, Oxford

OXFORD. The path near Merton College founded 1274.

Intuition tells me that we must have taken the ferry from Beachley, near Chepstow, to the tiny village of Aust in Gloucestershire. At the time it would have been an amazing experience, but the mind has an odd way of deciding which memories to keep and which to bury. Perhaps one day some incident or word will jolt it back.

On arriving in England we made for Bristol. Bombsites were not given a second glance. We had plenty of those at home. The empty shells of churches looked interesting, but we passed St Luke's church each time we took a tram into Liverpool city centre. One day I will go in to look around.

Dad waited for us to catch up at a spot where there was a good view of Clifton Suspension Bridge.

Harry had his pad and pencil out almost before we stopped. The tip of his tongue flicked from one side of his mouth to the other as his eyes flashed from one side of the gorge to the other and the towers were captured on the paper.

'Some years ago in the days of Queen Victoria,' Dad said, 'A young girl was jilted by her lover.'

This wasn't Dad's usual kind of story. We were expecting him to tell us who built the bridge, how long ago, and the problems they had to overcome. Yes, he told us stories from literature, *Romeo and Juliet*, *Lorna Doone* and so on, but this seemed to be a true story. He had our full attention.

'She had dressed in her finest clothes to meet him. Her skirt was so voluminous she had difficulty going through the doorway. As she was about to leave home she received a letter from her lover, telling her he wanted to end their love affair. Broken-hearted she walked to the bridge. She went right to the middle, where the water below was deepest, and jumped to her death.'

All of us, including Mam, drew in our breath in horror.

'Well, she intended to jump to her death,' he continued. 'But her skirt acted as a parachute. The wind carried her to the embankment, where she landed in the mud.' He was grinning broadly.

He knew no more, except that she was unharmed.

Did she marry her lover? What happened to her after this event? I didn't know then but, thanks to the internet, I do now. I will leave you to find out if the story interests you. Here are a few clues to start you off. Her name was Sarah Ann Henley. She was born 8th July 1862. This incident happened May 1885.

Arriving in Queen Square, Bath, we looked for somewhere to lock up our bikes while we ate, before taking a walk around the city. When I say a walk, I don't mean an aimless amble. Dad had studied maps, guide books and history books well in advance of our visit. We all enjoyed the interlude, but food was sustenance to keep us going on our journey. Fortunately Dad liked his food. If he hadn't he would have been hustling us to get moving.

The Georgian terraces on the north side of the square glowed in the afternoon sunlight. The architect, John Wood, was said to have based his design of the terrace on the Roman Baths built two thousand years earlier that gave the city its name and its fame. The seven houses, with their Corinthian pillars soaring up two storeys and supporting a frieze and grand pediment on the central house, give the illusion of being one majestic palace. Houses on the other side of the square were bomb damaged from the Blitz but the north side had come through unscathed. They were our first taste of Bath and filled us with joy.

While eating, Dad told us that Jane Austen had lived on the square. Two of her books, *Persuasion* and *Northanger Abbey*, had scenes based in Bath. She was an author I hadn't read, so I was under whelmed by talk of the house where she had lived and the Assembly Rooms where she had danced.

Dad was impatient to start the route march as soon as we finished eating. We made our way across a small park to The Circus. Two bombs had fallen on the oval during the Blitz on the city. One had buried itself into the soft earth while the other had stood on its nose unexploded. The houses in The Circus were undamaged. I won't bore you, dear reader, with a guided tour of Bath. It is sufficient to say that we looked at every architectural detail on every building of note in the centre of Bath, learned a little about freemasons, in Dad's disapproving tone, and little morsels of history. We had arrived in the city too late to visit the Roman Baths, but we passed the building on our walk. The visit to the baths couldn't be rushed. It was our treat for the following day. I'm sure it cost Dad more than half a crown for each of the children and a couple of shilling more for him and Mam. In a park, somewhere on that walking tour, we posed for a photograph beside a drinking fountain with the MacFetter family that we had gone camping with in previous years. Tom and young Tommy were Aryans of the first order, tall and blond. Mrs Mac must have felt proud of her handsome husband and son.

For over sixty years I kept that small, cracked, black and white picture, along with the other photographs from that holiday, in album number one of my family and friends photograph collection. The original number one album disintegrated some twenty years ago. I transferred the photographs into a new one. Over the years they have been taken out and copied for family events, made into slides, videos and DVDs.

A mammoth collection of early photographs have just been donated from my mother's family. The earliest one is Mam's grandma with Mam's eldest sister 'Nell' as a baby in about 1890. Once more I need to re-make album one.

When writing about this visit to Bath, I searched on the internet, through images, maps and the tour guides for parks or gardens with this specific drinking fountain. I had looked at the photo so often I would have recognised the fountain immediately. I asked my sister-in-law, who lived there until she married, whether she knew where it was. I also asked a friend who went to college there.

'I'll show you a photo,' I said.

The photos from 1950 were in a folder waiting to be filed in the new album. I rifled through them, and drew a blank. I looked on the shelf where the album had been, on the floor, through the collection taken out for a recent display. It was all in vain. All the actors on the stage have gone apart from me, and taken with them the memory of a fountain of Bath stone, one balmy summer's day in 1950.

We would willingly have woken at the crack of dawn to ride into town and wait at the doors to the baths until they opened. There was nothing to be gained from getting up early. We couldn't leave the hostel until we had completed our allotted task. If it meant sweeping the dormitory, washing the washbowls in the washroom, or helping to clean the kitchen we would be lucky to get away before 9am. Too excited to sleep, we washed, helped make breakfast and packed, then played outside until everyone else in the hostel was up and about. The warden checked that our work was done satisfactorily and stamped our cards. At last we could be on our way.

Going through the palatial entrance from the bright sunlight left us blinded momentarily. We were surprised to find ourselves outside again before our eyes had adjusted to the darkness. Below us water from the great bath glistened in the sunlight.

'Two thousand years,' I thought. 'Romans swimming down there.' I could feel it tingling through every nerve in my body. Pillars rose to the floor we were walking on. Above us, on plinths, stood statues of Romans in their togas.

'This great bath was only rediscovered recently,' Dad said.

I thought it must have been found because of the Blitz, when they were clearing away the bombed houses. That was eight years earlier, in 1942, so it would have seemed recent to Dad.

'It used to have a roof,' Dad said.

'Well the roof wouldn't have survived the bombing,' I thought. 'It is amazing that the statues are still in one piece, but we have made surprising discoveries in bombed houses. Delicate crockery sometimes survived without a crack.'

Leaving the balcony we wandered downstairs and along

191

alleyways and arcades where bits of stone frieze clung to walls leaving us to imagine how beautiful it must have been.

Somewhere we saw Roman coins. They had come from a fountain in a temple. I had seen some before in a small museum on Chester wall. They always fascinated me.

We saw small pools, hot rooms with underfloor heating and freezing cold pools, but I can't remember the order in which we saw them. We held our noses while we drank water that tasted like bad eggs. At last we arrived at the great pool, all of us except Harry, that is.

His attention had been captured by a mosaic, possibly the sea horses. He stood entranced before it, too excited to take out his sketchbook.

'Hells bells and damnation,' bellowed Dad in his ear. 'I have been looking everywhere for you.'

By the time they re-joined us beside the great bath, Dad had recovered his composure. Smiling happily he continued our guided tour.

Dianne and I were enjoying the day and had no idea about this incident.

Harry in a sulk at the great bath in the Roman Baths, Bath, Somerset, June 1950

Many years later, when looking at the photograph, he told us the story. 'I was in an ecstasy of delight. Bang! Out of nowhere this roar shattered my dreams. I was determined not to smile for him.'

Harry built up a mental dossier of resentment which lasted long after Dad had died.

Dad's shouting in the baths was from anxiety. Harry was a dreamer, always getting lost. The day-to-day drudgery of going to work fifty weeks in the year for a pittance and taking orders from others had worn Dad down. Harry wanted Dad to stand up for him when he came to see his headmaster at the secondary school but Dad regarded teachers with reverence. An opinion held by a teacher must take precedence over any thoughts he might hold. Dad started work at the age of fourteen. He was still having to find money for school uniforms, school books and school outings for Harry when he was in his mid-fifties. He wanted his own life and his own interests but he didn't have any time or money for himself.

Dad became a competent artist after he retired. The paintings were left to Harry but he refused to accept them.

Over forty years after Dad upset him in the Roman bath, Harry looked at Dad's paintings hanging on the walls of my sitting room.

'They're very good. He had a good eye for composition and colour.' Harry had been so angry that he had never been able to look at them before.

Shortly after this, in 1997, Freda's daughter Jan organised a family get-together at St Briavels Castle. Harry brought a bottle of champagne.

'This is for a toast to Dad,' he said. 'He tried his best, according to his culture, knowledge and ability. I doubt if I would have done half as well as he did.'

A month after the cycling holiday to Bath, Freda married Ernie in Southport on 22nd July 1950. I wanted to be a bridesmaid so badly that I convinced myself that it was guaranteed, almost. Each time I passed the photographer's

St Briavels Castle, Forest of Dean, 1997. L–R: Tom, Richard and Harry.

studio opposite St Michael's church I looked at the wedding photographs and imagined the kind of dress that would be chosen for me. The day drew near and I still hadn't been measured. Right up to the day before I didn't give up hope.

There was no church wedding and no big Smith family get-together. We weren't invited. I was very upset but I didn't talk to anyone about my disappointment. I didn't discuss it either with the family or my friends. The education authorities in the region had organised a major athletics event on The Wirral that day. I hadn't arranged to meet any of my friends there as I had expected to be at the wedding. This was half a century before mobile phones. We would call at the homes of our friends to make plans, or send a postcard if they lived too far away. I decided to go to the event to fill the day, so that I wouldn't be thinking about the wedding. It was a large arena with many different events taking place. None of the competitors were known to me. The crowd roared or cheered but I didn't see one familiar face amongst them all morning. I was alone and lonely. Dispirited, I left for home without seeing

Wedding of Freda and Ernie, Southport, 22nd June 1950

the afternoon competitions. I don't know where Harry and Dianne spent the day.

Three days later it was my thirteenth birthday. Maureen Mowatt and two of my school friends came to the party. Maureen had given me my first taste for Greek literature some years earlier. She was now at a grammar school. We belonged to different worlds.

Jill and Jack from the family next door were there for the birthday photo, so was the famous cake. Perhaps we ate it later. Jill was the one who chased Dianne with an axe. Jack was a pleasant boy. He played a leading role in the story of the day we were climbing the rock named Man's Face in Frodsham and I put my foot in a wasps' nest.

Later in the day their mother joined us in the back yard. I was wearing one of the dresses Aunt Mamie made for me.

Ever since going to live in Chesterton Street, we had kept hens. Throughout the year we hunted through the now obsolete air-raid shelter for their eggs and one or two of them we killed for Christmas dinner. Once or twice they managed to fly over the back yard wall and were brought back by neighbours. Dad bought half a dozen ducklings, but they all died. We had always had a cat and a dog. Now we had pet rabbits, including a beautiful chinchilla.

Two days after this photograph was taken the rabbits disappeared. On the following day the skin of the chinchilla rabbit was thrown over the back yard wall.

Dad had always suffered from insomnia. He was now

Beaty's 13th birthday, 25th July 1950. Martha and Alf's 25th wedding anniversary cake, Dianne, my best friend Maureen Mowatt, and two school friends, Doreen on my left and Thelma on my right. Harry and the axe girl, from next door, on Thelma's right.

working permanently on the night shift. The master bedroom overlooked the noisy street.

Dianne and I had bunk beds at the back of the house. The view from our window was the yards of our neighbours and the yards and houses of the next street. The man in the house behind us kept pigeons. I would often sit there watching the sky, following a soft cloud and listening to the sparrows and pigeons. There was an abundance of sparrows.

Dad took to sleeping in our bedroom. That caused problems for me. It was difficult to remember to take everything I needed for school out of the room before he went to bed. If I arrived in school without a particular book for a lesson, or my swimsuit when we were going to the swimming baths, I would get reprimanded. If I returned to the bedroom when he was in bed

I would be bawled out by him. I had no choice. I would creep in as quietly as I could, and he would bellow at me to get out. Unless I had found the item immediately I had to leave empty-handed. Then I had to face being chastised in school.

Mam had bought a stack of second-hand records at a jumble sale. Harry, Dianne and I were looking forward to an afternoon discovering a fresh collection of songs. With a cup of weak, milky tea beside us we changed the steel needle on the head of the gramophone and wound up the clockwork mechanism. The first record in the stack was Gracie Fields. This wasn't the kind of song Mam would have approved of. If she had been home it would have been off the turntable immediately and smashed so that it couldn't be played again. It was about a family of crooks.

An ear-splitting shout from upstairs alerted us that Dad was awake. There was a thump as he jumped out of bed. We raced out of the house as he started coming down the stairs.

'Turn father's face to the wall, mother,' sang Gracie.

We didn't dare to return to the house until Mam came home and called us to come in at tea time.

In my thirteenth year I flowered emotionally and intellectually. Perhaps it was because the man who had sexually abused me had gone out of my life. It could have been because of the form teacher for 3D or maybe that's when girls make the great leap forward.

Richard finally persuaded Dad to let him leave home when he was seventeen years old but he was very worried about him. It had been bad enough a year earlier thinking of him going to sea, but at least he would have come home. If he had been unhappy he wouldn't have been forced to go back. It was with a heavy heart that he signed his permission for Richard to go to Australia with the Big Brother Movement. If he wanted to return to Britain within two years he had to raise his own fare.

Uncle Tom fitted him out with everything he would need. Into a large, sturdy trunk he packed stacks of underpants, vests, stockings, handkerchiefs and shirts. Then there were smart tropical trousers and jackets, plus shoes and sandals. There was a toilet bag containing items he had never seen in his life before and had no idea of their use. There might have been an alarm clock, but that was probably in the inventory Uncle Tom gave to Harry when he left home. The trunk was in the bedroom above the living room, ready for Richard's departure.

Arriving home from school a few days later, I lit the fire in the living room as usual. It took some minutes to catch and I held a newspaper across the front of the grate to create a vacuum. As soon as the wood began to sizzle and crackle, I took away the paper before it caught fire. In no time the coals were glowing red and flames began to fly up the chimney. I put the fireguard around the grate and was about to start my next task when I heard urgent banging at the front door and Dad shouting from upstairs. The bedroom above the living room was ablaze. Somebody found a ladder to get Dad out of the window. The fire brigade arrived. All of the neighbours were out in the back entry watching, and Ada turned up from somewhere.

'Tell them somebody was smoking in bed,' she whispered to me.

'But nobody smokes,' I told her.

The only person in bed was Dad and he never smoked either in or out of bed. She seemed to think that telling this story would help us when we claimed the insurance. It made no sense to me. Perhaps there was a law against me lighting a fire at thirteen years old. Nobody ever blamed me for the fire. Years later I learned that the landlord was to blame because there was a fault in the chimney.

We had just been allowed back into the house when there was a knock at the door. It was the insurance man. He had just come for his money.

'You'll be paying us this week,' I said, suppressing a hysterical giggle.

Richard's trunk and all his splendid new clothes were ruined.

Family farewell party for Richard, June 1951. L–R, front: Great-uncle Harry, Richard, Grandma, Dianne; middle row: Martha, Dorothy, Freda, Beaty and Harry; back row: Evelyn with Meryl, Tom and Dad.

Elwyn, Richard and Evelyn with Meryl. Harry is peeping between Elwyn and Richard.

Richard and Mam outside
the Houses of Parliament,
June 1951

Uncle Tom fitted him out again but this time the clothes were
second hand.

All the family came home for a farewell party. We gathered
in the back yard for a photograph.

Richard was leaving from London. Mam and Dad went with
him to see him off.

They took an early train and arrived with plenty of time to
visit the Festival of Britain and make a tour of many of the
notable sights.

They were staying at the youth hostel in Earl's Court. Once
they arrived at the hostel the enormity of Richard's departure,
which they had managed to keep at bay while they were
occupied, shook them all. Dad was on edge. Richard was high
as a kite and couldn't stop talking, while wearing a groove in
the tiled floor from walking up and down. Mam was struggling
to hold back her tears.

'Will you shut up and sit down for God sake,' Dad yelled at
him. 'You're giving me a headache. And you're upsetting your
mother.'

'Don't bring me into it,' Mam said quietly, barely able to
speak. On top of everything else all the other hostellers had
stopped what they were doing to stare at them. She felt so
embarrassed she wanted to find somewhere to hide.

Richard shouted back at him, and in no time they were
having a fully-blown verbal feud. When it came to the use of

the English language either of them could have put Dr Johnson and Roget to shame.

Finally, Richard picked up his jacket and walked out of the kitchen and banged the front door behind him.

Fuming, he strode the streets of London, blind to all. After a couple of hours he had recovered some composure and made his way back to the hostel. The door was locked. It was after closing time. He rang the bell. Through the intercom he heard a voice telling him that he couldn't come in because it was too late. He pleaded in vain that he had nowhere to go. But rules were rules.

Mam and Dad knew nothing of his return. In their separate dormitories, one for men and another for women, they lay awake worrying about him out alone on the streets of London at night. Mam had to go to the toilets and make sure she closed the door before she allowed the tears to flow. She was afraid of disturbing the other occupants of the hostel. She was furious with Dad.

He, for his part, was overwhelmed with guilt. Why couldn't he, just this once, have controlled his temper? He was certain Richard would return. It didn't occur to him that the warden wouldn't let him in.

Meanwhile, Richard was walking the streets once more. He had enough money for a few cups of tea. He wandered from café to café, staying as long as possible in each one. For the most part the other customers looked homeless. It was the longest night of his life.

At 8am the door of the hostel was opened. All three of them were emotionally and physically wrecked. Dad decided to treat them all to a full English breakfast at one of the greasy cafés Richard had visited during the night. Mam only wanted egg on toast with her tea, so Dad and Richard shared the rest of her breakfast between them. Nothing was said about the row of the night before.

At the docks Mam and Dad stood on a viewing veranda with all the other relatives who were seeing off their loved ones.

There had been no hugs or kisses as they parted from him, any more than there had been that morning when they were reunited after he had walked the streets all night. We weren't a touchy, feely family. It took us many years to learn to hug each other. I started by hugging the children. When all of the siblings grew comfortable with greeting each other with a kiss, Dad was bemused. He called us a soppy lot.

One Saturday afternoon Dad and Mam took Dianne, Harry and me to the Plaza. This was a rare treat. The only other occasion I remember going there was to see *Pinocchio*. Unfortunately, that wasn't a happy occasion. I woke in terror for years afterwards. But this time we were going to see *The Red Shoes*.

In the foyer there was an exhibition about the Festival of Britain that was being held in London from May until September, telling the story of British achievements in art, industry and science. The photographs showed the Dome of Discovery and The Skylon.

We were cycling to the exhibition at the end of June. We soaked it all up, wanting to know everything about it. I wrote

Richard's photograph of Mam and Dad seeing him off to Australia, 1951

in my notebook that the dome was 365 feet in diameter, making it the biggest dome in the world. There was a plan of the eight exhibitions. They were: The land, about British exploration all over the world; The Earth, geology about the age of rocks and the use of minerals, and archaeology, the latter particularly interested us after our visit to Bath the year before; Polar Expeditions; The Sea, including Drake, Cooke and marine scientists: The Sky Exhibition, where a real weather forecasting station had been set up and experts showed how they predicted the weather; Outer Space, with astronomy from the old methods of Isaac Newton (all I knew of Newton was that an apple fell on his head) to the new methods of using radio; The Physical World, covering chemists showing what matter consists of and physicists saying how matter behaves (these were just words I copied down, they meant nothing to me, so what did it matter?) and, lastly, The Living World, which was about Darwin, the voyage of the *Beagle* and evolution.

Oh, The Skylon, I forgot to describe it. It was shaped like a cigar standing on end and rose 250 feet into the sky.

There is an apocryphal story that, on hearing that the Skylon had no visible means of support, King George said, 'It is an apt symbol for the British economy.'

The national debt, as defined by the Gross National Product, was 213.97% in 1948, so if he made this joke about the economy, the British people would probably agree with him. British debt had been in double figures or more since the end of the First World War, in 1918, but the Second World War had taken it over two hundred.

How did the government deal with this crisis? They launched the National Health Service, the Welfare State, and a massive housing project. These plans cost billions of pounds but gave work to doctors and nurses, builders, civil servants and other workers, from cleaners to administrators.

Dad was working as a window cleaner for a few years after the war. He was always very strict about paying his taxes.

'Our taxes are paying for the National Health Service,' he

told us. That was how the government planned to get us out of debt.

He instilled into us the need to pay our fare on the tram or bus. 'If we don't pay, Liverpool Corporation will think nobody is using the bus and they will stop running it on that route.'

The government also put on the Festival of Britain, to bring fun, fantasy, colour and pride into the lives of people after the devastation of their homes during the war, and the austerity which followed it.

The *Daily Express* kept attacking the Festival, saying it was a waste of money, but nobody took any notice. We were all enjoying the films and exhibitions being put on. Those who could raise the money made the trip to London. Eight and a half million people went for the day of their lives. They all remembered the atmosphere, while one or two events remained in their memories to be told and retold sixty years later.

The first film was about King George opening of the Festival. Flag-waving crowds six deep lined the route from Buckingham Palace to St Paul's cathedral to watch the royal family go by. At Temple Bar, in the City of London, the procession stopped and the king was offered the Pearl Sword of the City by the lord mayor. The lord mayor had authority over everyone, but it was a tradition to hand supremacy over to the king by giving him the sword. The royal family continued on their way to St Paul's cathedral for a special service for the Festival. The film showed them going up the steps. I was sad to see the king looking so tired and thin. The queen was plump and motherly. Philip, duke of Edinburgh, was as handsome as ever and the princesses were pretty in their summer dresses.

After the service King George stood on the steps of the cathedral and declared the Festival open.

We had heard the speech on the wireless on 3rd May. He said that he hoped future technology would be for peace. He must have said more, but that was what caught my imagination.

In the afternoon the royal family went to the South Bank and attended another service, this time at the Royal Festival Hall, which was conducted by the archbishop of Canterbury. They stopped to chat with the prime minister, Mr Clement Atlee, and Mr Winston Churchill, who had been prime minister during the war. Queen Mary, the mother of King George, went with them on a tour of the exhibits. She started the tour walking, but it was too much for her, so she was pushed around in a wheelchair.

After the *Pathé News* came the main feature film, *The Red Shoes*. If Dad thought he was bringing us to see the moral tale by Hans Christian Anderson he hadn't read the reviews.

The original, terrifying story was of a selfish little girl who cared more about her ballet shoes and dancing than her vows to God or her responsibility to her guardian. A sorcerer put a spell on her shoes. She couldn't take them off and couldn't stop dancing. Eventually somebody chopped her feet off with an axe and made her a pair of wooden feet.

Dad, in spite of his quick-tempered outbursts, was a gentle-natured person. *Pinocchio* growing donkey ears and a long nose, or the story of a little girl having her feet cut off, seem odd choices for him to have made as special cinema treats.

The film was a story of love and passion. The Hans Christian Anderson morality tale was a story within that erotic story.

From the first moment that the music and colour burst upon us, we were captivated as the ballet dancers moved gracefully across the stage.

Moira Shearer was playing the part of Vicky Page who suddenly and unexpectedly became the prima ballerina in a ballet based on the morality tale. She was totally under the sway of the director of the ballet company. It was as if she was hypnotised by him. The ballet of the red shoes was so successful that the company travelled all over the world.

In this heightened emotional state, she was bound to fall in love. The man she loved was the conductor of the orchestra.

She couldn't continue to perform once she married. This wasn't stated in the film, as far as I remember, but it was taken for granted in the 1940s that female teachers and nurses had to resign. Their place was at home, caring for their husbands and, when they arrived, the children. This situation must have been changing because there was a married teacher in my school.

The director of the ballet company was furious when he was told that they were courting. Her lover told the director he was jealous. That was true, the director told him. He wasn't in love with her. He was vigilant in guarding his art. Only the perfect prima ballerina could perform to the standard he aspired to. Nobody had ever danced like Vicky Page. He wouldn't let her go.

She had to choose between dance and the man she loved.

We were held in thrall by the exciting jumps and turns, by those moments when the dancers held sparkling, unexpected poses while the music soared and Moira Shearer pirouetted before us at an impossible speed.

When the national anthem played we stood automatically, but we were hardly aware that it was playing. We were still enveloped in the swirling colour of the ballet.

At the end of June, Mam and Dad took Harry and me to London to see the Festival. Dianne didn't come with us because Evelyn and Elwyn took her and Meryl. They went by train and stayed at a hotel. Harry and I imagined this would be really posh, and a memorable experience.

One part of it was certainly unforgettable. Many years later Dianne told me that they had a room in the hotel. There were comfortable sitting rooms and a restaurant, but she knew no-one apart from Evelyn and Elwyn. The couple went out for the evening leaving her to take care of 18-month-old Meryl. She had neither books nor a radio. There were no *en suite* rooms at that time. She was afraid to leave the room to go to the toilet. She couldn't leave the door jammed open in case something happened to the baby. If she closed it she couldn't get back in. More than anything, she was concerned because she didn't know how to get help if there was an emergency.

Perhaps Meryl was asleep and they just popped out for a takeaway of fish and chips, but in Dianne's memory she was

Evelyn, Elwyn, Dianne and Meryl, Trafalgar Square, 1951

totally deserted by them for the whole evening.

It had made such an indelible mark on her that she told me the story over fifty years later when I began to write this memoir. I was asking her about places we had visited. She had to keep reminding me that she wasn't with us in London.

'I would have given anything to have been with you two and Mam and Dad,' she told me.

Harry took Dianne's place on the back of the bike for three, while I had an old bike Dad had put together from bits he found on Garston shore.

We took more or less the same route that I will describe in chapter four so I won't be a bore and go through it all twice.

The only reason I remember being on a single bike was that while riding along, miles behind Mam and Dad, the bike frame suddenly disintegrated beneath me. It was fortunate that I was riding through flat countryside at my usual slow pace. Had I been freewheeling down a hill I would have suffered a serious accident. Fortunately, the wheels were not affected so I was able to walk pushing it. Eventually, Dad came back to look for me, leaving Mam and Harry at the hostel. He started his usual ballyhoo until he saw that the frame was broken in two.

Immediately he was contrite and asked whether I had been hurt. I told him I had come to no harm. He was at pains to assure me that the damage was not my fault. He thumbed a lift on a lorry. The driver helped him to lift both the bikes on the back and took us to a garage near the hostel. By the next morning the mechanic had done a temporary repair to make it roadworthy until the end of our holiday.

Nothing we had read about the Festival or seen on newsreels and exhibitions could have prepared us for the actual event. Each display in the Dome was a magical feast. In the first section, 'The Land', a giant relief map of the birth of Britain appeared from nowhere. After a few minutes showing the geology of the land, it disappeared. We would have liked more time to take it in and write down some of the information. We thought the film was over and went to look at another display when it came on again. We couldn't see the projector, then discovered it was disguised as a pillar of rock.

The first area had just touched upon geology while giving us a taste of the exhibitions. There was a whole portion called 'The Earth', devoted to mining and minerals. It showed how miners and mining companies all over the world were benefiting from these scientific discoveries.

In the part about 'The Sea', Captain Cook was standing beside his sailing ship HMB *Endeavour*. He was a very good mapmaker and discovered, amongst other places, Australia and the Hawaiian Islands.

In Hawaii he was feted as a god. When he returned they killed him and ate his heart. They realised he was a fake as there was no Second Coming in their religion.

We walked around a full-sized model of a white horse being ridden by a white knight, either Peter or Edmund from *The Lion, The Witch and The Wardrobe*, the story by C.S. Lewis. We leapt away in fright when the rider lifted his head.

'Dad, Mam, come and see this knight.'

They left whatever they had been looking at. The knight was still now. We didn't warn them of what would happen. Suddenly the knight moved. They nearly jumped out of their skins, while we laughed.

We would have stayed in the Dome all day, but at 1pm Dad and Mam came looking for us. We ate our sandwiches and went into one of the cafés for a cup of tea. Dad said it would cost an arm and a leg. We were thankful that he didn't suggest cycling to Greasy Joe's in Earl's Court.

There were leaflets and billboards everywhere advertising the other events. On our table we picked up one about the Telekinema, a cinema built specially for the Festival.

Over twenty films and documentaries were made especially for the Festival and selected by the British Film Industry (BFI). Most of the exhibits in the Dome were enlivened by a short documentary. Without film it would have been impossible to explain many of the complex ideas. Reading information or looking at photographs on display boards would have bored us quite quickly. Models, even moving ones, couldn't have shown us the fire in the centre of the earth, volcanoes, or how radio waves travelled.

Harry's eyes shone when he saw *The Red Shoes* listed as one of the films recommended by the BFI. A little more than decade later, in the Swinging Sixties, Harry and his wife lived in Finsbury and I lived in Bloomsbury. We went to the Royal Opera House, Covent Garden, to see the ballet once or twice a month. No ballerina ever compared with Moira Shearer. He carried *The Red Shoes* in his heart for the rest of his life.

There was a television studio in the foyer of the cinema, where stars were being interviewed. If we went in to see the films we would watch the interviews live and then see them on film. Very few people had television sets. There was also a 3D-film *A Solid Explanation*, where objects flew out from the screen.

Dad had already paid for us to come in to the Festival and he had bought a cup of tea. It was an extra two shillings each to go into the cinema! After a brief discussion, Dad and Mam decided to pay for the two of us to go in without them, if that was allowed.

A giraffe's head came right towards us. We ducked, then

looked sideways at our neighbours, feeling foolish, but they had all done the same.

It was late afternoon when we left the festival and made our way to Trafalgar Square. Before spending any time there we went to the post office to get stamps for our postcards. Dad probably had to draw out some of his savings. It was a massive building with on a corner with doors on two or three sides. People milled about all around us. There were twelve or more counters and we had to queue for ten minutes. When we were ready to leave there was no sign of Harry. Dad pushed and shoved his way through the crowd, annoying everyone. He found the head postmaster and one of the staff brought a chair for Dad to stand on. The postmaster phoned the police station. The police told Dad to go to where the bikes had been left to see whether Harry had gone there. If he wasn't there Dad was to go to the police station. Dad didn't wait to tell us what he was doing. He hared off leaving Mam and me trotting along behind. It was fortunate he didn't lose us as well. After a fruitless search in the area near the bikes we rode to the nearest police station. Mam was afraid to speak to him, he was so agitated, but she plucked up the courage to tell him that I had to know where they were going. She didn't want to lose me.

He wrote down directions. I think it was to Bow Street Police Station. It was rush-hour. The traffic was moving so slowly that I had no trouble winding my way through it to keep up with them. Whenever I needed to turn on my right I got off and crossed with the pedestrians.

After an hour or two at the police station, with no results to our enquiries, Dad gave the police the phone number of the hostel.

While we were preparing supper Dad looked crushed and tears glinted in Mam's eyes. Now and again the silence was broken by Dad repeating, 'but where could he have gone?' or 'I should have kept an eye on him,' or 'why does he always wander off?'

Nobody blamed me, but watching him should have been

more important to me than writing postcards for my friends. I knew he was a dreamer. My throat and stomach ached seeing Mam and Dad so unhappy. And it spoiled our holiday. However, I told myself he'll be alright. I was confident that nothing serious had happened to him.

Nothing ever put Dad off his food, but Mum had no appetite.

I passed the evening writing my notes about the festival. Scott and the Antarctic appeared to be a good subject for a poem.

Meanwhile, Mam and Dad were on tenterhooks. They couldn't concentrate on anything but listening to the phone ringing in the office of the warden and waiting for him to come to say Harry had been found.

While I slept soundly Mam lay awake. This was the second time in a month she had been in a bunk-bed in a dormitory full of strangers while one of her sons was missing in London. Occasionally she dozed off, disturbing everyone except me with her banshee wailing.

While saying my prayers before going to bed, the thought flitted through my mind that 'to lose one son may be regarded as a misfortune. To lose two looks like carelessness.' I suppressed a giggle, and gave myself a mental slap on the wrist.

A few years later Tom introduced me to a tale that showed the cunning of the devil in introducing wayward thoughts into the pure Christian mind. It was *The Screwtape Letters* by C.S. Lewis. The book was funny but it had an important objective. The theme was a senior devil giving instruction to his nephew on how to tempt humans into an immoral way of life. The family took the message very seriously.

While Mam and Dad had spent an anxious night worrying about him, Harry had occupied himself reading back copies of a comic he had never seen before, called *The Eagle*, and drinking hot chocolate. After sleeping in a cell in a police station he feasted on a full English breakfast.

Dad took a bus to the other side of London to pick him up.

Form filling and the journey took two or three hours. We were so late setting off that, even on a summer's evening, it was dark by the time we reached the village of Potters Bar which was barely on the outskirts of London. The doors of the hostel we were making for were well closed.

To Mam's embarrassment Dad knocked on the door of the village post office until somebody was roused and came to the window. Dad was very polite, and ever so humble, as he explained our plight. The postmistress gave us the name and house number of a widow who lived alone and might be able to put us up.

The widow answered the door in her nightclothes and Dad paraded Harry and me in front of her to plead for her help. Very unwillingly she allowed us in. I had to share her double bed with her. I was so afraid of touching her or disturbing her in any way that I lay awake all night, desperate for the morning to come.

In spite of a sleepless night the thought of a day in Stratford-upon-Avon gave me pedal power. Dad hadn't told me how far it was. If he had I would have lost heart. In two hours I had covered sixteen miles, only another fifty to go. After I rode through Hemel Hempstead I saw the family waiting for me. Dad thumbed a lift and a lorry took us all the way to Banbury.

The medieval town of Stratford put Ludlow into the shade. There was so much to see I couldn't resist bobbing my head from left to right, like a spectator at a ping pong match. The pavements were as crowded as they had been in London. Fortunately, there weren't any lorries thundering past me, but there were round-roofed Bedford charabancs in cream and red, and serious black Ford cars. I should have been keeping my eyes on the traffic. The three-seater was forging ahead. I knew Dad would have planned the visit to the last detail but when we left the thatched cottages behind I began to wonder if he had heard about a cheap mug of tea in the next town.

Anne Hathaway's cottage was first on Dad's schedule. We were familiar with the tied cottages in Hale. This was not a

Beaty, Mam and Harry at Anne Hathaway's cottage, 1951

cottage. It was the farmhouse that had been owned by Anne's father, Richard.

William Shakespeare had wooed her here. In the hall, where the family entertained guests, there was a wooden bench near the fireplace where they were said to have flirted. But, the evidence points to them having courted somewhere else and not on this bench. The seat was from a later period and she was pregnant when they married. I knew none of this during our visit and swallowed all the stories with relish.

We returned to the town and followed the tourist trail to all the places of historic interest. We started at Shakespeare's birthplace, then went in a circle, past the knot garden created on the land where he lived with his wife and children when he was home from London, visited Henry IV Grammar School and the Guild chapel, saw the house where his daughter Susanna lived with her husband Dr Hall and Shakespeare's grandchildren, and on to the Holy Trinity church, where he was baptised and buried.

The brick Shakespeare Memorial Theatre offended my senses after the mellow beauty of the thatched cottages and the warm stone of the churches. The river meandered and sparkled between smooth, green lawns and passed beneath the fourteen arches of the ancient Clopton Bridge. The river and bridge could not be appreciated because of this monstrosity.

The popular French writer Guy de Maupassant (1850–93) reportedly ate lunch in the Eiffel Tower restaurant every day for last few years of his life – not because he loved the great

213

iron monument but because, so the story goes, it was the only place in Paris where he could sit and *not* see the tower itself.

I hadn't heard of him at the time but his sentiments about the Eiffel Tower summed up my opinion about the theatre exactly.

It is unfortunate that this art deco building was not to my taste, because it was the first important work erected in Britain from designs by a woman architect. Her name was Elizabeth Scott.

I didn't object to art deco in its place. I think the Plaza Cinema was in that style. The theatre was out of character beside the river.

'See that old pub across the road from the theatre?' Dad said. 'Everyone has called it The Dirty Duck for hundreds of years,' he laughed 'Its real name is The Black Swan.'

As we continued along the river I told Dad and Mam about Hugh Clopton. The bridge was named after him because he paid to have it built. He was lord mayor of London from 1491 to 1492 and had the bridge built when he came back to Stratford.

Mr Clopton came into the story of Shakespeare quite a bit. Besides the bridge, he contributed towards the Guild chapel and the alms houses and grammar school built beside it. This was the school that Shakespeare attended.

One of the buildings we visited had a low whitewashed ceiling. In my memory it was the grammar school. Some of the adult tourists showed scant respect for this invaluable example of British heritage, as they wrote, 'I was here.' Their names were followed by the date of the visit. In our priggish judgemental way, Harry and I thought this was a shocking way to behave.

In 1597, Shakespeare bought the house Hugh Clopton had built a hundred years earlier. New Place, Shakespeare's family home, was built of brick, which was very unusual. It was the second largest house in Stratford. Shakespeare retired to Stratford in 1610 and remained there until he died in 1616.

A hundred and fifty years later, the house was demolished by its owner, Reverend Francis Gastrell, because he hated the constant stream of tourists coming to pay homage to the playwright.

John Hall, the son-in-law of Shakespeare, was famous in his own right as a doctor of medicine. He grew medicinal herbs, and discovered a cure for scurvy a hundred years before British naval physicians realised that citrus fruit would cure the disease.

Shakespeare made financial contributions toward the upkeep of the chancel in Holy Trinity church. He was also supposed to make sure that repairs were done. It was because he had made donations to the church that he had gained the right to be buried in the chancel, not in recognition of his fame as a poet and playwright.

I almost forgot to say, while I was scribbling facts and dates into my exercise book, Harry was drawing. We were very impressed with wood carvings in the church, particularly the special carvings under the seats in the choir stalls.

We always wanted to know the origin of place-names. Dad told us Stratford-upon-Avon was made from Celtic and Saxon words. 'Avon' is Celtic for river. 'Straet' is the Roman road, while 'ford' is a Saxon word for a place where the river is shallow and can be crossed on foot by people or animals, or from the Celtic, Ffordd, meaning way.

The following day we continued our journey north. In three days we were home.

Harry told me of his adventure in London with the police. Dianne said nothing about her interesting experience with Meryl until sixty years later.

Adrenaline rushing, I returned to school to take the end-of-year exams. Having done no revision and my head full of the Festival of Britain, Stratford-upon-Avon and the biography of Shakespeare I hit the ground running. I flunked arithmetic as usual but came top of the class in every other subject.

I was as high as a kite and kept asking the teachers in each subject where I was placed in the class, so that all the other girls would hear that I was top. The teachers became really irritated after a few days.

In the fourth year I left all my school friends behind when I moved up to the C stream. It was the first time in my ten years of schooling that I wasn't in the bottom stream.

Mam and Dad celebrated the birth of their first grandson in October 1951. The age-old tradition of naming male children after their father or grandfather was going out. Freda named him Alan.

There were four males in Alan's generation. None of them were called Price Tom after my paternal ancestors and none were called Richard after my maternal ancestors. Michael Joseph Hewitt was Dorothy's son. He is a traditionalist. He called his sons David, after his uncle, and Joe after his father. Peter Smith, Tom's son, was the only one of my three brothers to carry on the name Smith. He is Peter, not Price Tom Smith. Richard had a daughter, while Harry had no children. Andrew Gareth Peter Roberts called his son Evan in memory of Eve, his mother Evelyn. His second son is Gareth Lloyd. Gareth is possibly the name of a paternal uncle. Peter and his wife, Emelia, have returned to tradition, naming their son Thomas after his paternal grandfather and Emanuel after his maternal grandfather.

Descendents of great-granddad Price Tom Smith and his wife Martha, great-uncle Harry's children, are in Speke, Liverpool. The Richard McCarten family are also in the Liverpool area.

In the autumn of 1951 Dorothy married Joe Hewitt from Farndon, near Chester. Nobody is sure where or how they met. According to one family story she was nursing in Manchester when they married. Perhaps she continued to work in Manchester and that was why Michael was born there a year later. Joe was a coal man in the Farndon area at the time, as far as anybody knows. Another family story is that she was in the Land Army on a farm near Farndon before she started nursing in Ormskirk and met Joe then. She is said to have befriended

Wedding of Dorothy to Joe Hewitt, 1951. L–R: Joe's mum, unknown, Joe's brother Dave, Freda, Joe, Alf's head between Freda and Doe, Dorothy. End on right, from back to front: Tom, Harry, Dianne.

the wife of the farmer, and returned to the farm for a working holiday, possibly fruit picking.

Mam told Dorothy that she was too old at twenty-six to have a white wedding. Dorothy followed her plump maternal grandmother in stature. On her wedding day she looked elegant in her royal blue suit, with a knee-length jacket. I had never seen her looking so striking.

At the start of the spring term in 1952, I moved to the B stream. When the Christmas holidays arrived, half of the pupils had reached their fifteenth birthday and left. Perhaps the top year was reduced to three classes, but maybe, just possibly, I moved into the B stream because the school was beginning to recognise me as the child genius I had always known myself to be.

On the afternoon of 6th February 1952, one of the monitors interrupted the lesson to have a whispered conversation with the teacher. On the rare occasions when anything like this happened, the class would regard the interruption as an extra break. Something of the sadness in the face of the teacher caused us to stop talking.

217

'We are all to go to the hall,' she said, in hushed tones. 'Please form your usual line as quietly as you can.'

I had stomach cramps as I tried to guess what had happened. 'Had I done something to bring disgrace on the school?' I asked myself.

When all of the pupils were in the hall and the teachers, standing with bowed heads, were on the stage, the headmistress informed us, in a solemn voice, that King George had died. She said a prayer for the queen and the princesses. As we were saying The Lord's Prayer the girls around me began sobbing. The teachers were red-eyed and struggling to hold back the tears.

I liked the king a great deal but I didn't know much about dying. No matter how hard I tried I couldn't summon up any tears. To show that I cared I made a vow of silence. This worked very well until the teacher asked me to help her tidy the classroom at the end of the day. She tried to engage me in conversation. I just nodded or shook my head. This puzzled her as I was always a chatterbox. My friend Jean volunteered that it was probably because of the king dying. I nodded and she left me to complete my task.

For weeks afterwards I scoured the newspapers and cut out all the royal photographs for my scrapbook. The day after the king died there were pictures of Princess Elizabeth, dressed in black, coming down the steps of the aeroplane that had brought her from Africa, and trying to hide her face as she sat crying in the car. A few days earlier *Pathé News* had shown the princess and the duke at the Treetops Hotel in Aberdare National Park, Kenya, where they were watching the wildlife. The newspapers had pull-out sections about the life of the king, queen and princesses. Three hundred thousand people went to London and Windsor to watch the state funeral on 15th February 1952. *Pathé News* brought the whole procession to us. The coffin was carried on a gun carriage that was pulled by naval ratings. As I watched the ceremony, I pulled at my heart and my tears came at last.

To prepare the pupils for a life of work, we were taken to the bobbin works. It had been the main employer in Garston for over fifty years. Pupils from the senior schools had always been taken there and the girls from the secondary modern schools were their successors.

The factory wasn't the bustling energetic place we had been told about. I am surprised that the manager didn't cancel our visit but perhaps he, like his workers, was treading water and hoping that the situation would change. Morale was low and there was none of the banter we expected. Demand for cotton and, therefore, for bobbins had reached its post-war peak two years earlier. Suddenly the industry went into decline in 1952. There were a couple of false rises in business during the decade but the British cotton industry was in its death throws.

I loved school and happily would have stayed there forever. Ten places were offered at Mabel Flecher Technical College. The pupils were given the opportunity to vote for the fourth-year pupil they thought should be given a place. I have no recollection of voting. This was a most unusual and exceptionally democratic way to allocate the places. The first I knew about the vote was when the headmistress informed the assembly. The blackboard was revealed with the ten names written on it. My name was there white on black. I couldn't believe my good fortune. It might have been at the bottom of the list, I can't remember, but it was there. If it had been today I would have hugged and kissed everyone, but we didn't do touchy-feely things in 1952. I was going to stay at school. What I would be learning was of no consequence. At the college they learned to make hats and learned about nursing but I wasn't sure what other subjects were offered. Of the first two, I would have chosen nursing.

I cycled home with the wind at my back. I almost took flight.

'Mam, Mam. I've won a place at Mabel Fletcher,' I told her joyfully. 'I'm staying at school.'

'You're going to be fifteen next month,' she told me flatly. 'Your school days end when the school holidays start.'

Choking back the tears I said, 'but Mam, I've got a place at the Tech.'

'You're going to work,' she told me, and walked off.

Totally crushed, I didn't raise the matter again.

Next day I informed the school and my place was given to the next person on the list.

I worked in the stores in Woolworth's for twelve months. They were tolerant to keep me so long. I didn't contribute very much to the workforce. After that I went from a crummy job to crummier job for four years but I was never out of work for more than a few weeks at a time. That period was better than any education I would have received at college. It taught me to respect factory workers, men and women who spend hours sitting at a bench or beside a conveyor belt efficiently performing boring tasks. I was never any good at repetitive work. The foremen or women who were given the thankless task of telling us we were surplus to requirements tried to be kind. I particularly remember the forewoman at a fruit and nut factory who gave us notice when we finished the Christmas orders.

'You are not being sacked,' she said. 'You are redundant.'

As I walked through soulless industrial estates from one factory to the next in the bitter cold of winter, the name you gave to being out of work didn't seem to make much difference. Sometimes I would reach the door of a factory office and walk away, unable to take another rejection.

I read in the *Liverpool Post* or *Liverpool Echo* that the government admitted to Bessie Braddock, a Liverpool MP, that 4.4 per cent of the Liverpool population was unemployed in 1952, including school leavers who hadn't found work that year. Unemployment in Liverpool had increased by eight thousand, five hundred. Four years later thousands of 15 to 25 year olds had never worked.

Like St Paul, I had a revelation when I read those statistics.

I had thought there was something wrong with me because I couldn't keep a job. Most of the time I had been in work. Many of my contemporaries had never found work. They were not to blame. The system of running the country was to blame. On coming to this conclusion I began trying to re-invent the wheel.

Tom was a committed trade unionist and the Methodist church had discussion groups. Step by step I discovered that the wheel had already been invented I just had to find the blueprint.

One eye-opener came from Tom, when I complained about an interview I had at the employment exchange, which is now euphemistically named the Job Centre.

'Next time one of these clerks tries to put you down, remind him that he gets his wages from the taxes you have paid and will pay in the future. He has never produced anything in his life. You are paying him to help you to find suitable employment.'

According to the book, *1066 and all that*, history came to a full stop when Britain was no longer a top country.

Perhaps once I reached fifteen, and my schooldays ended, my childhood came to a full stop but I have decided to continue through my fifteenth year, to June 1953.

4

Biking to the Coronation, 1953

The Queen of Tonga
Crossed the ocean from faraway
The Queen of Tonga
Came to Britain for Coronation Day.

A big, fat, jolly woman in a summer dress and her hair worn in plats across her head, the Queen of Tonga was riding in an open carriage despite the rain, looking like a cross between Buddha and a sumo wrestler. We all jumped in the air waving and cheering as she went by. It was 2nd June 1953. The crowd of three million had waited all night on the London pavements in the constant drizzle to watch the Coronation procession pass by next day. Dad, Harry, Dianne and I had camped on the Green Park side of Piccadilly, handy for the temporary toilets.

But I'm rushing ahead. In June 1953 I was almost sixteen. I had been working in the storeroom in Woolworth's department store in Liverpool city centre for almost a year. Dad and I had taken our two weeks annual holidays to go to the coronation. Harry and Dianne were given leave from school to take holidays with Dad.

Harry was at a secondary modern school for boys. At eleven years old he found most of the teachers lacking in sensitivity. They were recently demobilised from the armed forces. He had served almost two years of his four-year sentence and was about to have a reprieve. There was one gentle teacher who recognised Harry's talent and encouraged him to take the Thirteen Plus examination to the small, friendly Liverpool School of Art.

Dianne was in her last year at primary school. She had just taken the Eleven Plus examination for grammar school.

The results would be waiting for both of them when they returned from holiday. They dismissed it from their thoughts, unaware that passing these examinations would divert them onto paths untrodden by Mam and Dad or their older siblings. Carefree and excited, we set off on our annual adventure.

We were cycling to London in seven days, sleeping in YHA hostels, staying in Highgate YHA in London for four nights plus one night on the pavement in Piccadilly and returning to Liverpool in three days.

Mam always found setting off for the holiday embarrassing. All of the neighbours would stand on their doorsteps or gather round to watch as the bikes were brought out, followed by the panniers holding our luggage. We were in our usual threadbare clothes. The panniers were in no better state. Tins of food would go rolling down the street as frayed bags burst open and had to be pinned or roped back together. A tyre would be flat and everything would be unloaded while Dad repaired the puncture. At last, we were ready and waved goodbye to the neighbours. A pedal fell off.

Mam didn't come on this holiday. Dad's mother was living with us. Mam had to stay home to take care of her, but that's a story for another time.

The first fifteen-mile cycle ride from Garston in any direction was boring, ugly and smelly. We were heading for Shrewsbury, sixty-five miles away, for our first night, and had to go through the dark satanic mills of either Widnes or Elsmere Port before we hit the open road.

From ten years old until he married, Dad lived with his Uncle Harry, his mother's twin. My great-uncle Harry's claim to fame was that he had been to the Shrewsbury show. He was a dandy in 1923 when Mam was taken home to Garston to meet the family. She particularly remembered his calfskin boots. We had heard the story of him going to the Shrewsbury show all our lives and thought that he had made this journey every year. In 1980 I learned that he had gone once. It was an unforgettable experience at the beginning of the twentieth century.

We were wearing the lightest of our patched shorts and tops. The sun broke through the cloud of dirt and smoke that hung almost permanently over houses, factories and gasworks. Looking toward the docks we could see clear blue sky over the river Mersey. Once we were away from Liverpool we knew it would be a beautiful, scorching hot day. The sun always shone for us when we went on our annual holiday.

Dad, Harry and Dianne were riding a bike for three. Dad had put together another bike for me, out of bits and pieces. I hoped it would survive the journey,

As I rode along Window Lane, the main shopping street, the bus to Woolton passed me, followed by a lorry and a horse drawn delivery van. The smell of baker's yeast mixed with the fresh meat from the butcher's. The pavements were crowded with women wearing flowered smocks over their blouses and skirts, hair curlers peeping out from headscarves or turbans. Some wore strong hairnets to keep waves and curls in place. My mouth watered as a boy came out of the baker's eating a hot barm cake. There was a bombed site of hard, red soil on the corner opposite the bakers that had become a short cut and a play area for the children. Eight years after the end of the Second World War, nothing remained of that block of buildings except the pub, with the remains of the interior decoration of a shop and house. Across the road a queue had formed in the Co-op. I passed sweet shops, the dairy, the post office and two more butchers. Looking along the side streets of a hundred houses, one or two cars might be seen. Coming out of the shopping street I turned away from the two gas tanks, the parish church of St Michael's and, six miles away, the city of Liverpool. Inhaling deeply as I pushed on the pedals, the taste of gas, soot, smelting iron, horse manure and petrol filled mouth, nose and lungs. Leaving behind the Methodist chapel, the redbrick county primary school, the Roman Catholic church and the claustrophobic terraced houses, I headed for Widnes, Runcorn, and the open road.

The river sparkled in the distance beyond the airport, with the gentle slopes of the Wirral peninsula beckoning me in the sunlight. Speke Hall was hidden in the trees near the spire of All Saints parish church. A broad, overgrown meadow stretched between me and the new housing estate, leaving the impression, even there, of space and purer air.

Now a patchwork of farmland surrounded me, blue-green wheat cheek to jowl with brown potato fields to one side and olive-green meadow on the other. The blazing sun drew the scent from the grass and early summer flowers in the hedgerow. Birds chattered in bush and tree. There was a great cloud of butterflies. Most of them were Cabbage Whites or Speckled Woods or other boring brown jobs but occasionally half a dozen Red Admirals would burst from a bush or Common Blues darted across my path. I became aware of the low buzz of insects. A grey squirrel darted out and ran along the centre of the road, afraid of a predator watching from the hedge, then escaped up a tree.

Too soon, fresh countryside scents were replaced by the stench of Widnes where sulphurous pools and ugly twisted pipes and chimneys supplanted trees and gentle streams. Gagging, eyes streaming and afraid to take a breath, I struggled for a mile through this infernal industrial landscape.

On reaching the town the smell began to disperse and became more tolerable the closer I came to the river.

The towers of the Transporter Bridge dominated the skyline. The family was waiting in the queue, hemmed in by cars and lorries. Every year at the start of our summer holiday we saw this amazing feat of engineering. We first saw it from the window of the train as we travelled to Frodsham for a camping holiday. For the past four years, we had admired it from the road as we waited to board.

Runcorn to Widnes
Transporter Bridge

From the gondola we marvelled at the latticework of steel girders and twelve-inch-thick steel ropes. Suspended by cables from an oblong steel table, we were carried slowly over the Mersey twelve feet below. We looked back along the sandbanks and shore as far as Hale.

When Tom and Richard were twelve and ten years old, they attempted to run across from Hale to the Wirral at low tide. They would have made it but the tide changed. As they ran back the sandbanks became submerged and sucked at their feet. Richard couldn't swim. Tom hoisted him on his back and swam the last fifty yards.

'This is great,' Richard said at the time, holding his arms tightly around Tom's neck and nearly throttling him.

The gondola cleared the wall of the Manchester Ship Canal by only four and a half feet. We arrived in Runcorn after a journey of less than three minutes.

As we headed for Chester I soon dropped behind. The tiny, white blossoms on the rowan trees lining the verges on each side of the road caught my attention. Late last summer, soon after I started work in Woolworth's, I had escaped here one Sunday and seen berries hung down, crimson, against the green foliage. Beyond the blossoming trees I looked across the flat expanse to the river on my right, while I pedalled towards the rock known as the Man's Face protruding from Helsby Hill.

I was tempted to stop for a cold drink as I cycled through the pretty village of Frodsham. We had spent long summer holidays there over many years. I pressed on, as I had barely gone a quarter of the way to Shrewsbury.

I looked up as I passed the Man's Face and remembered a couple of years earlier when I had been climbing with a gang of friends from our street in Garston. The eldest son of the family next door, was below me as I climbed. Taking my foot from a foothold, the air was filled with angry wasps. I had trampled a wasps' nest and they went straight for my companion. He hung on as they stung him all over his face and hands. We all climbed as fast as we could so that he could escape. I felt terribly guilty. Surprisingly he didn't suffer any serious effects from his ordeal. This was his first visit to the countryside and probably his last.

It was almost an hour later that I rode into Chester. We had often been there, walking the walls, visiting the tower that held a collection of the first Roman coins we had seen, and the King Charles Tower, where the king had watched his army defeated at the battle of Rowton Moor.

Dad waited impatiently for me on the cathedral green. They had finished their sandwiches by the time I caught up and he was itching to go for a cup of tea. Dianne lay on the grass, happily dreaming. Harry was sketching the cathedral. The tip of his tongue poked out between his lips and moved from one side of his mouth to the other as his pencil traced across the page.

If Mam had been with us the treat after eating sandwiches would have been to go to a café with tablecloths, delicate crockery with matching tea pot and milk jug. But maybe not. We were sweaty, dirty and scruffy.

As we continued our journey Harry looked back to me. He pointed to a café in a row of Elizabethan shops. It looked so inviting, with mouth-watering cakes displayed in the window. A few years earlier both of us had cycled to Chester on a tandem and treated ourselves to afternoon tea there. A smart waitress in black dress and white lace pinafore and cap had come to take our order. We were treated with smiling courtesy and kindness. At the time I accepted it as our due. We must have looked and smelled like a pair of ragamuffins but we were very well mannered and always had a high opinion of ourselves.

Mam always repeated the mantra whenever someone tried to put us down, 'You are as good as anyone.'

The sun had been beating down on us since we left home. It was fortunate that I had taken a drink of water at the cathedral. Chester was disappearing behind us before we saw the peeling hand-painted sign for the transport café. Dad was at the counter, picking up the thick white mugs of steaming tea, by the time I arrived.

The smoke from fried bacon and the heat from the stove hit me as I opened the door. Alma Cogan singing 'You belong to me' on the jukebox was practically drowned out by the lorry drivers arguing and joking as they crowded around the brown Formica tables. Their plates were piled high with mashed potatoes, meat and vegetables, drowning in glutinous brown gravy. A slice of white bread half-an-inch thick and plastered with margarine was on the side to mop up any food left on the plate when they had finished. This would be followed by suet or sponge pudding covered in semi-solid custard. The mugs were stained with tanning and the strong tea was a milky, orange colour. As they talked they ladled as many as six teaspoons of sugar into the mug.

Some day during the holiday we would enjoy a feast like this. Today we had to be satisfied with a mug of tea.

I sidled over to the jukebox to read the names of the records. There was one of Pat Boone singing 'April Love'. I had a major crush on him. That was in the days when actors had to keep one foot on the floor if the love scene included a bed. He was held up as a model of respectability as he was a married man and wouldn't kiss in films. I was tempted to part with my meagre holiday money.

'Is your money burning a hole in your pocket?' Dad asked. 'Get your tea drunk. We're not half way to Shrewsbury yet.'

The sky was unbroken blue. Flat fields of corn and meadowland stretched as far as the eye could see in every direction, broken only by hedgerows and the occasional stone wall. Here and there we passed farm houses with barns, old brick mansions, ancient churches where there didn't appear to be a community to make up the congregation, a hillock on the left looking strangely out of place in this flat landscape and, on the right, an old mill. On a slope was the ancient church of St Oswald's casting its shadow on the village of Malpas below. My rump was aching. Chancing the wrath of Dad, who was now out of sight, I stopped by the Llangollen canal to watch the water as I finished my sandwiches and took a drink from my water bottle. We had cycled to Llangollen often. As I looked along the canal toward Wales, I imagined going there in a barge along the waterway.

Break time over, I returned to the bike, stopped daydreaming and put some effort into catching up with the family. We were going straight through Whitchurch without stopping.

'You'll be late for your own funeral,' Dad grumbled as I came puffing up. 'I had to wait in case you missed the road and went halfway to Wolverhampton before you stopped dreaming.'

For the next few days our way followed the old Roman road which ran straight as an arrow through Shrewsbury continuing on to Hereford. At 5pm we still had twenty miles to go. The sun shone down from a clear blue sky. I passed a wooded area on the left. A signpost pointed to the pretty village of Grinshill with its Jacobean and Georgian houses less than a mile to the right. I remembered it well from two years earlier but I had no energy for detours.

My legs were shaking with exhaustion and my backside was numb when I finally reached the hostel.

There was still the luggage to unload and carry upstairs, then we would have supper to make. There would be potatoes, carrots and swedes to peel and cook, sausages to fry and gravy to make. I was falling apart with hunger and nothing would be ready for an hour.

Dad called to me from the dining room.

'Leave everything for now. Wash your hands. We're having a treat tonight. I booked in for supper but I only just arrived in time. They're still at table, thank the Lord.'

If Dad had arrived a few minutes later we would have lost our meal booking.

After supper, Dianne and I carried our panniers to a dormitory of about a dozen bunk beds. All the bottom bunks had been taken. The women's washroom was empty so we were able to strip off and have a good wash in private. I was always well endowed and never got used to washing in public.

Mam probably thought staying home with Grandma was the easier option. She hated everything connected with youth hostelling. Washing and dressing in public was an anathema to her. When she snored, which she did every night, she would wail like a banshee. Next morning she would almost die with embarrassment when she heard the other hostellers discussing her, referring to her as 'that poor woman'.

I climbed up to the top bunk, totally muscle weary, slipped inside my cotton sleeping bag and covered myself with the standard issue army blankets.

Downstairs, teenage boys and girls were laughing, shouting and singing but I hardly heard them. Within minutes I was asleep.

A bell rang to wake us at 7.30 in the morning but we were already up queuing for the toilet and washroom. I had woken to the sound of happy gossiping. Pretty blonde girls changing out of their feminine nightdresses into smoothly ironed blouses and perfectly fitting shorts as they discussed the boys they had met the night before.

Dad was down in the kitchen chatting to the other people preparing breakfast while he made the porridge. It was a spacious, well-equipped room with worktops all around the walls, plus a dozen or more cooking stoves. Pans and kitchen utensils hung from the walls above each of the worktops. The floor had cardinal red tiles. In the centre were two scrubbed wooden tables with benches.

I started cooking black pudding with fried bread. This was a typical breakfast. The hostel was near to the abbey and shops were close by. When we stayed at rural hostels the bread might be delivered still hot from the baker. Milk could have come from a milk churn being taken down the street on a handcart. We would chase after the cart with whatever container was to hand, a glass milk bottle if a clean one was available, a jug or a pan. Eggs from a farm were different shapes and colours with warm shells and the occasional brown feather stuck to them. After we had eaten the porridge I would add the eggs to the fry up.

Meanwhile, Harry cut great wedges from a freshly baked white loaf for our midday sandwiches. The bread was still warm and would have crumbled if he attempted to slice it thinly. Dianne spread the margarine with care. They wouldn't have had this problem making sandwiches with Mother's Pride sliced bread. While on the plate it had the smooth, firm texture of rubber, but once in the mouth it became as adhesive as chewing gum. Mam bought it only when we had run out of bread from the baker's. The one advantage to Mother's Pride was that it came in strong, greaseproof bags. These bags would be hoarded for occasions like this, to keep sandwiches fresh on a journey. We wouldn't have another cooked meal until we reached the next hostel.

All of us, including Dad, would have liked to set off as soon as we had washed up after breakfast. This wasn't allowed. Every hosteller had to contribute to the upkeep of the hostel by performing a simple task. You might be asked to brush the floor of the dormitory, wash the floor in the kitchen, empty the bins or polish the furniture in the common room. When the warden was satisfied with your work, your membership card would be stamped and returned to you. Then you could continue your journey.

EXTRACTS FROM
RULES AND REGULATIONS

1. Youth Hostels are for the use of members who travel on foot, by bicycle or canoe; they are not for members touring by motor-car, motor-cycle, or any power-assisted vehicle.

2. On arrival at a hostel:
   Hand this card to the warden.
   Pay the overnight charge.
   Sign the house book.
   Make up your bed.
   In the event of any complaint against the member the warden may retain the membership card and his decision will stand pending an appeal to the Regional Group to which the member belongs.

3. A sheet sleeping bag of approved type must be used.

4. Hostels are closed between 10 a.m. and 5 p.m. except on Saturday nights during November, December, January and February, and every night between December 15th and January 15th inclusive, when hostels are opened at 4.30 p.m.

5. Members must be in the hostel by 10 p.m.

6. Members must do their share of hostel duties.

7. Intoxicants are not allowed in the hostels and smoking in the dormitories is prohibited.

8. Y.H.A. members have gained a reputation for sensible behaviour in the countryside. You can help to maintain that reputation and encourage others to do likewise. Wanton damage is not likely to be caused by hostellers, but little thoughtless actions committed by many people may create a serious nuisance. Therefore, for the good name of the Y.H.A., you are asked to respect the privacy and property of local residents and to keep in mind the Country Code printed inside this card.

9. You should have a current National Handbook, which may be purchased from National or Regional Offices.

This card is the property of
the Youth Hostels Association (England and Wales)

YOUTH HOSTELS ASSOCIATION
(ENGLAND & WALES)
National Office: Welwyn Garden City, Herts.

JUVENILE CARD (9 and under 16 years of age)
Valid only for use by member to whom it is issued

Member of the International
Youth Hostel Federation

MERSEYSIDE YOUTH HOSTELS LTD
93a SCOTLAND ROAD, LIVERPOOL 3.

MEMBERSHIP No. M 7874
DATE: 23. 5. 53.

Miss B. Smith,
8, Chesterton Street,
Liverpool, 19.   R or N

Profession .... Date of Birth 25/9/38

DECLARATION
(This card is not valid until signed in ink by the member)

I agree to abide by the rules and regulations of the Association as printed in the current National Handbook and undertake not to use any hostel if I have recently been in contact with any infectious disease.

Signed *Beatrice Smith*

VALID ABROAD
ONLY IF
MEMBER'S
PHOTOGRAPH
IS AFFIXED

JUVENILES
UNDER 12
The holder of this card, if under 12, may only use hostels if accompanied by a parent or other responsible person who must also be a member of the Association.

JUVENILES
UNDER 10
The holder of this card, if under 10, may only use hostels in England and Wales.

DECLARATION BY PARENT OR GUARDIAN
I am the parent (legal guardian) of the holder of this card and certify that I am willing to allow him/her to stay at Youth Hostels.

Signed ....

OBJECTS OF THE ASSOCIATION
To help all, especially young people of limited means, to a greater knowledge, love and care of the countryside, particularly by providing hostels or other simple accommodation for them in their travels, and thus to promote their health, rest and education.

THE COUNTRY CODE

Avoid damaging crops (including mowing-grass) in any way.
Do not disturb cattle or sheep. Keep dogs always under control.
Protect crops, plantations, ricks, etc., against fire. Don't drop lighted matches or cigarette ends.
Close all gates, unless they are obviously intended to be left open.
Be careful not to damage trees, hedges, fences or walls.
Clear up all your litter, including glass.
Be specially careful never to foul pools or streams.
Pick wild flowers sparingly, if at all, and never dig them up.
Do not rob birds' nests.

Enjoy the countryside, but do not hinder the work of the countryman.

HOSTELS VISITED

1 SHREWSBURY	9 HIGHGATE LONDON
2 RUSHALL	10 Royal Leamington Spa
3 ST. BRIAVELS CASTLE	11 SHREWSBURY
4 DUNTISBOURNE ABBOTS	12
5 FILEY ... 28 MAY 1953	13
6 HIGHGATE LONDON	14
7 HIGHGATE — LONDON	15
8 HIGHGATE LONDON	16

New blanks for stamping obtainable from National or Regional Offices.

YHA membership card 1953

By 9am we were following the old Roman road again as we headed for Ludlow. The sun beat down on farmland of lush meadows and green corn. Occasionally, a slight wind rippled through the grass and the sun shimmered on the waving heads. Stretton Hills and The Long Mynd broke the flat horizon and before long I passed below the hill fort of Caer Caradoc where Caractacus is said to have made the last stand against the Romans. I would have liked to climb up to see the view but we had been promised the treat of a real visit to Ludlow. When we stayed there in 1951 we were on our way to the Festival of Britain in London. We didn't see the town as we arrived late and left early the following morning. I hurried on between the hills and through Church Stretton. Shortly after passing Craven Arms, I spotted the three-seated bike leaning against a hedge beside a caravan transport café. The family sat on a bench finishing mugs of tea.

Anticipation gave me pedal power and I was cycling immediately behind them when St Laurence church tower came into view. We all gave a shout of joy, including Dad. Traffic was barely moving in Corve Street, the main Shrewsbury to Hereford road through the town. Lorries, horse drawn wagons and the occasional car were weaving around each other in total disarray. We gave up trying to ride. Within a few minutes we were threading our way between the black-and-white Elizabethan houses of High Street where the ground floors were shops. In complete contrast to Corve Street, the High Street was almost traffic free. Pedestrians strolled along the road as though it was the pavement. Carefully dodging around them, I almost ran into a delivery boy on a bike with an enormous basket as I made for the castle.

Putting my bike against the wall, I chased after Harry and Dianne. They were already through the castle gateway taking in all that they could see, towers, turrets, arrow slits and enticing gateways. The two little princes lived here before being taken to the tower. Once in the tower they disappeared, murdered by order of Richard III, if the bad press Shakespeare gave him is to be believed. Any minute the ticket seller would call out to us from the office by the gateway and we would have to retreat. Dad would see the price and regard it as daylight robbery.

'Half a crown,' he'd say. 'I'm not paying half a crown.'

Castles were two a penny in the Marches. Although we were disappointed we knew we would soon find a deserted one where we would have the freedom to run about and let our imagination take wings.

Locking the bikes together, Dad left them with all of our luggage leaning against a wall. We had arrived soon after 1pm and couldn't go into the hostel until 5pm. By the time we had been chased from the castle gateway, he had taken the sandwiches out of the panniers and found a bench for us to sit on near the cannon.

We wandered back towards the High Street, feasting our eyes on a harvest of medieval, Tudor, Stuart and Georgian buildings. Everywhere we went Harry was rapidly recording Georgian doorways, details on a pillar, or an Elizabethan gable, in his sketchbook. Wandering along a narrow alley we found ourselves at the church. We counted the steps as we climbed up the tower but immediately forgot how many there were when we saw the views from the top. The castle was far grander from here than it had appeared when we had peered through the gateway.

We were ravenous as we cycled down majestic Broad Street, which had once been the 'Harley Street' of Ludlow, and through the narrow gateway of the old walled town. The turrets of Ludford Lodge, the youth hostel, appeared above a canopy of trees, high on the riverbank, across Ludford Bridge.

My most vivid recollection of our visit to Ludlow two years earlier was waking in the hostel and looking out upon an expanse of hyacinth-blue sky. Beside the bridge, the water appeared tranquil while about thirty yards downstream it fell into the weir.

Ludford Bridge

The weir at Ludlow

Grabbing my swimming costume, bathing cap and threadbare towel, I scrambled down the bank to the river. A few years earlier I would have dived straight in but after grazing my head in Southport outdoor pool and, on another occasion, landing head first in soft mud in the river Weaver, with my legs flaying in the air, I had become more cautious. I stepped into crystal-clear cold water, which barely reached my waist and wadded to the central arch of the bridge. After doggy paddling and floating on my back for a few minutes until I had acclimatised, I swam to the weir, sat down, and let the water swirl around. The dawn chorus was reaching a crescendo. The river bubbled and leaped fitfully down the slope and rapids rushed towards the once thriving woollen mill. On the far bank a mallard was attempting to lead her brood for the first swim of the day. One independent fellow repeatedly wandered away from the line. She would stop, gather them together, and wait for him to miss the family and come running. For half an hour or more I sat dreaming before making my way to the bank. Looking up to the bridge I discovered I had attracted an audience and hastily climbed up to the hostel.

By 1953 adolescence had brought reticence and self-consciousness. I was too embarrassed to wear a bathing suit and mess about in a river in the centre of a busy town. Thankfully, I soon outgrew all forms of reserve.

***

Dad had planned to go to St Briavels Castle in the Forest of Dean the next night. It would have been one of the highlights of the tour. Imagine his disappointment when he was informed that there were no vacancies.

A special ceremony, going back to the twelfth century, was held in St Briavels parish church every year to confirm the ancient rights of the mining community of the Forest of Dean to receive bread and cheese. It took place on the weekend we wanted. Crowds came from far and near to this annual event, in coaches, horse drawn wagons, bicycles, and on foot. In 1953 some came in family cars. They gathered at the walls to watch the bread being scattered.

Dad had been forced to change our destination. We made for the tiny hamlet of Rushall near Ledbury. Ludlow and the hills dropped away behind us and rich, open farmland spread in every direction.

Flags flew from the Victorian pile of the Town Hall of Leominster and buntings hung across the street.

'Dad, did you tell them we were coming?' I shouted to him.

'There's the town crier,' Harry laughed. 'He's going to announce our arrival. HO Yey, HO Yey.'

Leaving the Hereford road we made for Bodenham. We were heading into cider country. Apple orchards, in full blossom, were dotted here and there on the undulating landscape but it was mainly pasture. We climbed over a gate to sit in the shade of a beech tree to eat our sandwiches. The distinctive mahogany coloured cattle raised white faces from the lush grass and ambled slowly across to examine us but kept a respectful distance. The copper coloured earth of the next field made a potent contrast to the meadows and blooming apple trees. Two shire horses pulled a single plough. The farmer walked behind them making a perfectly straight furrow.

We were very impressed by his skill.

'But Dad, why is he planting? It's summertime.'

'He isn't planting,' he explained. 'He's covering the new potatoes. As the shoots come up they have to be covered by soil.'

We arrived in Ledbury with an afternoon to spare. The hostel was an hour away, near Much Marcle.

The small market town was a feast for our eyes. Everywhere we turned there were Elizabethan houses with gables protruding out over the narrow streets. We peered into cobbled courtyards of inns and envisaged fine carriages drawing up. The aristocracy would have arrived distraught more often than not, with a tale to tell of a highwayman. Harry could barely contain himself as he began sketching the 17th-century market hall which stood on chestnut pillars on the High Street. I tried to capture the essence of the place in a poem.

Much Marcle is hardly a metropolis but we traversed narrow, winding lanes, and followed signs to Much Marcle, until we came upon one to Rushall. An enormous post office that stood on the corner of the hamlet appeared to be the biggest building in the village, if you discount the farm that faced it across the road.

The hostel was a stone farm building. We put our bikes into a small outhouse. It was a relief to arrive at the hostel minutes before 6pm. We would have time to relax after the evening meal and make friends with the other hostellers.

Dianne and I were still too late to get bottom bunks. After claiming our beds by putting our sleeping bags, nightwear and panniers onto them, we made for the washroom. It was heaving with giggling teenage girls who were not in the slightest bit modest. After a quick wash we went to the kitchen and joined Dad in preparing our meal. A teenager using the next stove to ours borrowed lard from us. We had come without salt and borrowed from a woman across the room. We asked them where they had come from and about their plans, mainly out of politeness because we wanted to tell them that we were going to the Coronation. Many of the girls were Scandinavian or Dutch. They were tanned, blonde and elegant and from a different planet. All of us were deep in conversation by the time we sat down to eat.

After the meal the three of us went for a walk along a footpath. It was a pleasant relief to be walking. We were hoping to find a stream. I had brought my swimsuit with me in anticipation but we were out of luck. Away from the trees the evening sun still shone and we lay in the long grass amongst the buttercups to wallow in the gentle warmth.

Rushall YHA

The Garden

The irregular line of elms by the deep lane
Which stopped the grounds and dammed the overflow
Of arbutus and laurel. Out of sight
The lane was; sunk so deep, no foreign tramp
Nor drover of wild ponies out of Wales
Could guess if lady's hall or tenant's lodge
Dispensed such odours...

So wrote Elizabeth Barrett Browning, remembering with nostalgia the garden of the Barrett home in the Malvern Hills before the family moved to Wimpole Street, London where she was held a virtual prisoner until she eloped with Robert Browning.

I had wallowed in the first sentimental film *The Barretts of Wimpole Street*, while I was at school. It gave me a fresh drive to read her poetry. I didn't know then that her father, played by Charles Laughton, was a slave trader. He had to sell Hope House, Herefordshire, when slavery was abolished and he downsized to a Georgian mansion in Wimpole Street.

'How do I love thee? Let me count the ways' was the

239

poem that grasped my heart and left me breathless then, and whenever I was in love, but that summer's evening I saw 'The Garden' and imagined her as a joyful child running through the garden and out to the fields and lanes of Herefordshire.

There was a fire blazing in the hearth of the common room when we returned. Dianne and I found a stack of board games and were deciding which one to play when two teenage girls asked whether they could join in. We took out Monopoly. Two young men asked to play. As we played Dianne chatted pleasantly. The men weren't paying attention to the game as they flirted with the young women. Suddenly it dawned on them that Dianne had hotels all over the board and was raking in the money. Being beaten by an eleven year old, a female eleven year old, would have been a major blow to their male ego. They tried to appear indifferent as they concentrated on winning. Dianne battled it out with the men until 10. One of them was knocked out. Soon she was eliminated by the other man, to his relief. Our companions returned to the courtship rituals after Dianne and I had gone to bed. While we were engrossed in Monopoly, Harry had played Chopin on the tinny piano and Dad had read a Monmouthshire tour guide.

'You'll be glad to know we're not cycling far today,' Dad told us over breakfast next morning.

'How far's "Not far"?' Harry asked suspiciously.

'We're going to St Briavels Castle,' he said. His eyes were shining.

'St Briavels' we chorused. St Briavels was a complete castle, and we had stayed there overnight two years earlier.

Distance didn't matter. We had visited many castles when touring Wales, all in varying stages of decay. We loved them all. Dad would have read the history of each place we visited but if he attempted to educate us in Welsh history I didn't take it in.

Dad couldn't contain his excitement. 'But that's not all,' he said. 'You know that Henry VIII destroyed the monasteries and churches? The famous Tintern Abbey is near St Briavels and on our way there is a vantage place for superb views called Symond's Yat.'

We were always caught up by his enthusiasm. 'We know about Tintern Abbey,' Harry and I said together. 'And the spectacular views.'

'These waters, rolling from their mountain springs with a soft inland murmur,' we said in unison, and laughed.

Dad was delighted when we shared his joy of history and literature.

The bikes were checked for roadworthiness and our panniers packed. As soon as our allotted tasks had been completed and passed by the warden, she stamped our membership cards and we were free to head for Monmouthshire.

On every side as I cycled along I was overwhelmed by such treasures that I couldn't imagine how we could witness scenery more beautiful. The steeple at Ross-on-Wye beckoned but we didn't stop. The detour to climb the rock at Symond's Yat in the mid-morning sun seemed an unnecessary addition to our journey. Stunned, I stood on the rock, struggling to absorb the view before me.

Below a cloudless sky lay the Wye Valley. The river, sparkling in the sun, meandered between the verdant meadows and around the wooded hills, winding back upon itself in a horseshoe.

We were reluctant to leave but soon Harry put away his sketchbook and we descended to the road. The way we sped past the splendid Georgian houses and old coaching inns of Monmouth might be thought that we had become blasé. We would have loved to stop but we had all been there on previous cycle tours. Sandwiches and the possibility of a mug of tea tempted us to hurry on to Tintern.

Bordered by a gorge of wooded hills, the majestic abbey rose before us out of a heat mist, silhouetted against the open pastures and the gently flowing river. It appeared as a spectre floating in the air.

When we were within its walls, gazing up at the delicate

tracery of the windows, open to the sky for four hundred years, it still appeared more part of the heavens than of the earth. A shiver ran through me as I stood there. I could see the monks hurrying from their cells before the break of dawn, hear the plainsong as they proceeded down the grand, wide aisle. Through the unglazed windows I watched them in the flat, green fields digging, sowing, watering, and harvesting according to the season.

Replete in heart and eye, we tore ourselves away to continue our journey to St Briavels Castle.

This castle was every child's dream. It had a moat, a drawbridge complete with grill to trap the enemy while we poured boiling oil on them, and there was an oubliette, a dungeon. Food might be lowered down through a trap door, but not very often. Prisoners had no way out and would die of starvation. During the reign of Charles II, prisoners like John Hibbess had scratched their names into the jambs of the tower windows. They threatened to wreak vengeance upon their enemies when they escaped.

I had composed a poem about St Briavels during our previous visit. On returning home I had written it out in my neatest script, put my full name and address on it and placed it on a prominent shelf in the Walker Art Gallery in Liverpool and waited to be discovered as the next Elizabeth Barrett Browning. The cleaner probably dropped it into the nearest bin.

The dormitory was a grey stone cell. The window jambs were two foot thick. The cell also had slits for firing arrows.

Meals were taken in the Great Hall, where the baron once presided and law courts were held. A walkway with Gothic arches, probably for the servants to carry food from the kitchen, ran the length of the hall. We were knights in gaudy silken doublets and hose with great codpieces or we were ladies in flowing robes.

We ran through every room, up the spiral staircases, onto the battlements and down to the dungeons. By 8pm Dad decided we needed to quieten down and give the other hostellers some peace.

Replete, we settled to write and draw and dream.

Dr Foster
Went to Gloucester
In a shower of rain.
He stepped in a puddle
Right up to his middle
And never went there again!

So ran the school spelling rhyme. We were never satisfied with the words. We wanted to change 'Right up to his middle' to 'And got in a muddle.'

St Briavels Castle had been a detour. Now we returned to our route to London by way of Gloucester. We were heading for a tiny hamlet in the Cotswold Hills, Duntisbourne Abbots on the river Dun.

'The hostel is only six miles from the source of the Thames,' Dad said.

I felt really excited. We could already anticipate being in London.

I followed them through Lydney and continued beside the Severn to Gloucester. A feast of colour met my eyes as I passed the leaning tower of St Nicholas church and approached the Cross along Westgate Street. A magnificently decorated archway stood at the entrance to the city. Union Jacks flew from the upper windows of Georgian houses and half-timbered shops. Bunting hung across the street. City stores attempted to outrival one another with flamboyant Coronation displays in their windows.

A placard outside the newsagents didn't fit the optimistic mood of the nation. It proclaimed 'Ross-on-Wye blocks gypsy camp'. Forty years later I remembered this headline. I was in Lydney with a Socialist choir. We sang the travellers' song by Ewan McColl. It went down like a lead balloon.

The placard writer must have been in a truculent frame of mind that day in 1953, for the next placard read 'Pensioners don't want Coronation tea'.

Beyond the Cross, on Eastgate Street, another decorative archway matched the one on Westgate Street. I was tempted to dismount to take a closer look at the Fountain Inn but lunch had a stronger pull than architecture at that moment. The striking Norman cathedral dominated the skyline. We were having our sandwiches on the green.

On entering the cathedral precinct I was dumbfounded. A deep silence had fallen. The sounds of the city didn't reach this medieval sanctuary. Even Dad managed to lower the volume of his voice to a reverential tone as he greeted me. The green was encircled by a variety of houses, some of them impressive Georgian structures shining in the sun and surrounded by intricate wrought iron railings and gates, while others were so ancient they appeared about to tumble down. The roofs dipped, near to collapse, the timber looked rotten, and the wattle and daub hadn't seen a coat of paint in years.

We spent happy hours wandering around the cathedral and city. The shell of Greyfriars Friary brought Tintern Abbey back to my mind. The murder of Edward II horrified our tender minds. Thankfully, we didn't hear the gory details until many years later. Dad remained an innocent throughout his life. He wouldn't have understood the meaning of the red-hot poker even if he'd read it, despite having gone to sea at fourteen years of age. Nothing like that would have been in guide books in 1953.

As the evening began to draw in, we set off for the hostel at Duntisbourne Abbots. Even I managed to put a spurt on. We barely scraped in before the doors were locked at 10pm. Dad stood shamefaced as the warden read him the riot act.

There was a bath, the first we had seen in five days. Everyone in the hostel had gone to bed. The water was piping hot, filling the bathroom with steam. I sank into it, leaving only my mouth and nose above the water. The warmth crept through my aching muscles to my bones. I lay watching the steam condense and run down the yellow ochre walls and form rivulets down the windows. Dianne knocked as I began to doze. Reluctantly, I climbed out and dried on the threadbare towel we were sharing. I put the towel on the radiator to dry for her but it had been of little use to me. Already damp, it would hardly dry her at all. Fortunately, it was pleasant to slip into our cotton sleeping bags a little wet. The night was sticky and airless.

Duntisbourne Abbots nestled down in the wooded valley of the river Dun. It was a tiny unspoiled Cotswold hamlet with a Norman church and a post office. There wasn't even a village shop. Fortunately there was a store in the hostel that sold provisions, fruit and vegetables.

By morning Dad had charmed the warden. He chatted to us as we leaned the bikes against the wall to strap on the panniers. The pleasant stone building had once been the rectory.

'We often hold folk dancing evenings on the lawn in the summer.'

Duntisbourne Abbotts YHA

A mile from the hostel we turned onto the main road near Five Mile House. There was little to stir my imagination on the busy highway through Cirencester. The second largest city in Roman Britain lay buried beneath a modern urban sprawl. Nothing reminded me of its former glorious and romantic past. Riding in gutters and dodging buses and lorries, I longed for the countryside.

The houses became scarcer and garden lawns grander and more spacious until we reached the chequer-work of flat fields marked by dark green hedges. Sheep, picked out white against the meadows, called to their lambs. Streams meandered aimlessly. From the hedgerows a hectic humming and buzzing rose up as insects flew among the riot of flowers. The air tasted of nectar.

Occasionally, through a break in the hedge or over a farm gate, I would see an isolated church or farm. Three sheep with their lambs were straddled across the road ahead. A delivery van moved patiently behind them, waiting to pass. I dismounted and stood against the hedge to let them pass. Eyeing me warily, they walked by in a single file on the other side. I remounted and had barely gone fifty yards when I sensed something behind me. Looking back I found the sheep returning. They had realised the grass was no sweeter in the meadow before them than the meadow behind.

Desolate airport runways and hangars – relics of the war – stretched out behind a fence on the right. Sometimes I spotted something glistening in the sunlight far beyond this flat, deserted expanse and wondered whether it could be the elusive Thames.

On reaching the market place at Fairford, I dismounted and looked around, hoping the family would have stopped for a cup of tea. If tea had been sold at The Bull, the old coaching inn, it would have been beyond Dad's pocket. The square was surrounded by evocative old stone buildings but I couldn't see a café.

Half a century later in another life, a totally different world,

I returned to that airport in a vain attempt to stop the second Gulf War. The railings were twice the height they had been on that balmy May morning and topped by sharp spikes. Arriving at the airport by coach from Wales, I could have been anywhere in middle England. The name Fairford failed to awaken any memories. As we walked down the road from the airport gates, bombers roared over our heads to take the lives of innocent civilians in the Middle East. The old stone buildings hadn't lost their beauty but the coldness of the locals took away the magic. I was too late for food at The Bull and had to make do on pickled eggs.

On that pleasant summer's day in May 1953, I continued my journey to Oxford. There was a lake or a wide river to the right of the road. Etched against the sky stood a splendid tower and spire.

> Light sound and motion own the sway,
> Responding to the charm with its own mystery.

I found myself in a surprising village of wide Georgian streets. The three-seated bike leaned against the wall of Lechlade church. The family had finished eating. Harry and Dianne were splashing about in the river while Dad sat dangling his feet in the water. We had reached the Thames at last.

They lost me before we reached Farringdon. I rejoiced in occasional glimpses of the Thames, now far to my left, as I continued following the signposts to Oxford. The road became narrower and winding and I realised this wasn't a major highway. The level landscape that had stretched around me mile after mile gave way to pleasant undulating hills.

A woman coming through a farm gate was the first person I had seen in half an hour.

'Can I get to Oxford along this lane?' I asked in my best Liverpudlian English.

At first she regarded me with total incomprehension. Then she said 'Oxford?' in a warm dialect, rolling the R.

I nodded.

'Yes,' she said and pointed, indicating I should continue the way I was going. This was followed by intricate details and lots of gesticulating.

I listened carefully, nodding thoughtfully, hoping to catch a word here and there that would give me a clue as to what she was saying. She could have been telling me what she was having for tea. I didn't understand a word. In retrospect I congratulate her for understanding the question I had asked in unadulterated Scouse.

The asphalt road disappeared and I followed a dirt track with grass growing down the centre. I was alone on top of the world, with only the bees and butterflies to keep me company and the occasional lark rising up to sing its alarm as I approached. It was an hour of pure rapture.

As I descended I had a vision of the Holy City. The New Jerusalem could not be more beautiful. Before me, bathed in honeyed light, lay Oxford. Spires and turrets pierced the sky. Turquoise domes and blue slate roofs harmonised with the golden stone. Through gaps in the hedge, I caught glimpses of the city as I drew nearer and nearer.

I arrived at the hostel an hour before the family. Fortunately, I had the potatoes and vegetables and was able to start preparing the meal. Dad arrived looking anxious.

He was clearly relieved when he saw me. 'Where on earth did you get to?' he asked.

'I must have taken a wrong turning,' I told him. 'I followed the signposts to Oxford but ended up on a dirt road.'

'You weren't supposed to be coming direct to Oxford. We've been to Wantage.'

'We've been blowing King Arthur's blowing stone,' Dianne said. 'We were hoping to wake him up.'

'And the Knights of the Round Table,' Harry added. 'But I think they're still asleep.'

Later I told them about seeing Oxford from the hillside. I persuaded Harry to show me the picture he had drawn of King

Oxford

Oxford

Harry, The Blowing Stone,
Wantage

Dianne, The Blowing Stone,
Wantage

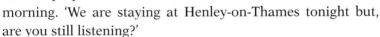

Harry drawing King Arthur, Wantage

Arthur's statue. We wandered through the city and sat beside the river to talk and watch young men and women in smart white clothes messing about in boats and flirting. As darkness fell we hurried back to the hostel before the 10pm curfew.

'Right, young lady,' Dad said, as we prepared to leave next morning. 'We are staying at Henley-on-Thames tonight but, are you still listening?'

'Yes, Dad.'

'We will be in Henley at 11am. We are riding straight through and on to Windsor.'

'Will we be going into the castle?' we all chorused.

When he answered in the affirmative Harry dared to ask, 'Even if it is half a crown?'

Harry jumped out of reach before he could receive the customary cuff around the ears.

Dad laughed. 'Even if it's three shillings.'

We were over the moon.

Across the flat meadowland to our left rose the Chiltern Hills with Ewelme, a whole village of black-and-white houses, etched against them, while the Thames snaked along on the right, sometimes close by, sometimes almost out of sight. Picturesque hamlets, villages and riverside resorts clung to her edges, famous names to conjure with. Dorchester with her 12th-century abbey was passed with hardly a second glance. History was seeping out of the very soil, but we had no time to stop. By 12.30 we wanted to be in Windsor, eating our sandwiches.

Friends Meeting House,
Henley-on-Thames YHA

Henley-on-Thames YHA

Henley hostel was behind the Friends Meeting House on the Oxford to Henley road and we passed it on our way into the town. It was a real tourists' town with lots of ye olde worlde tea shops in half-timbered buildings and tempting inns, like The Bull, with its cobbled courtyard. Dad was prepared to pay three shillings to go into Windsor castle if necessary. We weren't going to push our luck by asking for a cup of tea in a tea shop. Lorry drivers must stop somewhere even in this posh piece of England's green and pleasant land. We would carry on until we found a transport café.

The Victorian town hall dominated the market place. Workmen were hanging bunting as we passed. We turned down towards the river, home of the regatta for over a hundred years, and crossed the bridge. This one-and-a-half mile stretch of water encompasses the straightest section of river in the British Isles. Pleasure boats plied their way. Yachts sailed by. Young men with Brylcreamed quiffs, wearing cream trousers with creases that looked sharp as knives, shot through the water on single skiffs. Families patiently queued for the rowing boats hemmed in by houseboats moored on one side of them and Morrises, Austins, Fords and motorbikes parked on their other side. I envied the children sitting on the empty moorings, dangling their feet in the cool water, and promised myself I would be there that evening when we returned from Windsor.

There was a slight slope as we left Henley and headed for Maidenhead, the town made famous by the theatre set during the 1920s and 1930s. One could hardly describe this rise as a hill but it forced the river to loop around it in a horseshoe to our left.

After Maidenhead I was delighted to discover our route took us through Bray. This attractive Thameside village of black-and-white houses was pleasing to heart and eye.

'The Vicar of Bray' was the first political song I ever learned, when I was about fourteen years old. It told the story of a 17th- to 18th-century vicar who, during those turbulent times, remained in his post through the reigns of five different English monarchs by adjusting his beliefs to accommodate each changing tide. I had no idea where the vicar had his parish and was pleased to put a place to the name of Bray.

> In good King Charles's golden days,
> When Loyalty no harm meant;
> A zealous High-Church man I was,
> And so I gain'd Preferment.
> Unto my Flock I daily Preach'd,
> Kings are by God appointed,
> And Damn'd are those who dare resist,
> Or touch the Lord's Anointed.
>
> And this is Law, I will maintain
> Unto my Dying Day, Sir.
> That whatsoever King may reign,
> I will be the Vicar of Bray, Sir!
>
> When Royal James possessed the crown,
> And popery grew in fashion;
> The Penal Law I shouted down,
> And read the Declaration:
> The Church of Rome I found would fit
> Full well my Constitution,
> And I had been a Jesuit,
> But for the Revolution.

Soon the walls of Windsor, the largest castle in Britain, rose in gigantic splendour from the plain. We had eyes for nothing else as we cycled towards it. Half an hour later we sat beneath the curfew tower eating our sandwiches. At the crossroads, a policeman wearing white gloves and armbands, standing with his back to the statue of Queen Victoria, directed the traffic. Across the High Street stood the grand White Hart Hotel.

'Shall we go and have a look for a café for a cup of tea?' Dad asked when we had eaten.

We looked at him aghast.

'Only joking,' he laughed. He was as excited as we were. 'Let's have some Adam's ale and go in.'

I shivered with pleasure as we walked up the hill to the entrance. Dianne and Harry's eyes were glowing, looking everywhere. We could barely contain our excitement.

Once through Henry VIII's gate, we stood open-mouthed. Where should we start? What would we look at first? The warmth of the redbrick and timber houses, the homes of the choir of St George's chapel, were in sharp contrast to the austere stone perimeter walls of the castle on one side and the highly-ornate chapel on the other. The splendid architecture of St George's chapel left a lasting impression on me. High above us, at the top of a steep incline, stood the round tower.

We climbed towards it, gasping at the wonders that greeted us on every side. Arches, statues and delicate stone tracery caught the eye wherever we looked.

The moat around the round tower had been made into a beautiful garden with waterfalls and a pool giving relief from the endless stone at the centre of the castle.

An arch led to the North Terrace and the State Apartments where we found a massive cannon pointing over the ramparts. We would have loved to examine it more closely, touched it or, best of all, climb on it. It was girded with a chain. We were too well raised in Victorian good manners to step over the barrier. Over the ramparts was a wood about sixty feet below. The tops of the trees were as high as the castle walls.

'Now that is very rude,' I heard Dad say.

I turned to find Harry and Dianne standing with their heads bowed, looking very ashamed.

'Do you want us to be turned out of the castle?' he asked.

'Sorry Dad,' they muttered.

'Right. So don't ever do anything like that again.'

They skulked along, not sure what to do with themselves, while Dad walked ahead.

After a silence that seemed to last for an eternity he said,

'Look at that,' pointing at a peerless assembly of buildings across the river.

Despite themselves they couldn't resist the beautiful vista before them.

'What is it, Dad?' I asked.

'I think it's Eton College.'

We had almost reached the end of the royal apartment buildings when we heard thump, thump, thump and a guardsman appeared from the corner and marched before us across the North Terrace, turned smartly with much ceremonial stamping, before retracing his steps.

Whooping with joy we ran past the corner. He was standing in front of the sentry box. A pretty teenager stood smiling up at him while a youth took her photograph. Children, sailors, old men, and mothers stood waiting their turn to be photographed. Dad didn't give any indication that we should join them so we just stood to watch the fun.

After a while I wandered off to look at the formal garden and across the meadows to the river.

'Can we see Datchet and Runnymede from the castle?' I asked Dad.

I had read of Datchet in *Three Men in a Boat*. The men couldn't find suitable accommodation in Datchet and had to sleep in beds that were too short for them. My only other recollection from the story is of them having nothing to eat but a tin of beans and trying to open a tin without a tin opener.

Runnymede was far more significant. It played an important part in English history.

'Datchet is just out of sight on our right. Runnymede is directly opposite to Eton but we aren't allowed onto that side of the castle.'

'What scenes have passed since first this ancient yew / In all the strength of youthful beauty grew! / Here patriot Britons might have musing stood, / And planned the Carta for their country's good,' I quoted.

Dianne and Harry listened with looks of admiration. They

were always appreciative of the way I learned poetry by heart.

'Can we go to see Runnymede, Dad,' Harry asked.

'Sorry son. It's too far. We have to go back to Henley tonight. Time is already pressing.'

Returning the way we had come, we took a last look at St George's chapel, where Henry VIII was buried beside Jane Seymour, and went out through the arch.

When we had arrived in Windsor we had eyes for nothing but the castle. Now we were aware of the narrow cobbled streets opposite the castle with tiny cafés and a public house on the corner.

'Dad what are those steel hoops for on the road?' Harry asked.

'They are from the days when horse drawn carriages used to wait on Castle Hill for fares. The hoops held the carriages.'

We were about to walk to the bikes.

'Come this way for a minute,' he said, crossing the road behind the statue of Victoria. 'Do you see the building with arches that comes out as far as the road?'

We nodded.

'That's the Guildhall designed by Sir Christopher Wren. Some of the councillors said it wasn't safe. They insisted it needed more pillars to support the ceiling. He put the pillars in as instructed. Many years later it was discovered that there was a two-inch gap between the pillars and the ceiling.'

I don't know where he collected these snippets of information from but we loved them.

When we retrieved the bikes we waited because the policeman was holding up his hand to the traffic coming down Castle Hill. Soon he waved us across and we rode down Peascod Street, past the Regal cinema, then found ourselves in streets of terraced houses. We could have been back in Garston and couldn't get away quick enough as we headed out of town towards Maidenhead.

The tower of Henley's parish church, St Mary's, was a

welcome sight and we freewheeled down the hill and over the bridge much earlier than we had expected. Crowds flocked along the landing area and towpath. Skiffs, rowing boats, and yachts were so numerous they appeared in danger of colliding.

When the hostel opened at 5pm we were impatient to get in, have supper, and get down to the river. As soon as we had bagged our beds, I rushed to the kitchen to put the kettle on. We hadn't had a cup of tea since breakfast.

We made short work of cooking and eating our meal and were on our way to the river before 7pm. Taking off our shoes and socks, it was a joy to sit on one of the wooden jetties, dangling our feet in the water. Dianne and I were lazily watching the bustling world around us. Harry was industriously recording everything, river, boats, people, bridges and buildings in his sketchbook.

The bells of St Mary's chimed 8.30. The sky remained the brilliant blue but we decided it was time to walk through the town to the hostel. The section of the church walls nearest the river had a chequered pattern. Our interest was aroused by the sight of an ancient roof and we went around the church and through the graveyard. Finding a 15th-century building, Chantry House, which had once housed the school, I peered in through the window.

'Now, that is very rude,' Harry said, imitating Dad. 'Do you want the vicar to turn you out of the graveyard?'

Dianne looked shamefaced, but went into a fit of giggles.

I hadn't had a chance to ask them why Dad had chastised them when we were at Windsor castle. By the time we were alone for the evening it had gone from my mind until Harry mimicked Dad.

'What did you do?' I asked now, full of curiosity.

Dianne's eyes were shining with excitement as she remembered. 'We found a door open into one of the state rooms, so Harry pushed it wider. I had a dekko over his shoulder.'

'What was it like?'

'There was a crystal chandelier, but it wasn't lit. Curtains hung from floor to ceiling. There was a beautiful painting above an ornate fireplace. The room was much smaller than I expected.' Dianne answered. 'There were two or three people in there but they were dressed like ordinary office workers.'

'Then Dad caught us,' Harry said. 'And that was the end of our adventure.'

'What can you see through the window, Beaty?'

Dianne felt guilty enough to resist joining us for about two seconds, then we all stared in through the window at the large hall with strong oak beams and a dimpled wooden floor shining from the patina of centuries.

Throughout our lives we could resist anything except the temptation to creep into private courtyards in Spain, peer into the living rooms of poor villagers in Greece, push open grand wrought iron gates to enter the gardens of Napoleon's home on Elba, or try ornately carved doors in Italy and step inside magnificent chambers with frescoed ceilings and a cornucopia of beauty tastefully displayed.

We continued past the almshouses, rubbernecking whenever we found a curtain or door carelessly left open, and made our way up New Street by Brakespear Brewery. As we turned the corner by the theatre, we were drawn by the lights illuminating the foliage in the courtyard of The Bull. It was one of the oldest inns in Henley, with walls up to three feet thick. Tradition has it that it is haunted by the ghost of a young woman. It is also claimed that you can also smell tallow candles. There were two plaques on the wall for fire insurance. Until 1868 Henley had two fire brigades and The Bull was insured with both of them.

It had gone 9pm and Dad would be coming out to look for us if we didn't arrive at the hostel soon. Curbing our need to pry into every alleyway, we hurried back to the hostel.

Henley and South Oxfordshire Standard, the local weekly rag, was lying on the table in the common room. The main picture was of the carnival queen for Coronation day. I grabbed it eagerly, to read anything about the Coronation.

The carnival was going to be starting from the market place at 4pm. The star of the carnival would be the carnival queen, Silvia Hirons. She was chosen by eight judges in front of a crowd of four hundred.

Everyone would be able to listen to the Coronation broadcast on the radio or watch it on television. Many people, even in Garston, bought televisions especially for the Coronation. The Henley carnival would begin when the broadcast of the Coronation procession ended.

But we wouldn't be watching a carnival queen. We would be in London listening to the radio broadcast of the Coronation ceremony relayed over the public address system. We would watch the procession and marvel as the pageant unfolded before us. The queen of England would wave to us from her golden coach.

***

Next morning we said goodbye to Henley, crossed the tranquil Thames and retraced our journey to Maidenhead. Windsor castle arose like a mirage on the horizon as we continued on to Slough.

Lorries thundered by reeking of petrol fumes and throwing up dust in my eyes and mouth. As we approached London the cars, lorries and buses were nose to tail and barely moving. I was moving faster than the traffic but once more I was consigned to the gutters and had to negotiate grids. It was a relief to see the turn off to Kew, where I was meeting Dad for lunch. As I cycled towards Kew Gardens I spotted one or two cheap cafés where we could go for a mug of tea after we had eaten, and I was ready for it. I couldn't see anywhere to lock the bike outside the botanical gardens. Dad had locked his to a post, so I attached mine to the three seater and followed them in through the gigantic gates. I found them sitting beside the lake near the Palm House. As soon as we had finished eating, we dashed along the avenue of trees to the glasshouses. At the far end of the avenue was a Chinese pagoda. Inside the Temperate House we looked with amazement at the exotic and beautiful flowers and fruit from the Pacific Islands, Africa and the Mediterranean, places we had heard of in Sunday school.

After a pleasant interlude, including a mug of tea in Kew village, we returned to the busy Great West Road and were soon cycling along Kensington High Street, looking in wonder at five-storey-high shops, each vying with the other to have the most spectacular Coronation decorations.

Our route passed along Piccadilly but Dad, bursting with excitement, waited for me at the crossroads.

'Let's go and take a peak at The Mall,' he said.

We thought nothing could be more spectacular than Kensington High Street but the most impressive decorations were those on the Coronation route. Over The Mall there were three ceremonial arches of lions and unicorns, each one sixty feet high. Suspended from each was a princess's coronet. It took our breath away.

Returning to Piccadilly we stopped while Dad pointed out the pavement where we were going to camp out on Monday night.

'I think I prefer the opposite side of the road.' I said, looking at the enclosed boxes for spectators facing us.

'I bet they cost more than half a crown,' Dianne commented softly.

Dad laughed. 'A king's ransom. More than a year's wages for one seat I should think, let alone a whole box.'

'Enough boxes have been erected to seat over one hundred thousand people,' he said, awed by the magnitude of this achievement.

We gasped when we saw the statue of Eros. It was enclosed in a gilded cage, fifty feet high. The steps around the statue had been boxed in to protect it from over enthusiastic subjects climbing up for a better view of the procession.

Ogling, ooing and aahing, we made our way through the centre of London, across Euston Road and into the more down-to-earth world of Kentish Town Road. Here the decorations strung across the side streets were red, white and blue bunting like the ones we had in Garston. Many of them were home-made and had that slightly jaded look of old friends that had been brought out on many previous occasions.

Turning up Highgate Road, we climbed beside Parliament Hill to the rambling Georgian edifice of Holmeswood, the hostel at the top of Highgate West Hill, beside the cemetery. The square, yellow-brick buildings had two of the windows bricked in and we wondered whether that had been done during the days of the window tax. While approaching the hostel, I was relieved to see a wide expanse of grass and trees softening the landscape. Ponds sparkled in the evening sunlight.

As soon as supper was over, we made our way to Parliament Hill and wandered beside the Highgate ponds to the grounds of Kenwood House.

Over a decade later I found the ponds again, and watched men peacefully and studiously sailing model yachts there.

***

Sunlight blazed into the dormitory, broken into a dozen squares by the crisscrossed panes in the tall windows. It heralded another glorious day.

Dad wanted to take us to the art galleries and museums or the Tower but it was Sunday. Nothing was open until the afternoon, except the zoo and Madame Tussauds. The waxworks was one of the most expensive attractions in London but it was special to London. We had often visited Chester Zoo. Going to London Zoo seemed like time filling. After Dad had done some soul-searching and mental calculations, we cycled back down Kentish Town Road, past Regent's Park and along Marylebone Road to Madame Tussauds.

There was a policeman in the doorway and Dad asked

him if it would it be alright to leave the bikes locked to a post outside. He was halfway through his question when he roared with delighted laughter. It was a waxwork.

We descended to an Aladdin's cave of wonders and could hardly believe that they weren't flesh and blood. I was looking at Sleeping Beauty and screamed when I saw her breathe.

Everyone came rushing over asking what had happened. She was as still as all the other figures and they thought I had imagined it.

As they were about to turn away I said, 'Look, look quickly.'

'Well blow me,' Dad said, as she breathed again.

We waited for it to happen once more and we all burst into helpless giggles. Harry rolled on the floor, hugging his legs as he laughed and laughed. After that shock, the chamber of horrors seemed quite tame.

We came out into the glare of the morning sun.

Dad pointed out Baker Street, where Sherlock Holmes had lived on the Edgware Road. We were about to go running across the road to see number 221B when Dad stopped us. He told us there was no such house. It was a fictitious address.

The second big treat of the day was the Tower of London. We took in some of the route of the procession on our way. As we cycled up the Edgware Road, we were met by the sight of the majestic Marble Arch festooned in flags of St George. The central arch is reserved for the Sovereign to use on State occasions. The massive gates were closed.

On the previous day we had viewed the decorations in Oxford Street from the other end. Now we saw the wonderful displays on the shop fronts in Oxford Street from Marble Arch before we crossed to Park Lane.

'Wait a minute,' Dad said, as I was about to ride on. 'Let me look at the plan of the procession. Where did I put my specs?'

This was a rhetorical question. We waited while he searched through all of his pockets. 'Oh I see,' he said, looking at the plan. 'Come and have a look.'

All of us loved maps. We had studied this one diligently and thought we knew it by heart. When we gathered around he pointed out the matter bothering him.

'I thought the procession came along Park Lane. It comes through the park from the arch at Hyde Park Corner to Marble Arch along a way called East Carriage Drive. I didn't know the roads in the park had names.'

We wanted to see Whitehall, Westminster Abbey and the Houses of Parliament, so we headed down Piccadilly again and made for Trafalgar Square.

I wasn't impressed with the decorations in Whitehall. They looked like ladders and lacked the lightness and fairy-tale quality of the delicate arches and crowns in the Mall and didn't have the joyful explosion of primary colours that we had seen in the bunting in the streets of terraced houses in north London. Attached to these ladders in Whitehall were standards, household cavalry helmets, and heraldic motifs.

Big Ben chimed as we stood in Parliament Square examining the functional looking annexe that had been built at the west end of Westminster Abbey. The queen's beasts were wrapped up. Above the circular entrance stood a fifteen-foot-high royal emblem.

Many of the stands for onlookers lining the route were fairly basic, with occasional coats of arms, flags or bunting, but those on Parliament Square must have been for dignitaries who hadn't quite made it to the ceremony. These stands were decorated with attractively painted emblems of the Commonwealth.

Cycling beside the river we looked to where the Festival of Britain had thrilled us two years earlier. The Skylon and the Dome of Discovery had gone. All that remained was the Royal Festival Hall. The sight of the Gothic towers of Tower Bridge increased my pedal power. Ahead I saw the signals and lights that gave warning if Tower Bridge was closed to traffic. This happened when the drawbridge opened to allow ships to pass along the Thames. A year earlier, in 1952, a bus ignored the stop signals and was caught on the bridge as it opened.

It had to leap across the gap. Turning onto Tower Hill, I arrived at the Tower right on opening time. There was a long queue. Fortunately for me, Dad had almost reached the ticket office.

We hurried through the arch in the Middle Tower and across the bridge over the dry moat into the Byward Tower. There above us was the lifting machinery and the portcullis. The Bell Tower stood before us, where Elizabeth once walked for exercise along the ramparts when she was held as prisoner during Bloody Mary's reign. Spotting an open green through an archway, we raced through, skidding to a halt at the sight of men dressed in Tudor uniforms, navy blue trimmed with red embroidery, strolling across the grass. They were Beefeaters, Dad told us. Visitors posed with them to have photographs taken but Dad didn't encourage us to follow their example. Perhaps his film was expensive and he was keeping it for the Coronation, or maybe he was too reserved to ask for permission.

First on the guided tour came the Bloody Tower and we giggled shyly to each other knowing that we wouldn't be able to get the word 'Bloody' out without blushing no matter what the context. Neither could Dad. But I found myself humming the Stanley Holloway song.

The guided tour over, we stood on Tower Green soaking up the atmosphere while listening to the blue black ravens cawing. The backdrop to the lawn was the 12th-century Norman tower, dazzling white against a cloudless sky. Beside it stood the Bloody Tower. We had left Dad admiring St Peter's chapel.

Bundling his jacket into a ball, Harry put it under his arm and started skulking around singing:

With her head tucked underneath her arm
She walks the Bloody Tower
With her head tucked underneath her arm
At the midnight hour.

He could always guarantee that Dianne and I would be an appreciative audience.

For the next two hours we peered into every nook and cranny and were transported to Tudor England. We conveniently forgot that had we lived then, we would have been the lowest drudges. The unfortunate wives of Henry VIII must have been turning in their graves as we three urchins tramped across their burial ground.

On leaving the Tower, Dad led us down a side street for a closer look at Tower Bridge.

'I can't believe our luck,' he exclaimed. 'By Jove, come and see this.'

'What is it, Dad?'

'Look at the bridge. It's opening in the middle to let a ship through.'

We were all so engrossed in watching this wonder that we didn't notice Harry wasn't with us.

'Hell's fire. Where has that boy disappeared to this time?' he groaned.

Harry spent his life daydreaming or exploring while the family spent theirs searching for him.

I spotted Harry coming towards us through the crowd that had gathered to watch the ship pass. He was flushed, his eyes radiant. He had obviously been up to something.

When we were away from Dad he told us he had sneaked to the middle of the bridge while nobody was looking. He wanted to see how it worked.

'I had just stepped across the join,' he claimed. 'When the bridge started to rise up and I had to jump over the gap to this side.'

Half an hour later we had escaped the worst of the petrol fumes.

Cycling beside Parliament Hill the volume of traffic had thinned enough for us to ride on the road instead of circumnavigating grids in the gutters.

For all the wonder and excitement of London, I could only

cope with the roads, stone, brick, and slate, as far as the eye could see because I knew I would return to a tranquil island of green at the end of each day.

**

Clouds careered across the sky on Monday morning, the first rain clouds we had seen in over a week. We were full of optimism. The weather would improve during the day.

The sandwiches were made and wrapped with extra care that day. They had to last thirty-six hours, until the end of the Coronation procession at 3pm the following afternoon. The Mother's Pride greaseproof bags we had been using since the start of the holiday were badly creased and losing their preservative qualities. We used them for the sandwiches for Monday lunch. Fresh bags had been kept especially for Monday night and Coronation day. The packets were further protected by placing them in biscuit tins.

Instead of taking our usual route beside Parliament Hill, Dad turned left to go through Highgate village and down Highgate Hill. He had something to show us. Opposite Whittington Hospital he stopped and we dismounted. I couldn't see anything of interest but he took out his camera. Dianne and Harry were examining a milestone when I joined them. It was unremarkable and we would have passed it by if he hadn't drawn our attention to it.

'This is said to be the milestone Dick Whittington was sitting on when he heard Bow Bells ring out, "Turn again, Whittington, Once Mayor of London." It was the curfew bell in the City of London and used to ring 9pm and tolled again at 5.45am to wake local Cockneys.'

We had cycled from the City and we doubted that anyone could hear a bell from there. It was about four miles.

'It wouldn't be like today,' Dad said. 'There wouldn't be all this traffic roaring by. If the wind was in the right direction the sound might have carried in the silence of the night.'

Half a century later when I lived in Roath, a suburb of Cardiff, and heard the bell on Cardiff City Hall chime out, I realised that Bow Bell could have been heard on Highgate Hill.

When we entered the thick of the traffic on the Euston Road it was already after 9.30am and the rush hour was supposed to be over. Even from our disadvantaged position in the gutter, we were still passing everything. Half an hour later we were skirting Hyde Park and could see the spire of the Albert Memorial and the dome of the Albert Hall.

Dad turned down a side road but I had to stop and take a closer look at the monument. The spire, which rose from a roof of four arches supported by pillars, was unlike any I had seen before. It had brightly coloured mosaics that shone as though they had just been polished, and gilded borders that glistened. The spire was surmounted by a cross. Four wide flights of granite steps led up to the platform and arches. A frieze of hundreds of tiny figures surrounded the platform. In the centre of the platform sat a fourteen-foot-high statue of Prince Albert.

'Oh, there you are,' Dad said, sounding more relieved than irritated.

He had locked up their bike and come back to look for me.

'I'll have to put you and Harry on a leash each.'

I followed him along the road beside the Albert Hall to the Natural History Museum and entered a neo-Gothic cathedral celebrating life. Grand staircase led to lofty rooms of rocks, minerals, gemstones and meteorites. I had no wish to look at the dead butterflies mounted on boards and glass display cabinets of stuffed birds. For over a week I had enjoyed them in their full enticing flight.

A colossal suspended skeleton of a whale captured my attention. On examining its structure I discovered that the bones of whales appeared to bear a close correlation to those of humans. This was a total revelation. The idea had never occurred to me.

The wind had risen when we left the museum and clouds were moving across the sky.

Looking up, dismayed, I commented on how quickly the wind was blowing the clouds.

'The clouds are scudding across the sky at a tremendous rate,' Dad said, with a grave smile. 'But they are being drawn into a vacuum.'

There was no arrogance in his manner when he dropped these jewels into our laps. He knew. It gave him great pleasure to share his knowledge and we were eager recipients.

For the first year that Richard was in Australia he wrote to Dad whenever he needed to know anything because Dad was the fount of all knowledge. Sadly the answers to his queries took twelve weeks or more to arrive by which time he had forgotten the question. He realised the time had come when he must solve his own problems and have confidence in his own bank of knowledge. In later years, when Dad was no longer there to answer our questions, we turned to Richard, in the sure knowledge that he would have squirreled away every fact, and every face and name of every person who ever touched his life, however briefly.

When the family cycled to London for the Festival of Britain, Dad made us ride four miles across the City to Earl's Court where a café sold mugs of cheap tea. Fortunately, we weren't required to ride across London to the café in Earl's Court after our visit to the Natural History Museum on the eve of the Coronation because the café was close at hand.

Fat and cigarette smoke billowed out through the door as we entered a yellow ochre room with beige peeling notices. The dark brown ceiling was wreathed in smoke. Despite the stifling heat, many of the men wore caps while eating and the few women present were wearing head scarves or felt hats. The only touch of colour was provided by the still life fruit on the oilcloth table covers.

Eating in a café, any café, was a luxury and a major adventure. We would be living on day-old sandwiches by this time next day. This was our last cooked meal for more than twenty-four hours. The juke box competed with the conversation shouted all around us as we tucked into mashed potatoes and the biggest bangers we had ever seen.

Our water bottles were refilled by the owner of the café. We called at a greengrocer for a bag full of apples. The time had now come. We made our way to Piccadilly.

By three in the afternoon crowds were already beginning to gather and we had to dismount as we made our way towards Green Park. Locking the bikes in a side street, we carried the panniers to the spot on the pavement Dad had chosen for the night vigil. Spreading a groundsheet, we anchored it at the corners with the bags to mark our territory. This was a time of community good manners. No latecomer would consider disputing our claim. As long as one of us remained, it was quite safe for the others to leave from time to time as necessity demanded.

We were amongst the first to sit on the pavement but others took their cue from us. Soon families settled down on either side of us. Pedestrians passed to and fro on the ever-narrowing passageway between the park and the campers on the pavement.

The sky was a sheet of grey and we hurriedly covered ourselves in our canary yellow oilskin cycling capes and sou'westers.

I had parted with some serious money for a book about

Buckingham Palace guard in sentry box. A quiet day before the Coronation.

the royal family with lots of glossy photographs, but I barely looked at it as I didn't want it to get wet. Not being able to read wasn't a great problem as crowd watching held my attention for hours at a time. Between showers, Harry took out his sketchpad to record the wealth of personality in the characters around us, the flowering unblemished beauty of the children and young people, and the stories revealed in the faces of the old. A memorable drawing was of a family who had erected a canvas canopy above them to keep off the rain.

As the evening wore on somebody started singing the songs we all knew 'Down at the Old Bull and Bush' and 'Let's All Go Down The Strand'.

Soon Piccadilly Circus to Hyde Park Corner echoed with voices of the people. The sound was magnified as is bounced off the tall buildings opposite the park. From music hall we moved on to nationalistic songs such as 'The British Grenadiers' and 'There'll Always Be An England'.

> Land of hope and glory, Mother of the free,
> How shall we extol thee, who are born of thee?
> Wider still and wider shall thy bounds be set;
> God, who made thee mighty, make thee mightier yet.
> God, who made thee mighty, Make thee mightier yet.

We were drawing from a never ending fund, sea shanties and playing songs from childhood: 'What shall we do with a drunken sailor' and 'The Grand Old Duke of York'. At that time most people remembered hymns from school assembly or Sunday school, although attendance at church and chapel was in steep decline.

As the Revd Dr Donald Soper was to note about ten years later, 'Most people have forgotten which church they don't go to.'

'Jerusalem' was sung with gusto, followed by 'Underneath the Arches'.

By midnight most of us had sung ourselves hoarse. Dad had

great trouble getting the Primus stove to light in the rain. He pumped away at it until eventually he succeeded and we were able to have an enamel mug full of tea. Dressed in every item of clothing we had brought with us and covered by our capes, we lay on the groundsheet with our bags for pillows and tried to get some sleep. Despite the rain on my face and the hard pavement for a mattress, I slept for a couple of hours, then had to give it up. I'm never at my best in the early hours of the morning. I was cold, tired and stiff. Recumbent or sitting bodies of the sleeping or fitfully dozing appeared incongruous beneath the streetlights. Those in the crowd around me who were awake were full of bonhomie, including a cheerful American youth who had manoeuvred himself to sit back-to-back with me.

Too tired to hide my grumpy mood, I stood up and made my way to the temporary toilets in the park. Here masses of jolly revellers were in holiday mood. This was the biggest party in the western hemisphere and none of them had wasted it by sleeping. Swilling my face with freezing cold water from the stand pipes, I felt slightly more human. I had already queued twenty minutes in the rain for the toilets but the smell of hot dogs and onions tempted me and I joined another endless queue.

Food and a mug of tea began to melt the cold and stiffness from my bones. I left the merrymakers and returned to my concrete bed and a few more hours of restless tossing and turning.

Dad's booming voice roused me at around six and I was grateful for the steaming mug of tea.

The sky was leaden. A cold wind whistled through the trees in the park. It was more like November than June. Nevertheless there was daylight and my good spirits returned. I took a walk in the park. The frolicking mood had gone from the people to be replaced by a quiet cheerfulness I found easier to cope with at that hour.

Soon after I returned from my walk, we heard clapping and laughing from the crowd. It was coming as a wave towards us.

271

Police eating sandwiches on Coronation Day in Piccadilly

Soldiers at dawn in Piccadilly, marching to line the Coronation route

Soon a road sweeper came into view with his handcart. He was grinning from ear to ear.

Although there were thousands of people, there was very little litter. Everybody conscientiously kept their refuse with them until they could find a bin.

More clapping rolled towards us, this time coming from Hyde Park Corner. A dark square moving along the otherwise empty road was gradually recognisable as a squadron of servicemen. The thumping of their boots reverberated off the buildings. They wore flat white caps. If they were wearing ceremonial uniform we couldn't tell. Their outfits were covered in drab oilskin capes, protecting them from the fine penetrating rain. Perhaps they were making their way to the abbey to be part of the procession. So early in the morning it is more likely that they were going to line the route. The procession route was five miles long and was lined by over fifteen thousand men from the Army, Navy and Air Force. There were also fifteen thousand policemen from all over Britain. Many wore the traditional helmet but those near us had flat caps.

Like the crowd, they were relaxed and enjoying the day. I don't know whether they had brought lunch with them, but one of those in front of us was eating a bread roll. Perhaps one of the families near us had taken pity on him.

The stands on the buildings facing us were now packed with paying visitors. Below them crowds filled the narrow pavement. I wondered where they would go for toilets or water but no doubt something had been organised for them in the side streets. It could be that temporary toilets were erected on Berkeley Square.

A public address system had been set up along the route of the Coronation procession and the BBC radio coverage for the day was transmitted to the crowds.

Early in the day the announcement was made that Edmund Hillary had conquered Everest. A Sherpa guide might have been mentioned.

There was a rousing cheer from the crowd and my shout of joy joined with theirs. I assumed that Hillary was an Englishman. Later I discovered he was a New Zealander. I don't remember hearing the name of Tenzing Norgay, the Napalese Sherpa until years later. Together they had become the first people to reach the summit of Mount Everest. How did this tap into the feast of nationalism that had gathered millions to the Coronation? The connection appeared to be that it was a British expedition led by Colonel John Hunt. Perhaps he was English.

Just before 8am the lord mayor of London left the Mansion House in the City of London to start his journey to Westminster Abbey. The great state coach was drawn along the Embankment by six magnificent greys attended by footmen, Richard Dimbleby informed us over the tannoy. Beside and behind the lord mayor's coach marched a platoon of pikeman in traditional medieval uniform.

Royalty arrived at the abbey in a queue of cars from Buckingham Palace, followed hard on their heels by representatives from eighty nations.

The commentator barely had time to give a brief biography of those entering the abbey when the coaches began arriving from Buckingham Palace. First came colonial rulers, followed by prime ministers. Next came princes and princesses. The sergeant-at-arms, bearing the mace, travelled the short journey from the Houses of Parliament along Parliament Square to the abbey by coach, accompanied by the speaker of the House of Commons.

273

Queen Salote of Tonga in the Pacific was one of the first colonial rulers to arrive at the abbey. Her name was just one among a long list. We neither knew who she was nor where Tonga was. By the end of the day she had won so many hearts; she would be remembered when the rest of the pageant had become a distant memory.

At ten in the morning Queen Elizabeth, the Queen Mother, left Clarence House. Her brief but eventful time as Queen Consort had been unexpected. Her husband, King George VI, had been elevated to the throne when his brother Edward abdicated in 1936.

The hours had disappeared as we listened in wonder to the momentous day unfolding.

The queen descended from her golden coach and entered Westminster Abbey for the Coronation service.

The cry of 'God Save the Queen' echoed through the abbey and was carried to the waiting crowd. We heard a cacophony of bells from all the churches near Piccadilly. Cannon boomed so close behind us that everyone jumped and turned their attention to the park. The bang seemed to come from there. Trumpets sounded in the abbey, recalling us to the ceremony. The archbishop knelt at the feet of the queen to be the first to pay homage to her, followed by the duke of Edinburgh and all the royal dukes, and peers. The crowd were inspired to join in the singing of 'All People That On Earth do Dwell' remembered from school assemblies and prompted by the congregation in the abbey if they faltered.

This spectacular event was not only heard over loudspeakers by the crowd of three million people lining the five miles of the procession. It was also carried to every home in the land by radio and television. On and on it spread right across the globe, out in the bush in Australia, and far into the remotest parts of Rhodesia. Where television wasn't available they had to wait to see it on a newsreel, but they heard the broadcast as it happened, sitting up through the night, if necessary. Before this event nothing of this magnitude had ever instantly spread across the world.

The procession through the streets was led by four army bands we were told over the tannoy. They were playing familiar marching tunes. Many of us hummed along but there was no loud singing as there had been the evening before. With the daylight, self-consciousness and habitual English reserve had returned or, perhaps we didn't want to miss any of the commentary.

Detachment after detachment, rank upon rank, ten thousand servicemen (and a few token women) from the armies, navies, and air forces of the colonies were marching towards us. They had come from the far corners of the earth, from the whole British Commonwealth.

Behind the servicemen came the carriages. When the event was being planned there weren't enough carriages. Britain had been scoured for every available suitable carriage. There had been an even greater shortage of horses trained to pull carriages in a dignified manner. Stables, large and small, throughout the land loaned horses of an acceptable quality. The cortège now stretched for two miles and would take three-quarters of an hour to pass, the commentator informed us.

Clamorous applause from across Green Park told us that we would soon be witnessing the extravaganza of the age. The pictures that the commentator had painted were as nothing compared with the display that we were about to see.

Marching down Piccadilly came the four army bands, a great splash of colour in their ceremonial uniforms, in marked contrast to the drab khaki raincoats worn by the squadron of servicemen at 7am that morning. Next came the colonial

A Trinidadian squadron in white tunics and helmets

police, their colourful uniforms unbelievably surpassing the uniforms of the bands. They were followed by a Trinidadian squadron in white tunics and helmets.

Dad started taking photographs but was overwhelmed by the enormity of recording the merest portion of the events passing before us: Fijian soldiers with their abundant hair swept up in a style which would later be called an Afro; servicemen from Pakistan; Pathan tribesmen with long oiled hair or wearing tufted turbans; southern Rhodesians in broad-brimmed hats and shorts; men from every continent sporting extraordinary hairstyles, boasting a fez, a bush hat, and every other kind of headgear known to man; and exotic clothes beyond our wildest dreams. The Australians were there in force but didn't wear dress uniform.

A great cheer swept through the crowd. The men of the Ghurkha Rifles Regiment were approaching. They had a proud record of service during the Second World War and everybody loved and admired them. We clapped and applauded as they went by in their dull green uniforms. Except that they didn't go by. As the rain sliced down relentlessly, they stood waiting before us for almost half an hour. They looked small, desolate and far from home. There is only so much cheering you can do. Singing would probably have helped.

Thunderous applause with whistling and clapping erupted from the loudspeakers as the crowds around the abbey greeted the queen when she emerged. We became aware of the broadcast again. We joined in the cheering although we couldn't see her. The driving rain could not dampen our spirits for long.

Until the Ghurkhas had stopped marching, we had been so engrossed in the feast passing before our eyes that the commentary from the loudspeakers had been forgotten. Information about the occupants of each carriage, as they took their place in the train, had been drowned out by the crowd, exalting at the scene before them. The parade was two miles long and the queen and her immediate retinue were just leaving Westminster Abbey.

The saturated Ghurkhas came to attention smartly and marched forwards.

The Royal Canadian Mounted Police led the Canadian contingent. Dressed in pillar-box red jackets and broad-brimmed hats, they brought a bright splash of colour to the grey day as they rode by on their splendid black steeds.

The coach procession turned off St James's Street onto Piccadilly and we strained forward eagerly to see them. Seven sultans and the Queen of Tonga rode in the first four coaches. The sultans could have been wearing the most extravagant attire. Nobody noticed them. Queen Salote of Tonga, larger than life, smiling broadly as she waved to us, was the favourite of the crowd. Dressed for a hot summer's day, her braided hair uncovered, she rode in an open landau, oblivious to the torrential rain.

Winston Churchill rode in the last of the nine coaches for prime ministers. I viewed him with mixed feelings. He was the great hero who had led the country to victory in the war but I admired the Labour Party, particularly Nye Bevan, founder of the National Health Service.

I had been obsessed with the royal family since I was seven or eight years old, particularly the princesses Elizabeth and Margaret. I read about them in Mam's magazines, *Woman* and *Woman's Own*, and any other books or papers I could lay my hands on. Now they passed less than four yards from me and I peered inside the carriages as they passed, waving to us. Some I thought I recognised but, even at the slow pace of the procession, it wasn't possible to see everything. The Household Cavalry rode beside them and this sometimes obscured the view. Everyone gave an extra big cheer to the Queen Mother. We missed the king. I was very upset on the day I heard he had died. She must have found it very hard to cope with this Coronation day.

Now the moment had arrived. High-ranking officers of the Army, Navy and Air Force and a woman brigadier from the WRAC, representing the services, led the last part of the procession. Many of them were household names but the only one familiar to me was Monty, General Montgomery of Alamein.

The beefeaters arrived in a blaze of red and gold, far more impressive in their ceremonial uniforms than they had been the Sunday before at the Tower, when they had been wearing navy blue with red embroidery.

The golden coach was approaching. It was straight from a fairy tale. The roar from the crowd ricochetted off the tall buildings. No film producer could have created a coach so beautiful. Exquisite golden plants framed the sides of the windows, golden cords looped across the doors. Three golden cherubs on the roof held aloft a crown.

Eight fine grey horses drew the coach. They were mounted by four red-coated riders. Beefeaters and footmen walked beside it. Accompanying the coach, one on either side, were two horsemen, the red saddlecloths matching the plumes of their helmets and in sharp contrast to their grand dark steeds.

The coach moved so smoothly it appeared to float towards us. Now it was level and we were looking straight at the queen. She was smiling broadly as she passed by. The ecstatic crowd shouted and clapped their applause as the coach disappeared from view, followed by the Household Cavalry.

The crowd began to disperse and we made our way to a quiet alley near St James Street to collect our bikes. Harry and I were dawdling, taking a last look at the street traders. When we reached the bikes Dianne couldn't contain her excitement. She had been standing with Dad in the empty street when one of the pageboys from the abbey, dressed in all of his finery, had walked past her with his father. We had watched thousands of the great and noble parading before us for three hours or more but this one boy made us realise it wasn't a dream or a film. It had happened here and now and we were a part of history.

Dad thought of taking us for a hot meal to warm us up but decided that the quicker we rode the four miles back to the hostel and changed into dry shoes and clothes the better. We hadn't planned for rain. It was by sheer chance that we had washed our clothes and left them in the drying room two days earlier.

By the time we had taken a steaming hot bath we began to feel more human. It was cold in the kitchen but we made a cup of tea to warm us up and then knuckled down to peeling potatoes. Dad had bought sausage on the way back. Sausage and mash was the quickest meal we could make. We hardly had time to talk as we shovelled it down so quickly it gave us indigestion.

There were no radiators on as it was supposed to be summer, but a coal-fire was burning in the common room. We gathered around it, talking excitedly as we tried to steam the damp out from of our bones. By the time the other hostellers came in and we were expected to share the fire, we were almost thawed out.

We floated through Wednesday, barely taking anything in. Shaking the rain from our cycle capes and sou'westers, we went to the British Museum. I would have looked at every spearhead in every display cabinet if Dad hadn't dragged me away. The Egyptian mummies, with their leathery brown bodies in foetal positions thrilled and appalled me.

The joy of the visit was the reading room, a circular room beneath a great dome. There were twenty-five miles of shelves full of books. We entered this silent cathedral of learning and Dad led us to his special treasures. The dry but important manuscripts came first, Magna Carta and the Codex Sinaiticus.

'What is the use of a book,' thought Alice (in Wonderland), 'without pictures or conversations.'

But we knew the story of the barons forcing bad King John to sign Magna Carta. It was, after all, the time of Robin Hood and the sheriff of Nottingham. We had all the pictures we needed in our heads. Britain was the best country in the world. Everyone was equal under the law. Nobody could be locked away in prison without trial because of Magna Carta.

There was nothing in the austere appearance of Codex

Sinaiticus to stir me. It was brown parchment with darker brown Greek script. But I was thrilled to imagine the scribe sixteen hundred years ago recording the familiar stories from the New Testament. Six hundred years before Normans invaded Britain, over a thousand years before Tudors and Stuarts ruled here, this book was being written.

Alice in Wonderland had her own glass case where we could gaze in amazement at an open page of the first edition and see one of the original pictures.

Dad had kept the most impressive and radiant to the last, the Lindisfarne Gospels. The magnificent manuscript was open on the first page of one of the Gospels. The first letter of the Gospel had brightly illuminated interlacing and spiral patterns. This astonishingly beautiful work of art, created by a monk in the eighth century, was beyond words. Fifty years later I visited Lindisfarne Priory, on a tidal island off the coast of Northumbria. My heart was filled with the same wonder and joy I had known the first time I beheld an illuminated text. I savoured the bleak, damp atmosphere and thought of Eadfrith creating his extravagant masterpiece.

After eating our sandwiches we wandered around the galleries in a haphazard manner for a couple of hours, gleaning disconnected gems of information until Dad insisted we must get back to the hostel before 5pm.

The sky was leaden as we said goodbye to London next morning and cycled through the pretty Tudor town of Hemel Hempstead and on to Aylesbury. The rain was a thin drizzle. I looked longingly down the narrow Tudor alleyways knowing there would be no time to explore.

I have no recollection of sitting in a lorry but logic tells me that we must have had a lift a good part of the way. The journey would have been about eighty-seven miles and we arrived at Warwick castle at about quarter to three. Dad promised we could visit the castle if we reached it by 3pm.

Harry and Dianne beat me to the winding staircase up to the highest tower. We started running up but after the first floor we began to slow down. Up and up we climbed, peering through narrow slits and the occasional door. The roofs of the state rooms lay below us and still we climbed. I followed them through a small wooden door and gazed in wonder at the panoramic view. At the foot of the castle were narrow streets of half-timbered houses. The river Avon ran past castle and town and out of sight amongst the trees to our left. A church spire rose from the centre of a village across the river. Beyond the village, olive-green and blue-green cereal fields stretched to the horizon.

Dad found difficulty containing his excitement when we came down. He led us off to one of the state rooms where the death mask of Oliver Cromwell was displayed.

'When he was having his portrait painted the artist was going to leave out the warts on Cromwell's face,' Dad told us. 'Cromwell told the artist to paint him "Warts an' all".'

The portrait may have been in Warwick castle. I saw it somewhere.

We joined the official tour of the grand rooms and the dungeons and the guide gave us a brief summary of the castle's history from when it was built in the 14th century.

Harry and Dianne rushed back down to the dungeon as soon as the tour was over, while I wandered from room to room examining tapestries, reading the information beside paintings, admiring the needlework on curtains and screens, and taking pleasure in the design and beauty of the Georgian furniture and fittings.

I returned recently to find it had been taken over by Madame Tussauds and turned into a theme show with waxworks.

There was no sign of Cromwell's death mask. This had been the highlight of my visit to Warwick castle in 1953. Fifty years later I had to ask one of the guides where it had been placed. It was hidden in an inconspicuous corner. Unless a visitor knew it was in the castle they would come and leave without their attention being drawn to it. I want my history 'Warts an' all'. So do today's children. I enjoy waxworks but they are for entertainment.

281

Dianne, Harry and Beaty at Warwick castle

The castle guides flushed us out at 5pm, jangling their keys and locking the doors to the dungeons and state rooms behind us.

Dad took so long to compose a photograph that we all had jaw ache from trying to keep smiles on our faces. Harry gave up and stared over Dad's head at a leaden sky.

Soon we were cycling through the narrow streets of Warwick towards Leamington Spa. We looked eagerly along The Parade in Leamington, bedecked with bunting and flags. We had seen decorations for almost two weeks but we hadn't become blasé. Before turning away from The Parade at the post office, we spotted the Pump Rooms and made a mental note to return for a closer look after supper. The original spring for the spa was in a stone building in the grounds of All Saints' church. There was no charge for going in.

The attractive Georgian youth hostel caught the eye immediately. We were very aware of the rare privilege we had, being able to stay in attractive buildings that had been town houses for the rich and their servants just fifty years earlier. The impressive portico and double bay windows were crowned by a balustrade.

When we were in the dormitory Dianne and I heard Harry call to us from outdoors. This was puzzling, as we had just left him going into the room next door.

'Come to the window,' he called.

From the dormitory windows he had stepped out onto the balcony above the bay windows and was standing beside the balustrade. At the sound of Dad's voice from the stairs, he gave us a mischievous grin and dived back into the men's dormitory.

We found the kitchen in the basement, where it would have been when servants worked below stairs. The basement rooms had bay windows but very little daylight reached us when we were preparing supper, as only a quarter of the window was above ground.

Dad obtained special permission for us to leave at eight next morning without carrying out our tasks. We had an impossible ride ahead of us. Skirting Birmingham we were making for Shrewsbury by way of Kidderminster.

From Warwick we took a B road through miles of undulating hills. I would puff my way up, standing on the pedals until I was barely moving, then I would get off and walk. Downhill I sped along, ruining the brake blocks as I skidded around corners. It was pure joy as the wind whipped past my ears and stung my face. Sometimes I could see the three seater ahead of me on a straight stretch of road. Occasionally I thought I

Leamington Spa YHA

might catch up with the family. The downward thrust would carry me up the next slope if it was a short one and down I rushed again. A long uphill patch would leave me struggling once more. Two hours later I was pedalling along the long main street of Henley-in-Arden, looking out for the bike and hoping for a tea break. I saw little to whet my aesthetic taste buds, apart from the Guildhall, but perhaps my need for food and drink effected my judgement. I stopped to take a drink of water then pressed on uphill and down dale, delighting in spinning down and facing going up with stoicism.

Far to my right rose the ruins of Bordesley Abbey. An elegant church spire drew my attention to a tiny village in the distance to my left. I cycled through Redditch, passed over the Worcester and Birmingham canal and on to Bromsgrove. The sign to Tardebigge Locks had tempted me but there was no time for sightseeing.

Half an hour later I spotted the bike in the shelter of a splendid chestnut tree. It was leaning against the wall of an ancient church. I turned into Chaddesley Corbett, a village of half-timbered cottages, Georgian houses, inns and a Victorian school. Dad was sitting outside a café drinking tea and looking totally relaxed. He smiled and waved cheerfully when I cycled up and continued talking to a gaunt old man in his late forties or early fifties. We still had almost forty miles to ride but he didn't appear to be rushing us. Dianne and Harry came out off the post office, their hands full of postcards.

'Dad said we can stay here for an hour,' Dianne said. 'I think we're having a lift in that man's van.'

I could have cried with relief. Hardly sitting down to drink my tea, I joined them in an exploration of the village, eating my sandwiches as I walked.

At first glance it had looked like a picture postcard. The few shops, the Victorian redbrick vicarage with yellow lozenge-shaped patterns, the Swan Inn, the Georgian and Victorian houses and some of the cottages were attractively kept. There was a youth hostel in a pristine black-and-white corner house.